THE
SELECTED LETTERS OF
LADY MARY
WORTLEY MONTAGU

EDITED BY

ROBERT HALSBAND

PENGUIN BOOKS

Penguin Books Ltd, Harmondsworth, Middlesex, England
Viking Penguin Inc., 40 West 23rd Street, New York, New York 10010, U.S.A.
Penguin Books Australia Ltd, Ringwood, Victoria, Australia
Penguin Books Canada Limited, 2801 John Street, Markham, Ontario, Canada L3R 1B4
Penguin Books (N.Z.) Ltd, 182–190 Wairau Road, Auckland 10, New Zealand

This selection first published by St Martin's Press, Inc., New York, 1971
Published in Penguin Books 1986

Reproduced, printed and bound in Great Britain by
Hazell Watson & Viney Limited,
Member of the BPCC Group,
Aylesbury, Bucks

LIVES AND LETTERS

A series of diaries and letters, journals and memoirs

THE SELECTED LETTERS OF

LADY MARY WORTLEY MONTAGU

Mary Pierrepont was born in London in 1689, the first child of Evelyn Pierrepont and his wife, Lady Mary Fielding. In the following year, when her father became Earl of Kingston, she acquired her courtesy title, Lady Mary. In 1712, against her father's wishes, she married Edward Wortley Montagu, and when, in 1716, he was appointed Ambassador to Turkey, she accompanied him on the arduous journey to Constantinople. She remained in Turkey until 1718 and her letters give a vivid picture of life there. In England she enjoyed a reputation as a traveller and wit, and actively engaged in contemporary social and political debate. Her marriage was unsuccessful and in 1736 she met and fell in love with a young Italian writer, Francesco Algarotti. In 1739 she left England for Italy in the hope of finding happiness with him, but their meeting, two years later, ended in disappointment. Lady Mary returned to England in January 1762, where she died in August of that year. One of the great letter writers of the eighteenth century, ranking with Walpole, Johnson, Chesterfield and Cowper, she also has other claims to importance and distinction: as a traveller and expatriate, as a feminist concerned with women's education and marriage, and as a writer who expressed her views in a wide range of literary forms.

Robert Halsband, born and educated in the United States, is Professor Emeritus of English at the University of Illinois and currently Adjunct Professor at New York University. He has held Guggenheim Fellowships in 1968–9 and 1982–3 and an N.E.H.-Huntington Fellowship in 1981–2. He is the author of *The Life of Lady Mary Wortley Montagu* (1956), *Lord Hervey, Eighteenth-Century Courtier* (1973) and *The Rape of the Lock and its Illustrations 1714–1896* (1980). He has edited *The Complete Letters of Lady Mary Wortley Montagu* (three volumes, 1965–7), and co-edited Lady Mary's *Essays and Poems* (1977).

Editorial Note

This selection is based on my edition of Lady Mary Wortley Montagu's *Complete Letters* (3 volumes, Clarendon Press, 1965–67). From the approximately nine hundred of her known letters I have chosen one hundred and ninety-seven varied ones that seem to me to be the most interesting and lively. Each one is printed in its entirety; but the spelling, capitalization, and punctuation are modernized, annotation is minimal, and French is translated. Readers whose curiosity extends beyond what this volume offers can consult the complete edition.

I am grateful to the Oxford University Press for permission to make use of that edition. For my introduction I have drawn upon my biography of Lady Mary (1956) and two essays: in *PMLA* (1965) and *History Today* (1966). In preparing this volume for publication I have had valuable assistance from Arnold Cragg.

Contents

Principal Correspondents

✣

*ALGAROTTI, Francesco (1712–64), cosmopolite, poet, and writer of miscellaneous works; friend of Voltaire and of Frederick the Great.

BUTE, Countess of (1718–94), Lady Mary's only daughter; 1736 married to Bute (Prime Minister 1762–63); mother of a numerous family.

HEWET, Frances, née Bettenson (1668–1756); a country neighbour of Lady Mary's in Nottinghamshire.

*MACKENZIE, James Stuart (1719?–1800), Bute's only brother; received a succession of important government appointments through Bute's influence.

MAR, Countess of, née Frances Pierrepont (1690–1761), Lady Mary's sister; married in 1714 to the Jacobite Earl who was attainted in 1715 and lived abroad; she became insane in 1728.

*MICHIEL, Chiara, née Bragadin (d. 1780), met Lady Mary in 1740, and remained her intimate friend; her husband was Venetian Ambassador to Spain 1741–44.

*MUNDY, Philippa (1689–1762), of a Derbyshire family; married in 1714 to Burrell Massingberd after a long courtship.

POMFRET, Countess of, née Henrietta Louisa Jeffreys (1698–1761), Lady of the Bedchamber to Queen Caroline, after whose death (in 1737) she lived for three years in France and then Italy with her husband and two of their daughters.

STEUART, Sir James (1713–80), married in 1743 to Lady Frances Wemyss; trained as a lawyer; implicated in Jacobite rebellion of 1745; fled and lived in France and then Germany; published learned works; was pardoned and returned to Scotland in 1763.

WORTLEY, Anne (d. 1710), daughter of Sidney Wortley (Earl of Sandwich's second son).

WORTLEY MONTAGU, Edward (1678–1761), second but eldest surviving son of Sidney Wortley; educated at Westminster School and Trinity College, Cambridge; called to the bar in 1700; on Grand Tour 1700–3; M.P. 1705 until (with one interruption) his death; married Lady Mary in 1712.

*Printed for the first time in 1965–67.

Introduction

❧

Although Lady Mary Wortley Montagu is chiefly famous as one of the great letter-writers of the eighteenth century she has other claims to importance and distinction: as a traveller and expatriate, as a feminist concerned with women's education and marriage, and as a writer who expressed her ideas in a variety of literary forms other than the informal letter.

In 1716, four years after her marriage to Edward Wortley Montagu, she accompanied him to Turkey, where he was to take up his appointment as ambassador from the Court of St James to the Sublime Porte. Her earlier travels had been negligible – dutiful journeys from Nottingham or Yorkshire to London for the social season; now she traversed the entire continent of Europe to penetrate the strange, mysterious world of Islam. Her route took her over the frozen plains of Hungary, across the Danube, through what are now the Balkans, to the very shores of the Bosporus. Then, two years later, as she returned to England she sailed through the Dardanelles and the Aegean and Mediterranean Seas, going ashore to see the remains of ancient Troy and Carthage; and she disembarked in Italy to scale the Alps and cross France to the English Channel.

As a traveller Lady Mary had two great advantages (beyond her exceptional wit and intellect): being an ambassadress she could meet and converse with ducal and imperial monarchs, and partake of their elaborate hospitality; and being a woman, in Turkey she could share in a social life forbidden to men – she visited the luxurious baths for women and called on sultanas in their own palaces to observe an opulence that matched what she had read in Oriental tales.

Free of narrow insularity, she was receptive to any idea that seemed useful and sensible. In Hanover, when she saw that houses could be comfortably heated in the winter, she reflected on the obstinacy of the English in shaking with cold six months of the year, and vowed to use a stove at home, even if it were not the fashion. The same pioneering impulse led her, in Adrianople, to take careful notice of smallpox inoculation, which was virtually unknown in western Europe; and she bravely had it performed on her young son in Constantinople, and on her infant daughter after she returned to England. Her practice and her advocacy helped to popularize that method of avoiding one of the most dreaded and deadly diseases of the time. It remained the most effective method of immunization until about eighty years later when Edward Jenner discovered smallpox vaccine.

Twenty years later (in 1739) Lady Mary set out on her travels again, this time along the well-worn path of the Grand Tour in Italy, but her reason for going there was neither education nor economy; it was to keep a romantic rendezvous with Francesco Algarotti, a young Italian *littérateur* whom she had met in London three years before, and had fallen in love with. Although her journey to what she called the Elysian fields failed of its purpose – her meeting with Algarotti two years later was a dismal disappointment – she remained abroad, finding unexpected contentment in her expatriation.

In Venice, where she lived longer than in any other city abroad, she found that its social life, cosmopolitan society, and steady stream of visitors made life most agreeable. In other cities she sought out newly discovered antiquities, and near Naples tried to explore the city of Herculaneum, then being excavated by the King of the Two Sicilies. During the four years that she lived in Avignon, then a Papal posses-sion, she investigated its Roman remains (though she scoffed at its Gothic ones); and she travelled alone without a servant on the public passenger boat to Toulouse by way of the great canal of Languedoc, one of the engineering marvels of the day. Fortunately she had the stamina to sustain her curiosity.

The most distinctive phase of her expatriation was her residence in the Italian lake country. During the ten years (1746–56) that she lived in Brescia, a Venetian province, she stayed mostly at a house and near-by farm on the banks of the Oglio, about eighteen miles south of the town. She made extended visits to Lovere on the Lake of Iseo, and to Salo, on the Lake of Garda. An historian of that region has called her the 'discoverer' of Iseo, for it was unknown to other English travellers. Lady Mary's descriptions of this paradisal region, when they were published in the next century, persuaded English and other foreigners to visit that part of northern Italy.

By reason of her practice as well as her preachment Lady Mary deserves a place in the history of women's emancipation. As an organ-ized movement, feminism did not win its main goals until the end of the nineteenth century (when the word itself came into being), but Lady Mary was one of the pioneers concerned with the status of women in a world where they were second-class citizens. She is, so to speak, one of feminism's founding mothers.

Mainly through education, she believed, women could avoid the pit-falls of ignorance and folly. As a girl she had strenuously educated her-self. Her father arranged for her to be taught the genteel accomplish-ments suitable to a young lady of her social class – including French, Italian, and drawing; and as his eldest daughter she was taught to carve a joint of meat at table by a carving-master who came three times a week to instruct her. But on her own initiative she ranged through her father's extensive library, reading a prodigious number of romances and plays in French and English. With the aid of dictionaries and grammars she taught herself Latin, and practised translating the Roman poets into

English. At the age of fifteen she was so studious that her ambition was to establish a convent for learning, with herself as abbess. Certainly she was not the first learned Englishwoman; in the previous century there had been such female polymaths as the 'wise, wittie, and learned' Duchess of Newcastle, and Lady Conway, the friend of the Cambridge Platonists. But Lady Mary's learning was uncommon enough to impress her future husband, who had received a formal classical education; she collaborated with Alexander Pope and John Gay in imitating Virgil's eclogues; and in Constantinople the French Ambassador thought she knew Virgil and Horace by heart. When the Elector of Hanover came to London to reign as George I, Lady Mary set about learning German to make her court to him; and in Turkey she carefully studied Turkish soon after she arrived in that territory. Her intellectual ambition was inexhaustible and boundless.

Her self-education influenced her point of view. Girls should be taught Latin and even Greek, she believed, so that they would be able to read the classics in the original, and they should be familiar with English poetry as well. But she cautioned that whatever learning a girl acquired should be concealed as though it were a physical blemish lest it arouse envy and hatred. At the same time that she advocated learning and reading, she believed girls should mix in society for a 'public education' that would give them a realistic knowledge of the ways of the world. Her ideas are comparable to Lord Chesterfield's on the education of his son, in his famous series of letters.

In any society the institution of marriage is a touchstone for determining the status of women. Lady Mary's courtship, which lasted more than two years, is a classic situation for its time, when marriage between landed families involved hard bargaining – to strike a balance between the bride's dowry and the groom's settlement on her and their prospective children. Wortley refused to agree to her father's requirement that a large part of his capital should be entailed on his first son. The engagement was broken off, and the proud father cast about for another eligible but complaisant suitor for Lady Mary. She sided with Wortley; love seemed more important to her than financial settlements.

In her idealistic view of marriage she was in the vanguard of social thought in her time. What she calls her romantic scheme of marriage is one of mutual love, with her husband not thinking it unreasonable to enjoy her conversation and not regarding tenderness as an affront to his intelligence. When she finally eloped with Wortley she made a considerable sacrifice, not only alienating her father but putting herself entirely in her husband's power, without the customary safeguards of a specified allowance and provisions for her support should she outlive him. Her courtship, based on considerations other than financial, occurred during the time that Richard Steele was propagandizing similar notions in his *Tatler* essays. This changing status of marriageable women, from being commodities to companions, was an important advance in the history of marriage and of feminism.

In her various roles so far sketched Lady Mary is prominent as an intrepid traveller, an appreciative tourist and a contented expatriate in Italy, and as an advocate of feminism, education for women, and enlightened marriage. She was, besides, the foremost woman of letters to have appeared in England up to her time.

She began her career as a wit and poet in 1716 when three of her town eclogues achieved the dubious honour of publication by Edmund Curll, the piratical printer, who entitled them *Court Poems*. Lady Mary's other important published poetry was also stimulated by Pope, though in a different sense. Her *Verses Address'd to the Imitator of Horace*, in 1733, was a blunderbuss aimed at Pope, who had turned from admirer to enemy and hurled a succession of poisonous couplets at her. In his endless warfare with dunces and non-dunces, from Grub Street to St James's, he considered Lady Mary one of his most formidable opponents; and it is difficult to think of any of his other victims, men or women, who could boast of her gift for retaliation. In a more genial vein she wrote skilful and delicate verse that, as assayed by George Saintsbury, may not be pure diamond but at least 'flashes with the very best paste' in Dodsley's *Collection*.

With her forthright energy, Lady Mary felt impelled to disseminate her notions through essays that would reach an audience beyond her circle of friends and correspondents. Since as an aristocrat she could not appear in print publicly – in fact, not a single one of her publications during her lifetime bore her name – her essays were all printed anonymously. The earliest was an essay in the *Spectator* in which she relates the trials of a widow who has outlived six husbands. Far more vigorous than this gentle satire was the essay she contributed to a newspaper in 1722, during the controversy over smallpox inoculation. In it she pretends to be a Turkey-trading merchant who defends inoculation and attacks physicians with equal ferocity.

Her most ambitious activity as a periodical essayist, at the end of 1737, thrust her into the hurly-burly of politics. As Sir Robert Walpole's ministry was drawing to its end, he was opposed not only by the Tory opposition but by dissident Whigs, including Wortley. But Lady Mary remained Walpole's admirer, praising him in a poem for his 'cheerful smile, and open honest look'. He was at this time under violent attack from the opposition paper *Common Sense* when suddenly and unannounced there appeared a new periodical entitled *The Nonsense of Common-Sense*. In each issue the anonymous journalist states: 'To be continued as long as the Author thinks fit, and the public likes it.' Lady Mary was that author. Only nine issues were published because, evidently, the public did not support it sufficiently to persuade its author to continue it.

The nine spirited essays in *The Nonsense of Common-Sense* tell us something of Lady Mary's ideas on political and social problems. Since the author posed as a non-partisan commentator, her polemics had to be oblique, sometimes even humorous. Walpole's enemies accused him of threatening the freedom of the Press; yes, it is threatened, Lady Mary writes, not by him but by unscrupulous printers. In foreign affairs his most vulnerable policy was his refusal to take belligerent action against Spanish interference with British ships; Lady Mary gently ridicules the war-mongers by supposing they would declare war against Spain because Farinelli, the famous *castrato* singer, had taken up residence in Madrid. Her most eloquent essay, the sixth, was closest to her heart; devoted entirely to feminism, it praises women as rational creatures capable of as much nobility of character as the great heroes of antiquity. Although her essays could not have been of much political service to Walpole's ministry, they at least show her versatility in political journalism; and as her contemporaries could not have known, they were the most convincing proof of her feminist arguments.

Her interest in literature extended to still another *genre* – the drama. When her young cousin Henry Fielding began his career in London as a playwright he dedicated his first comedy *Love in Several Masques* to her as the 'Lady, whose accurate Judgment has long been the Glory of her own Sex, and the Wonder of ours'. A few years later, after trying his hand at a new kind of serious comedy, *The Modern Husband*, he read it to her in order to profit by her opinion. When Edward Young, who later won fame with his lugubrious *Night Thoughts*, wrote a tragedy he submitted it to Lady Mary, and then obsequiously thanked her for her suggestions. But her most startling activity in dramatic writing, only recently discovered, is her translation and adaptation of the popular comedy by Pierre de Marivaux, *Le Jeu de l'amour et du hasard*. She could have seen it on the London stage during the season of 1734–35, when a French troupe played at the Haymarket Theatre. She entitled her adaptation *Simplicity, a Comedy*, translating its rococo French spirit into a sturdier English as native as roast beef and Yorkshire pudding. Although bold enough to attempt a new literary form she was unwilling to make it public, and it was neither printed nor produced on the stage.

Lady Mary's versatility in exploiting different literary forms is paralleled by the great variety in her informal letters, for she was remarkably sensitive to her correspondent, the occasion, and of course herself. She wrote gossipy, pert, or grave letters to girlhood friends (Anne Wortley, Philippa Mundy, and Mrs Hewet); sober, businesslike ones to her husband about household or political affairs; courtly, stuffy ones to the dull Lady Oxford during the same years that she sent witty and spicy ones to the more sophisticated Lady Pomfret. Her letters to the Venetian Madame Michiel (in French) are affectionate and debonair, written during the same period she dutifully corresponded with her husband, distant in space and feeling, about their disobedient son. And in her final years, when she befriended Sir James Steuart, an erudite political economist, she sent him a series of strenuously clever letters that are like a sunset burst of intellectual fire. Yet all these correspondences, varied as they are, do not exhaust the range of her epistolary art.

Lady Mary's courtship correspondence with Wortley is one of the most extensive prenuptial negotiations on record, extending over two and a half years. Judged by its immediate goal it was a success, for the pair eloped and were married; but judged by its ultimate outcome it was a sad failure, for in spite of its laborious analyses of their temperaments and tastes they were thoroughly unsuited to each other. Their marriage dwindled into a formal arrangement, and during the last twenty years of their lives they lived on opposite sides of Europe. Perhaps Lady Mary's cleverness, subtlety, and rhetorical effectiveness proved to be self-defeating – she won Wortley (against her father's strong will) and lost her chance for happiness in marriage.

Her very first letter to Wortley sets the dominant tone: it is plain and unadorned, saved from flatness by a crisp clarity, and obviously pitched to appeal to the hard-headed M.P. and coal tycoon. Of course the correspondence has no formal design beyond an inherent pattern of a beginning, a long middle (interrupted by several pauses), and an end. But its subject matter is far from epic. The main themes are: financial – Lady Mary's dowry and Wortley's settlement; their meeting at friends' houses and at receptions; their future life together (love, solitude, and economy); his jealousy and her denials; her father's choice of a husband and her possible defiance; and complicated, everchanging plans for an elopement. The correspondence is perhaps susceptible to musical analysis as themes are announced, developed, varied, modulated, fragmented, set off by contrasting sub-themes, recapitulated *ad libitum*, and finally resolved in a triumphant coda before a parson.

Lady Mary is a virtuoso in manipulating these themes. 'I am incapable of art,' she writes in an early letter, 'and 'tis because I will not be capable of it. Could I deceive one minute, I should never regain my own good opinion, and who could bear to live with one they despised?' Another trait she emphasizes is her freedom from emotion. 'If you expect passion,' she writes, 'I am utterly unacquainted with any. It may be a fault of my temper. . . . I have no notion of a transport of anger, love, or any other. I here tell you the plain state of my heart. . . .' She wore her humility with becoming grace: 'I have not the usual pride of my sex. I can bear being told I am in the wrong, but tell it me gently. Perhaps I have been indiscreet; I came young into the hurry of the world.'

Her arsenal of rhetorical weapons includes one that can be called 'negative suggestion' – as when she writes, 'I have neither folly nor vanity enough to suppose you would think of running away with me'. She later reinforces that suggestion with a rare literary allusion: that not since the romantic tales of Mademoiselle de Scudéry has any heroine sacrificed a dowry by eloping. She pursues her epistolary campaign with vigorous prose, using such pungent phrases as 'Let us both be at liberty till the parson puts an end to it', and such concrete details as 'I shall come to you with only a nightgown and petticoat, and that is all you will get with me'.

For a romantic courtship the correspondence is terribly earthbound, as one can see when comparing it with Dorothy Osborne's courtship letters. Lady Mary rarely relaxes from her pose of sensible reasonableness – it is, in the main, a correspondence of plain thinking, plain dealing, and plain writing. Only near the end of the courtship does she betray emotion. 'My family is resolved to dispose of me where I hate. I have made all the opposition in my power; perhaps I have carried that opposition too far. . . . I am compelled to submit. – I was born to be unhappy, and I must fulfil the course of my destiny – ' But then, as though remembering her claim of being without passion: 'You see, Sir, the esteem I have for you. I have ventured to tell you the whole secret of my heart.' Another of the late-courtship letters begins: 'I tremble for what we are doing. – Are you sure you will love me for ever? – Shall we never repent? I fear and I hope.' But it concludes: 'You shall hear from me again tomorrow, not to contradict, but to give some directions. My resolution is taken – love me and use me well.' She starts with trembling doubts and questions; she ends with firm commands.

When Lytton Strachey read this correspondence in 1907, when it was published only in fragments, he thought them 'strange love-letters' of the 'deepest interest'. It is not difficult to see why.

About twenty-five years after the termination of the courtship by marriage, Lady Mary was again involved in a love affair – but this time of a most astonishing kind, with Francesco Algarotti, the Italian savant and writer. As 'literary documents' her love-letters to him are remarkable for their emotional abandon and extravagance. Even though their literary origins may have been the French romances and letter-writers of the seventeenth century, Lady Mary needed no models; the frantic pulsation clearly came from her own heart. If, in her courtship letters, plain feelings engendered plain prose, in these, extravagant feelings bloomed as extravagant prose. 'What has become of that philosophical indifference that made the glory and tranquillity of my former days?' she asks (in French). 'My feelings are too ardent; I could not possibly explain them or hide them.' In another letter, still early in her infatuation, 'How timid one is when one loves!' – and she concludes that letter with: 'I am torn by a thousand conflicting feelings that concern you very little. . . . All that is certain is that I shall love you all my life in spite of your whims and my reason.' In another (still in French): 'You must believe that you possess in me the most perfect friend and the most passionate lover.'

To express this intense emotion she usually wrote in French, though Algarotti could read English, for she found in that language a freedom from her customary inhibitions. (We can observe the same quality of relaxation and intimacy in Swift's French letters to Vanessa.) Besides French prose, she frequently fell into 'the extravagancies of poetry, which indeed are only fit to attempt the expressing my thoughts of you or to you'. In one letter, after complaining of winter weather and a tormenting toothache, she tells Algarotti that she looks forward to the spring when he and the sun shall return:

> You, lovely youth, shall my Apollo prove;
> Adorn my verse, and tune my soul to love.

In another borrowed effusion – this time from Dryden – she assures him she would prefer him to any man as great as the first Caesar and as young as the second. No hyperbole is too elevated – or grotesque – and her reading in Restoration heroic tragedy no doubt helped her.

Her use of literary characters as symbolic of her own state of mind reinforces her generally high-flown style. (In her courtship letters to Wortley, the few she cited were generally satiric; and she never erupted into verse.) In one letter she calls herself Don Quixote to Algarotti's Dulcinea (the inversion of sexual roles is appropriate for him at least); her other character identifications are classical: she is Dido, the 'soul-racked' Queen of Carthage, bemoaning the departure of her little Aeneas; or she is the Penelope of his absence; or she prepares to leave London to meet him in the Elysian fields – on the Grand Canal.

Besides this serious imagery, she frequently uses religious wit, of the kind affected by the *libertins* and seventeenth-century poets. She is thus able to lighten her declarations of love, and to appeal to Algarotti's *esprit*. 'The Enthusiasm you have infected me with is as violent as ever', she tells him (two years after they had met), meaning Enthusiasm in its religious sense. When she waits for him to call on her, she compares herself to the martyrs who have been canonized for less suffering; and she claims the Blessed Virgin does not have so sincere a votary as Algarotti has in her. But when she is about to begin her journey, the religious imagery loses its ironic edge; her journey is a pilgrimage, at the end of which he may grant her prayers; and she departs from England 'with the resolution of a man well persuaded of his religion and happy in his conscience, filled with faith and hope'.

When her faith and hope in Algarotti (as her saviour) collapsed, how would she 'compose' the denouement of the drama that had begun five years earlier? Instead of assuming the role of a classical heroine (or hero) she calmly tells him (in French) that she has studied him as carefully as Sir Isaac Newton has dissected the rays of the sun, and she elaborates the comparison. Her letter is a *tour de force*; its central imagery is especially apt when we remember that Algarotti's most famous book, published three years before, was a set of graceful dialogues on the *Optics*, entitled *Newtonianism for the Ladies*. Lady Mary had assured him, 'I have read, I have re-read, and I shall re-read your book. I shall always find new beauties; none of its charms escapes me.' She could not have foreseen its usefulness in dramatizing her disillusion.

When Byron read a few of these love-letters in manuscript he called them 'very pretty and passionate . . . the *French* not good, but the sentiments beautiful'. Taken as a group they extend our knowledge of Lady

Mary's emotional and literary powers far beyond the boundaries previously charted. They uncover new dimensions in her personality and art.

Lady Mary's letters to her sister Lady Mar in the 1720s are famous for their brilliant, occasionally malicious picture of upper-class English life. Because of her sisterly affection, the letters are intimate and unrestrained. Lady Mar, who lived in Paris with her exiled Jacobite husband, suffered from melancholia that later deepened into insanity; hence Lady Mary tries to cheer her up by pointing to what was most ridiculous in the *beau monde* they both knew.

The scandal she deals with at greatest length is, in fact, her own. It is the dismal history of her involvement with a blackmailing Frenchman named Rémond – an affair which *his* letters prove to have been purely financial and not amatory. But when she turns to the scandal of other people she elevates gossip to art.

Yet from beneath the sparkling surface of these letters sometimes emerge darker feelings. She suffered the deepest despair when her runaway son remained lost – he was on a ship bound for Gibraltar – and she allowed herself to slip into philosophical depression. But not for long. In the same letter, she advises her sister – and herself, we can be sure: 'One should pluck up a spirit, and live upon cordials when one can have no other nourishment.' She was not an unregenerate pessimist.

Her moments of happiness are felicitously expressed. From her country retreat at Twickenham she wrote: 'My time is melted away here in almost perpetual concerts.' In the same setting she gloated over how well she felt 'in this dear minute, in this golden now'. Besides, sturdy common sense kept her from losing her perilous equilibrium. When told that she looked better than ever in her life, she reflected that it was 'one of those lies one is always glad to hear'. In the same mood of comfortable disenchantment, after witnessing the absurd airs of elderly ladies at the Coronation of George II, she, who dreaded 'growing wise more than anything in the world, was overjoyed to observe one can never outlive one's vanity'.

'Egotism is the god that inspires the letter-writer,' George Moore once remarked, 'and good letters are all about the letter-writer.' Lady Mary frequently writes about herself, but with refreshing detachment, free of cloying vanity. No matter how often she philosophizes she is never boring, for she avoids those *longueurs* that so easily infect introspective writers.

Her mind and style have a consonant keenness. Among the critics who have analysed her style, Walter Bagehot awarded her 'the highest merit of letter-writing – she is concise without being affected. . . . She said what she had to say in words that were always graphic and always sufficiently good, but she avoided curious felicity. Her expression seemed choice, but not chosen.' Lytton Strachey praised her for being 'absolutely frank and absolutely sensible. . . . Her wit has that quality which is the best of all preservatives against dullness – it goes straight to the point.'

The most varied and interesting of her informal correspondences is that with her daughter Lady Bute, carried on most abundantly during the decade near the end of her life when she lived in comfortable retirement in northern Italy. Lady Bute served as the focus of a benign affection (unlike the hysterical passion of Madame de Sévigné for her daughter); and Lady Mary took full advantage of what she called her 'maternal privilege of being tiresome'. She practises what George Saintsbury defines as the art of letter-writing – a mosaic or *macedoine* of nearly all departments of general literature: description, narrative, argument; pathos, perhaps; wit, if well managed; and the greatest negative virtue of not being *obviously* 'written for publication'.

As a descriptive artist Lady Mary felt the full beauty of the landscape in the Italian lake country before that region was invaded by tourists armed with albums and water colours. The village of Lovere resembled Tunbridge Wells, she writes, and its gardens, those on Richmond Hill: she frequently makes such comparisons to bring the scene to her correspondent's eye. At other times she is forced to be poetical, and evoke all the 'delightful ideas of romance' or fairy tale. But her description is more effective in concrete terms: near her farm was a little wood 'carpeted, in their succeeding seasons, with violets and strawberries, inhabited by a nation of nightingales, and filled with game of all kinds, excepting deer and wild boar'.

As a social historian she tells of the local gentry, peasants, and artisans, of their diversions on the lake, at the carnival, their opera and theatre productions. Along with her finesse in description – more effective through its casualness – she practises the art of narrative. Here her worldly detachment and wisdom keep her tales from being tedious. Her longest story is 'an adventure exactly resembling, and I believe copied from, *Pamela*'; she sketches it in five (printed) pages, though, she says, it would in Richardson's hands 'furnish out seven or eight volumes'.

It is a masterly narrative; in it the true-life Pamela is depicted as virtuous, modest, and deserving; yet at the end Lady Mary accuses her of 'artifice' and a 'designing head'. This ambivalent attitude, her sympathy and cynicism towards the sentimental, is typical of her opinion of Richardson's novels. Her daughter in England supplied her with books, mostly fiction; and Lady Mary repaid her with (besides drafts on her London bank) long critiques of those books that particularly struck her. As she read *Clarissa Harlowe* and *Sir Charles Grandison* she wept; but then she called them mean, miserable stuff, and violently attacked their picture of upper-class life. 'This Richardson is a strange fellow,' she confessed; 'I heartily despise him, and eagerly read him, nay, sob over his works in a most scandalous manner.' Many years before, she had assisted her cousin Henry Fielding in his career as a playwright; now she commented on his novels and on his sad death, and on Smollett's novels and Johnson's *Rambler*. She read voraciously, and her letters mention more of the ephemeral novels of the 1750s than are listed in modern bibliographies. Here, then, is her literary criticism – fragmentary and disorganized perhaps, but valuable for its acuteness.

Lady Mary also indulged in what she calls 'reflections'; in effect, brief essays on almost any subject. She drew her observations from her surroundings, from her past life so rich in activity, and from the constant reading with which she 'sweetened her solitude'. The theme of retirement naturally engrossed much of what she calls 'thinking upon paper'. 'It was formerly a terrifying view to me, that I should one day be an old woman. I now find that Nature has provided pleasures for every state. Those are only unhappy who will not be contented with what she gives, but strive to break through her laws, by affecting a perpetuity of youth.' She resigned herself to old age and even to death with a stoicism worthy of Epictetus, whom she had once translated.

She looked beyond her own philosophical threshold to generalize on society and mankind. 'I have never in all my various travels seen but two sorts of people, and those very like one another; I mean men and women, who always have been, and ever will be, the same. The same vices and the same follies have been the fruit of all ages, though sometimes under different names.' In her utilitarian view, religion is 'a comfort to the distressed, a cordial to the sick, and sometimes a restraint on the wicked'. As she surveys the history of man she finds great progress since its infancy, but remembers 'the many palpable follies which are still (almost) universally persisted in' – especially war.

She does not set forth any strikingly original philosophical position, but rather what oft was thought but ne'er so well expressed-in-prose, particularly on the topic that engaged so many other minds at this time – the nature of happiness. No real happiness is to be found or expected in this world, and to think it can be secured is as childish as running after sparrows to lay salt on their tails. Lady Mary will never be enrolled among the philosophers of the Enlightenment (particularly since some of her precepts are so unenlightened); but her clear and vivid exposition of the basic assumptions of her time and of her social class gives these casual letters an interest much broader than their modest intent.

All the letters discussed so far are clearly personal and informal; the Turkish Embassy ones, which tell of her experiences and observations while accompanying her husband on his two-year Embassy to Turkey, are relatively impersonal and formal. These, fifty-two in number, were Lady Mary's first published collection and the basis of her initial fame. The problem is whether they can be considered informal letters when they were compiled, and transcribed into an album, by Lady Mary herself. Are they, in other words, a narrative in the form of letters, a very popular form of travel literature since the Renaissance?

They are evidently extracts from her journals (now lost) *and* revisions of actual letters. In one of the letters addressed to her sister she says: 'I am resolved to keep the copies, as testimonies of my inclination to give you, to the utmost of my power, all the diverting part of my travels, while you are exempt from all the fatigues and inconveniences.' And she headed her transcript 'copies'. She altered them, however, removing purely personal references and transposing sections from various letters. As in real letters, the contents are usually appropriate to the correspondent: for example, to Sarah Chiswell, a girlhood friend, Lady Mary addresses a homely description of a Dutch town that resembles Nottingham; to the Princess of Wales, a pathetic account of oppressed peasantry; to Pope, a gracefully modest and clever discourse on Turkish poetry; to the savant Abbé Conti, a witty analysis of the religious sects of Islam; to her 'dear sister', as she repeatedly addresses Lady Mar, her observations of the fabulous luxury surrounding Turkish ladies. The letters, then, are neither actual nor artificial, but something of both; altogether they are virtuoso letters in which she exploited her rich opportunities.

Taken as a whole the collection does have structural elements. It starts with her departure from England, and ends with her return to Dover. The most pervasive pattern, growing out of the nature of her subject matter, is a series of contrasts between western Europe and Turkey; and of contrasts within Europe and within Turkey. The scope of her observations, with their attendant commentaries, is immense; besides such obvious material of tourism as landscapes and buildings (from mosques and palaces to cottages and tree-houses), it includes social life, history, women's dress, religion, marriage and divorce, feminism, and poetry and fable.

In Vienna she observes the mode of gallantry where married ladies are 'served' by men not their husbands (sub-marriage is what she calls it); and at the end of her journey, the same custom in Genoa, under the name of *cicisbeismo*; and in between, she discourses on Turkish marriage, concubines, divorce, and gallantry. In Adrianople she visits an old, devout lady – boring, of course, except for the splendour of her establishment – and then a young, amusing beauty; in Constantinople she again contrasts two such visits. In Sofia she visits a ladies' bagnio and then in Constantinople another. (Her depiction of beautiful Turkish ladies at their bath-ritual inspired the French painter Ingres to compose *Le Bain Turc*.)

Far from showing the smug righteousness of so many travel writers, Lady Mary is unabashedly open-minded. After describing Viennese sub-marriages, she concludes: 'Thus you see, my dear, gallantry and good-breeding are as different, in different climates, as morality and religion. Who have the rightest notions of both, we shall never know till the day of judgment. . . .' The most enlightened Muslims, she also discovers, are no different from sensible English Deists; and after describing a religious sect who go to mosque on Friday and church on Sunday because 'not being skilled in controversy, [they] declare that they are utterly unable to judge which religion is best', she approves of the modest opinion they have of their own capacity. She continued to apply this comparative attitude to everything she observed on her journey; that she was not committed to any standard except reason and common sense allowed her to exploit in full her gift for witty paradox.

One of her striking paradoxes was that the Sultan of the great Ottoman Empire was himself the slave of the military Janissaries. (Voltaire borrowed this observation directly from some of her verse.) Slaves in Turkey were better treated and happier than free servants in England, she notes; and women's confinement in the harem allowed them greater opportunity for infidelity when they emerged effectively disguised by heavy veils and shapeless garments in what she calls 'perpetual masquerade'.

To such unifying themes as religion and feminism, in the Embassy letters, Lady Mary added her literary interests, particularly in those letters addressed to Pope. In Vienna she describes the theatre and opera. In Adrianople she observes the manners and customs of Theocritus and Homer still flourishing; and after translating a Turkish love poem literally, she transposes it freely into equivalent English. Her most elaborate literary letter is a long one (addressed to the Abbé Conti) about her voyage through the Mediterranean. It is in that latter that she exclaims: ' 'Tis impossible to imagine anything more agreeable than this journey would have been between two and three thousand years since, when, after drinking a dish of tea with Sappho, I might have gone the same evening to visit the temple of Homer in Chios, and have passed this voyage in taking plans of magnificent temples, delineating the miracles of statuaries, and conversing with the most polite and most gay of human kind.' This passage may conjure up an amusing tea-party, but it also shows how vitally and intimately she felt the force of classical civilization.

In general, she did not use automatic devices to begin and end her letters. She did not rely on formulas, but adapted the form to the occasion and the recipient. Her salutations and conclusions are so casual and spontaneous that they escape attention. She is fond, however, of ending on a humorous note. One of her frequent conclusions is a variant of: 'This letter is of a horrible length, but you may burn it when you have read enough.' This warning always comes, not at the beginning or middle, but at the very end of the letter.

Compared to her unequivocally actual letters, these Embassy ones may seem exhibitionistic and self-conscious; but how well she succeeded in her purpose: to amuse and instruct her correspondents – and ultimate readers! For we, more than two centuries later, are spared moral qualms – if we have any – about whether it is proper to read other people's private letters. Lady Mary wished these to be published – and thus to be read by a wider circle than friends and family; indeed to be enjoyed by readers not confined to only one continent and one generation. The reader today can equally enjoy her many personal, informal letters not known to readers of previous generations.

PART I

❦

Girlhood and Courtship
1708—1712

❦

Mary Pierrepont was born in London in 1689, the first child of Evelyn Pierrepont and his wife, Lady Mary Fielding. The next year, when her father became Earl of Kingston, she acquired her courtesy title, and for the rest of her life was known as Lady Mary. When she was only three years old her mother died, having borne in rapid succession two other daughters and a son. The children then moved to their grandmother Elizabeth Pierrepont's manor house near Salisbury, where they stayed until her death in 1698; they were then brought up under the supervision of their aunt Lady Cheyne.

When Lady Mary's surviving correspondence begins, in 1708, she was a nineteen-year-old, high-spirited girl whose life followed the conventional pattern of her social class. During the London 'season' she lived at her father's house on Arlington Street, off Picadilly, or at his suburban villa in Acton; and she enjoyed a full share of operas, plays, parties, balls, and visits, as well as attendance at the Royal Drawing Room in St James's Palace. The rest of the year she spent in the country – either at Thoresby, the Pierrepont family seat near Nottingham, or at West Dean, the estate in Wiltshire her father had inherited.

As a young lady whose father was wealthy and prominent (he had been elevated in the peerage as Marquess of Dorchester) Lady Mary was ready for the marriage market – an attractive girl, with bright, dark, animated eyes and a clever wit. Of the suitors who applied for her hand the one whom she regarded most seriously and who became her partner in a long correspondence was her friend Anne Wortley's brother Edward. Their father, Sidney Montagu, had changed his name to Wortley after marrying an heiress of that name, but Edward preferred to use both family names.

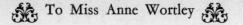

To Miss Anne Wortley

Thoresby, Nottinghamshire, c. 25 August 1708

I am convinced, however dear you are to me, Mrs Anne Wortley, I am no longer of any concern to you; therefore I shall only trouble you with an insignificant story, when I tell you I have been very near leaving this changeable world, but now, by the doctor's assistance and heaven's blessing, am in a condition of being as impertinently troublesome to you as formerly. A sore throat, which plagued me for a long while, brought me at last to such a weakness, you had a fair chance for being released from me, but God has not yet decreed you so much happiness, though I must say this, you have omitted nothing to make yourself so easy, having strove to kill me by neglect. But destiny triumphs over all your efforts; I am yet in the land of the living, and still your

M.P.

To Miss Anne Wortley

Thoresby 8 August 1709

I shall run mad – with what heart can people write, when they believe their letters will never be received? I have already writ you a very long scrawl, but it seems it never came to your hands. I cannot bear to be accused of coldness by one whom I shall love all my life. This will, perhaps, miscarry as the last did; how unfortunate am I if it does! You will think I forget you, who are never out of my thoughts. You will fancy me stupid enough to neglect your letters, when they are the only pleasures of my solitude; in short, you will call me ungrateful and insensible, when I esteem you as I ought, in esteeming you above all the world. If I am not quite so unhappy as I imagine, and you do receive this, let me know it as soon as you can, for till then I shall be in terrible uneasiness; and let me beg you for the future, if you do not receive letters very constantly from me imagine the post-boy killed – imagine the mail burnt – or some other strange accident; you can imagine nothing so impossible as that I forget you, my dear Mrs Wortley.

I know no pretence I have to your good opinion but my heart desiring it. I wish I had that imagination you talk of, to render me a fitter correspondent for you, who can write so well on everything. I am now so much alone I have leisure to pass whole days in reading, but am not at all proper for so delicate an employment as choosing you books. Your own fancy will better direct you. My study at present is nothing but dictionaries and grammars.[1] I am trying whether it be

[1] Lady Mary taught herself Latin in this way.

possible to learn without a master. I am not certain (and dare hardly hope) I shall make any great progress, but I find the study so diverting, I am not only easy but pleased with the solitude that indulges it. I forget there is such a place as London, and wish for no company but yours.

You see, my dear, in making my pleasures consist of these unfashionable diversions I am not of the number who cannot be easy out of the mode. I believe more follies are committed out of complaisance to the world than in following our own inclinations. Nature is seldom in the wrong, custom always. It is with some regret I follow it in all the impertinencies of dress; the compliance is so trivial it comforts me. But I am amazed to see it consulted even in the most important occasions of our lives, and that people of good sense in other things can make their happiness consist in the opinions of others, and sacrifice everything in the desire of appearing in fashion. I call all people who fall in love with furniture, clothes, and equipage, of this number; and I look upon them as no less in the wrong than when they were five years old, and doted on shells, pebbles, and hobby-horses.

I believe you will expect this letter to be dated from the other world, for sure I am you never heard an inhabitant of this talk so before. I suppose you expect, too, I should conclude with begging pardon for this extreme tedious and very nonsensical letter – quite contrary, I think you will be obliged to me for it. I could not better show my great concern for your reproaching me with a neglect I knew myself innocent of, than proving myself mad in three pages.

My sister[2] says a great deal about Mrs K[atherine],[3] but besides my having forgot it the paper is at an end.

[2] Lady Frances Pierrepont, one of Lord Dorchester's three daughters.
[3] Probably Anne Wortley's sister.

❧ To Miss Anne Wortley ❧

I am infinitely obliged to you, my dear Mrs Wortley, for the wit, beauty, and other fine qualities you so generously bestow upon me. Next to receiving them from Heaven you are the person from whom I would choose to receive gifts and graces. I am very well satisfied to owe them to your own delicacy of imagination which represents to you the idea of a fine lady, and you have good nature enough to fancy I am she. All this is mighty well, but you do not stop there. Imagination is boundless — after giving me imaginary wit and beauty you give me imaginary passions, and you tell me I'm in love. If I am, 'tis a perfect sin of ignorance, for I don't so much as know the man's name. I have been studying these three hours, and cannot guess who you mean. I passed the days of Nottingham races[1] at Thoresby, without seeing or even wishing to see one of the sex. Now if I am in love I have very hard fortune to conceal it so industriously from my own knowledge and yet discover it so much to other people. 'Tis against all form to have such a passion as that without giving one sigh for the matter. Pray tell me the name of him I love, that I may (according to the laudable custom of lovers) sigh to the woods and groves hereabouts, and teach it to the echo. You see, being I am in love, I am willing to be so in order and rule; I have been turning over God knows how many books to look for precedents. Recommend an example to me, and above all let me know whether 'tis most proper to walk in the woods, increasing the winds with my sighs, or to sit by a purling stream, swelling the rivulet with my tears; may be, both may do well in their turns. But to be a minute serious, what do you mean by this reproach of inconstancy? I confess you give me several good qualities I have not, and I am ready to thank you for them, but then you must not take away those few I have. No, I will never exchange them. Take back the beauty and wit you bestow upon me; leave me my own mediocrity of agreeableness and genius, but leave me also my sincerity, my constancy, and my plain dealing; 'tis all I have to recommend me to the esteem either of others or myself. How should I despise myself if I could think I was capable of either inconstancy or deceit! I know not how I may appear to other people, nor how much my face may belie my heart, but I know that I never was or can be guilty of dissimulation or inconstancy. You will think this vain, but 'tis all that I pique myself upon. Tell me you believe me and repent of your harsh censure. Tell it me in pity to my uneasiness, for you are one of those few people about whose good opinion I am in pain. I have always took so little care to please the generality of the world that I am never mortified or delighted by its reports, which is a

---

[1] The horse racing at Nottingham was a popular summer diversion for what Daniel Defoe called an 'Illustrious Company', including gaily dressed ladies.

piece of stoicism born with me; but I cannot be one minute easy while you think ill of your faithful

M.P.

This letter is a good deal grave, and, like other grave things, dull; but I won't ask pardon for what I can't help.

To Miss Anne Wortley

Thoresby, 5 September 1709

My dear Mrs Wortley, as she has the entire power of raising, can also, with a word, calm my passions. The kindness of your last recompenses me for the injustice of your former letter; but you cannot sure be angry at my little resentment. You have read that a man who with patience hears himself called heretic can never be esteemed a good Christian. To be capable of preferring the despicable wretch you mention,[1] to Mr Wortley is as ridiculous, if not as criminal, as forsaking the Deity to worship a calf. Don't tell me anybody ever had so mean an opinion of my inclinations; 'tis among the number of those things I would forget. My tenderness is always built upon my esteem, and when the foundation perishes, it falls. I must own, I think it is so with everybody – but enough of this. You tell me it was meant for raillery – was not the kindness meant so too? I fear I am too apt to think what is amusement designed in earnest – no matter; 'tis for my repose to be deceived, and I will believe whatever you tell me.

I should be very glad to be informed of a right method or whether there is such a thing alone but am afraid to ask the question. It may be reasonably called presumption in a girl to have her thoughts that way. You are the only creature that I have made my confidante in that case; I'll assure you I call it the greatest secret of my life. Adieu my dear, the post stays. My next shall be longer.

M.P.

[1] No 'wretch' is named in any of Anne Wortley's surviving letters.

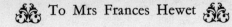

To Mrs Frances Hewet

Arlington Street, London, 13 February 1710

I hope my dear Mrs Hewet does not believe I follow my inclination when I am two or three posts before I return thanks for her most agreeable letters, but in this busy town there is very little time at one's own disposal.

My greatest pleasure is Mrs Selwyn's;[1] I come from thence just now, and I believe am the only young woman in town that am in my own house at ten o'clock tonight. This is the night of Count Tarouca's ball,[2] to which he has invited a few barefaced and the whole town *en masque*. I suppose you'll have a description of the ball from some who were at it; I can only give it at second hand and will therefore say nothing of it.

I have begun to learn Italian and am much mortified I cannot do it of a signor of Monsieur Rasigade's recommendation, but 'tis always the fate of women to obey and my papa has promised me to Mr Casotti. I am afraid I shall never understand it as well as you do, but *laissons cela*, and talk of something more entertaining.

Next to the great ball, what makes the most noise is the marriage of an old maid that lives in this street, without a portion, to a man of £7,000 per annum, and they say £40,000 in ready money. Her equipage and liveries outshine anybody's in town. He has presented her with £3,000 in jewels, and never was man more smitten with these charms that had lain invisible this forty year. But with all this glory, never bride had fewer enviers; the dear beast of a man is so filthy, frightful, odious and detestable I would turn away such a footman for fear of spoiling my dinner while he waited at table. They was married Friday and came to church *en parade* Sunday. I happened to sit in the pew with them and had the honour of seeing Mrs Bride fall fast asleep in the middle of the sermon and snore very comfortably, which made several women in the church think the bridegroom not quite so ugly as they did before. Envious people say 'twas all counterfeited to oblige him, but I believe that's scandal, for she's so devout I dare swear nothing but downright necessity could make her miss one word of the sermon. He professes to have married her for the devotion, patience, meekness and other Christian virtues he observed in her, his first wife (who has left no children) being very handsome and so good natured to have ventured her own salvation to secure his. He has married this to have a companion in that paradise where his first lady has given him a title. I believe I have given you too much of this couple, but they are not to be comprehended in few words.

My dear Mrs Hewet, remember me and believe nothing can put you out of my head.

---

[1] Mrs Hewet's sister Albinia, widow of Major-General William Selwyn.
[2] Conde de Tarouca, Portuguese ambassador to the Netherlands, was in London for diplomatic negotiations.

❧ To Mrs Frances Hewet ❧

ᵀis so long since I had a letter from dear Mrs Hewet I should think her no longer in the land of the living if Mr Rasigade did not assure me he was happier than I, and had heard of your health from your own hand, which makes me fancy that my last miscarried, and perhaps you are blaming me at the same time that you are thinking me neglectful of you. Apropos of Mr Rasigade – we are grown such good friends, I assure you, that we write Italian letters to each other, and I have the pleasure of talking to him of Madame Hewet. He told me he would send you the two *tomes* of Madame du Noyer's *Memoirs*.[1] I fancy you will find yourself disappointed in them, for they are horridly grave and insipid; and instead of the gallantry you might expect they are full of dull morals.

I was last Thursday at the new opera, and saw Nicolini strangle a lion with great gallantry.[2] But he represented nakedness so naturally I was surprised to see those ladies stare at him without any confusion that pretend to be so violently shocked at a poor *double entendre* or two in a comedy, which convinced me that those prudes who would cry fie! fie! at the word *naked* have no scruples about the thing.

The marriage of Lord Willoughby goes on, and he swears he will bring the lady[3] down to Nottingham races. How far it may be true I cannot tell. By what fine gentlemen say, you know it is not easy to guess at what they mean. The lady has made an acquaintance with me after the manner of Pyramus and Thisbe – I mean over a wall three yards high, which separates our garden from Lady Guildford's.[4] The young ladies had found out a way to pull out two or three bricks, and so climb up and hang their chins over the wall where we, mounted on chairs, used to have many *belles conversations a la dérobé* for fear of the old mother. This trade continued several days, but fortune seldom permits long pleasures. By long standing on the wall the bricks loosened, and one fatal morning down drops Miss Nelly, and to complete the misfortune she fell into a little sink and bruised her poor self to that terrible degree, she is forced to have surgeon's plasters and God knows what, which discovered the whole intrigue; and their mamma forbade them ever to visit us but by the door. Since that time all our communications have been made in a vulgar manner, visiting in coaches, etc. etc., which took away half the pleasure. You know, danger gives a *haut goût* to every thing. This is our secret history – pray let it be so still – but I hope all the world will know that I am most entirely yours,   M.P.

[1] Anne Marguerite Petit du Noyer's *Mémoires* (1710).

[2] The famous *castrato* singer, whose real name was Nicolo Grimaldi, had been in England since the autumn of 1708. He won his greatest success as the hero of Francesco Mancini's *Idaspe fedele*, first produced in March 1710, in which he killed a sham lion.

[3] Lord Willoughby (later Duke of Ancaster) was engaged to marry Margaret Brownlow, who lived with her sisters and widowed mother.

[4] Born Alice Brownlow, she was married to Baron Guildford.

✨ To Wortley ✨

Perhaps you'll be surprised at this letter. I have had many debates with myself before I could resolve on it. I know it is not acting in form, but I do not look upon you as I do upon the rest of the world, and by what I do for you, you are not to judge my manner of acting with others. You are brother to a woman I tenderly loved.[1] My protestations of friendship are not like other people's. I never speak but what I mean, and when I say I love, it is for ever. I had that real concern for Mrs Wortley, I look with some regard on every one that is related to her. This and my long acquaintance with you may in some measure excuse what I am now doing.

I am surprised at one of the *Tatlers* you sent me. Is it possible to have any sort of esteem for a person one believes capable of having such trifling inclinations? Mr Bickerstaffe has very wrong notions of our sex.[2] I can say there are some of us that despise charms of show and all the pageantry of greatness, perhaps with more ease than any of the philosophers. In contemning the world they seem to take pains to contemn it. We despise it, without taking the pains to read lessons of morality to make us do it. At least I know I have always looked upon it with contempt without being at the expense of one serious reflection to oblige me to it. I carry the matter yet farther. Was I to choose of £2,000 a year or £20,000 the first would be my choice. There is something of an unavoidable *embarras* in making what is called a great figure in the world that takes off from the happiness of life. I hate the noise and hurry inseparable from great estates and titles, and look upon both as blessings that ought only to be given to fools, for 'tis only to them that they are blessings.

The pretty fellows you speak of, I own entertain me sometimes, but is it impossible to be diverted with what one despises? I can laugh at a puppet-show at the same time I know there is nothing in it worth my attention or regard. General notions are generally wrong. Ignorance and folly are thought the best foundations for virtue, as if not knowing what a good wife is, was necessary to make one so. I confess that can never be my way of reasoning. As I always forgive an injury when I think it not done out of malice, I can never think myself obliged by what is done without design. Give me leave to say it (I know it sounds vain): I know how to make a man of sense happy, but then that man must resolve to contribute something towards it himself. I have so much esteem for you I should be very sorry to hear you was unhappy, but for the world I would not be the instrument of making you so, which (of the humour you are) is hardly to be avoided if I am your wife.

---

[1] Anne Wortley had died since the previous autumn.
[2] Isaac Bickerstaffe was the character Steele assumed in the *Tatler*. His essay on women's frivolity appeared on 9 March 1710.

You distrust me. I can neither be easy nor loved where I am distrusted, nor do I believe your passion for me is what you pretend it; at least I'm sure, was I in love I could not talk as you do.

Few women would have spoke so plainly as I have done, but to dissemble is among the things I never do. I take more pains to approve my conduct to myself than to the world, and would not have to accuse myself of a minute's deceit. I wish I loved you enough to devote myself to be for ever miserable for the pleasure of a day or two's happiness. I cannot resolve upon it – you must think otherwise of me or not at all.

I don't enjoin you to burn this letter; I know you will.[3] 'Tis the first I ever writ to one of your sex and shall be the last. You must never expect another. I resolve against all correspondence of this kind. My resolutions are seldom made and never broken.

[3] Not only did Wortley not burn the letter; he made a careful copy.

❧ To Wortley ❧

Acton, 25 April 1710

I have this minute received your two letters. I know not how to direct to you, whether to London or the country, or if in the country to Durham or Wortley. 'Tis very likely you'll never receive this. I hazard a great deal if it falls into other hands, and I write for all that.

I wish with all my soul I thought as you do. I endeavour to convince myself by your arguments, and am sorry my reason is so obstinate not to be deluded into an opinion that 'tis impossible a man can esteem a woman. I suppose I should then be very easy at your thoughts of me. I should thank you for the wit and beauty you give me and not be angry at the follies and weaknesses, but to my infinite affliction I can believe neither one nor t'other. One part of my character is not so good nor the other so bad as you fancy it. Should we ever live together you would be disappointed both ways; you would find an easy equality of temper you do not expect, and a thousand faults you do not imagine. You think if you married me I should be passionately fond of you one month and of somebody else the next. Neither would happen. I can esteem, I can be a friend, but I don't know whether I can love. Expect all that is complaisant and easy, but never what is fond in me. You judge very wrong of my heart when you suppose me capable of views of interest, and that anything could oblige me to flatter anybody. Was I the most indigent creature in the world I should answer you as I do now, without adding or diminishing. I am incapable of art, and 'tis because I will not be capable of it. Could I deceive one minute I should never regain my own good opinion, and who could bear to live with one they despised?

If you can resolve to live with a companion that will have all the deference due to your superiority of good sense, and that your proposals can be agreeable to those on whom I depend – I have nothing to say against them.

As to travelling, 'tis what I should do with great pleasure, and could easily quit London upon your account, but a retirement in the country is not so disagreeable to me as I know a few months would make it tiresome to you. Where people are tied for life 'tis their mutual interest not to grow weary of one another. If I had all the personal charms that I want, a face is too slight a foundation for happiness. You would be soon tired with seeing every day the same thing, where you saw nothing else. You would have leisure to remark all the defects, which would increase in proportion as the novelty lessened, which is always a great charm. I should have the displeasure of seeing a coldness, which though I could not reasonably blame you for, being involuntary, yet it would render me uneasy, and the more because I know a love may be revived which absence, inconstancy, or even infidelity has extinguished, but there is no returning from a *dégoût* given by satiety.

I should not choose to live in a crowd. I could be very well pleased to be in London without making a great figure or seeing above eight or nine agreeable people. Apartments, table, etc. are things that never come into my head. But I will never think of anything without the consent of my family, and advise you not to fancy a happiness in entire solitude, which you would find only fancy.

Make no answer to this. If you can like me on my own terms, 'tis not to me you must make your proposals. If not, to what purpose is our correspondence?

However, preserve me your friendship, which I think of with a great deal of pleasure and some vanity. If ever you see me married, I flatter myself you'll see a conduct you would not be sorry your wife should imitate.

To Wortley

Your indiscretion has given me so much trouble I would willingly get rid of it at the price of my fever's returning. You employed the foolishest and most improper messenger upon earth.[1] She has prattled all she knows, and all she supposed, which goes a great deal farther. 'Tis not her custom to make secrets of names. Everything is known but my innocence, which is never to be cleared. I could justify myself in part by showing your letters. I could not resolve to do what I thought not right, and burnt them to prevent their being seen, which was otherwise unavoidable.

How unhappy am I! I think I have been scrupulously just to my duty. I cannot so much as call to mind an expression I have cause to blame myself for, but I am not the less unfortunate. All commerce of this kind between men and women is like that of the boys and frogs in L'Estrange's *Fables*. 'Tis play to you, but 'tis death to us – and if we had the wit of the frogs we should always make that answer.[2]

I am mighty happy in Mr Steele and his wife knowing this affair. He over a bottle and she over a tea-table has (I don't question) said many witty things upon this occasion. My answers have not (by great good fortune) passed their hands. On second thoughts I half wish they had. To be sure, they do you justice in supposing I would answer them, and perhaps me the injustice in supposing them other than they was, without authority for it. I find 'tis in your power to exclude me the town. If I was as fond of it as you think me, I should be very angry at the cause of my going into a frightful solitude[3] instead of returning to London, where my family is now persuaded I have behaved myself very ill. Were I disposed to tell the whole story it would do me no good. They have reason to believe my vanity or worse has been more the cause of this business than any honourable design you had on me.

Your last letter (which came safe to me by miracle) I don't understand a word of, nor what letter you speak of. I writ you one to the Deanery of Durham. It had no name to it, and was in the same hand as the first. I fear you never received it. I know of no other.

My sickness was more dangerous than you think it. I have not lived very long in the world, but begin to be weary of it, and in the situation I am in, am very sorry I'm recovered.

---

[1] Betty Laskey, a servant in Lady Mary's house, was kept busy carrying messages between her and Wortley.

[2] 'A company of waggish boys were watching of frogs at the side of a pond, and still as any of them put up their heads, they'd be pelting them down again with stones. Children (says one of the frogs) you never consider, that though this may be play to you, 'tis death to us' (Roger L'Estrange's version of Aesop's fable).

[3] At West Dean, near Salisbury, a manor house owned by her father.

[*Postscripts*] By an indiscreet resentment to the foolish creature you employed, do not expose me to her tongue.

Make no attempts of writing. Either think of me no more, or think in the way you ought.

🎕 To Wortley 🎕

West Dean, Wiltshire, 20 July 1710

Thursday

I received two letters from you this afternoon. The first I opened was dated Saturday noon and pleased me so well I wish I had not opened the second, writ from Hartford Bridge, which seems out of humour with me. How can you be so? Perhaps I am to blame, but is there nothing to be forgiven to a woman's fears? I own I am a coward; I tremble at everything. Forgive me; if I injure your fortune any way, I do not deserve you should. You speak of losing £20,000. Lose nothing for me. I set you free from any engagement you may think yourself under. 'Tis too generous that you take me with nothing; I can never deserve even that sacrifice. You shall not however have to reproach yourself or me that I have lessened your fortune. You do not know how much I think myself obliged for what you have already done. I would make you any return in my power. I beg you sincerely if you find that the disobliging your father will be of consequence to you, and that it is unavoidable if you do it, leave me. I shall blame nothing but my own fears, that to silly niceties sacrificed all my happiness. Perhaps that understanding you compliment me with, should we come to be better acquainted, you would find yourself deceived in, and the silly woman appear in many instances. But I am honest; I would do right. I am naturally generous, though I have no opportunities of showing it, and I could never forgive myself (of all mankind) an injury to you.

I cannot answer that part of your letter which regards Mr ——. There is no judging what fools are capable of, and in what manner he will behave himself upon any occasion. As to my father, 'tis just the same thing how I do it. He will never see me more, and he will give me nothing, let me do it in what way I will. Your next letter shall guide me. I once more entreat you to do nothing but entirely with your own consent. Put me out of the case, and think what is best of yourself. After that point is settled consider me a little. Think if you can always speak after the manner you do in your Saturday's letter. Were you always to be so kind to me I should always think myself happy. Should you ever be uneasy with me, should you ever give me reason to think you repented, there would be nothing more unhappy than me.

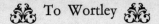

West Dean, Wiltshire, 20 August 1710

I never thought to hear from you more. 'Tis impossible to tell you my surprise. What would you have me say? There is a great deal of generosity and good nature in your letter, but I know not how to answer it.[1]

I will show you a confidence that will convince you I am at least very sincere in my friendship. I am told my brother is going to marry a great fortune.[2] £10,000 is to be settled on me, without its being possible to be recalled by anyone. A single woman may live very well on that money. The dispute I have at present with myself is whether I will or will not marry at all. Now in my opinion you are very much obliged to me that it is a dispute. I should not hesitate upon many proposals. Was I sure that you would live after a way agreeable to me, I should not be long in making my answer. But if instead of travelling, the fancy should take you to confine me to the country, I could bear solitude, but perhaps not when it was for life, and I had much rather be my own mistress as long as I live. If you really intend to travel, as it is the thing upon earth I should most wish, I should prefer that manner of living to any other; and with the utmost sincerity I confess I should choose you before any match could be offered me.

I think I have said a thing so favourable I ought to be ashamed of it. If you expect passion I am utterly unacquainted with any. It may be a fault of my temper. 'Tis a stupidity I could never justify, but I do not know I was in my life ever touched with any. I have no notion of a transport of anger, love, or any other. I here tell you the plain state of my heart, and more than I shall ever think it worth my while to tell another. I believe if I could dissemble I should please you better, but you must have some esteem for a woman that will not dissemble though to please.

I think I have said enough, and as much as ought to be expected. Flights of passion I neither know how to feel or to counterfeit. I have no hand in the making of settlements. My present duty is to obey my father. I shall so far obey blindly as not to accept where he refuses, though perhaps I might refuse where he would accept. If you think tolerably of me, you think I would not marry where I hated. As for the rest, my father may do some things disagreeable to my inclinations, but passive obedience is a doctrine should always be received among wives and daughters. That principle makes me cautious who I set for my master. I ought, and I hope I should, obey a severe one, but severity

---

1 Before sailing off for a long holiday at the Spa in Belgium, Wortley had written to Lady Mary informing her that his negotiations with her father had finally broken down, but asking her to write to him in his absence.
2 Lady Mary's only brother, William, Earl of Kingston, was married in May 1711.

is never so terrible as where it meets with a temper not made to resist. I have a softness that would make me perfectly wretched.

My letter is already very long. Adieu, Sir. If you think me worth your taking, it can be on no other terms than those of my father. If not, I wish you all the happiness imaginable, and that your future wife (whoever she is to be) may not be one of those ladies so very free of their expressions of tenderness, at best withering, generally false. You would like her manner better than you do mine till time convinced you of your mistake, but I rather choose to wish you a happiness more lasting.

You did very right in directing to that maid; any other way it would have miscarried. It is not from severity I beg you to write no more. I should think your correspondence a pleasure if it was among the number of the permitted. But you know it is forbidden, and I am in pain when I do anything that must be a secret.

You conclude yours with something about power. I know none that I have, or if that was possible would I use it to your prejudice.

✂ To Wortley ✂

West Dean, Wiltshire, c. 22 August 1710

Reading over your letter as fast as ever I could, and answering it with the same ridiculous precipitation, I find, one part of it escaped my sight, and the other I mistook in several places. Yours was dated the 10th of August; it came not hither till the 20th. You say something of a pacquet boat, etc. makes me uncertain whether you'll receive my letter and frets me heartily.

Kindness, you say, would be your destruction. In my opinion this is something contradictory to some other expressions. People talk of being in love just as widows do of affliction. Mr Steele has observed in one of his plays, the most passionate amongst them has always calmness enough to drive a hard bargain with the upholders.[1] I never knew a lover that would not willingly secure his interest as well as his mistress, or if one must be abandoned had not the prudence (amongst all his distractions) to consider, a woman was but a woman, and money was a thing of more real merit than the whole sex put together. Your letter is to tell me you should think yourself undone if you married me, but if I would be so tender to confess I should break my heart if you did not, then you'd consider whether you would or no, but yet you hoped you should not. I take this to be the right interpretation of: – even your

---

[1] In Steele's comedy *The Funeral: or, Grief A-la-mode* (1701) an undertaker (upholder) remarks that sorrowful widows drive hard bargains.

kindness can't destroy me of a sudden, I hope I am not in your power, I would give a good deal to be satisfied, etc.

As to writing, that any woman would do that, that thought she writ well; now I say, no woman of common good sense would. At best 'tis but doing a silly thing well, and I think 'tis much better not to do a silly thing at all. You compare it to dressing. Suppose the comparison just: perhaps the Spanish dress would become my face very well, yet the whole town would condemn me for the highest extravagance if I went to court in't, though it improved me to a miracle. There are a thousand things not ill in themselves which custom makes unfit to be done.

This is to convince you I am so far from applauding my own conduct, my conscience flies in my face every time I think on't. The generality of the world have a great indulgence to their own follies. Without being a jot wiser than my neighbours I have the peculiar misfortune to know and condemn all the wrong things I do.

You beg to know whether I would not be out of humour. The expression is modest enough, but that is not what you mean in saying I could be easy. I have already said I should not be out of humour. But you would have me say I am violently in love. That is, finding you think better of me than you desire, you would have me give you a just cause to contemn me. I doubt much whether there is a creature in the world humble enough to do that. I should not think you more unreasonable if you was in love with my face and asked me to disfigure it to make you easy. I have heard of some nuns that made use of that expedient to secure their own happiness, but amongst all the popish saints and martyrs I never read of one whose charity was sublime enough to make themselves deformed or ridiculous to restore their lovers to peace and quietness. In short, if nothing can content you but despising me heartily, I am afraid I shall be always so barbarous to wish you may esteem me as long as you live.

Indeed I do not at all wonder that absence and variety of new faces should make you forget me, but I am a little surprised at your curiosity to know what passes in my heart (a thing wholly insignificant to you) except you propose to yourself a piece of ill-natured satisfaction in finding me very much disquieted. Pray, which way would you see into my heart? You can frame no guesses about it from either my speaking or writing, and supposing I should attempt to show it you, I know no other way.

I begin to be tired of my humility. I have carried my complaisances to you farther than I ought. You make new scruples, you have a great deal of fancy, and your distrusts being all of your own making are more immovable than if there was some real ground for them. Our aunts and grandmothers always tell us men are a sort of animals, that if ever they are constant 'tis only where they are ill used. 'Twas a kind of paradox I could never believe. Experience has taught me the truth of it. You are the first I ever had a correspondence with, and I thank God I have done with it for all my life. You needed not to have told me you are not what you have been. – One must be stupid not to find a difference in your letters. You seem in one part of your last to excuse yourself from having done me any injury in point of fortune. Do I accuse you of any?

I have not spirits to dispute any longer with you. You say you are not yet determined. Let me determine for you and save you the trouble of writing again. Adieu for ever. Make no answer. I wish amongst the variety of acquaintance you may find some one to please you, and can't help the vanity of thinking, should you try them all, you won't find one that will be so sincere in their treatment, though a thousand more deserving, and every one happier. 'Tis a piece of vanity and injustice I never forgive in a woman to delight to give pain. What must I think of a man that takes pleasure in making me uneasy? After the folly of letting you know it is in your power I ought in prudence to let this go no farther, except I thought you had good nature enough never to make use of that power. I have no reason to think so. However, I am willing, you see, to do you the highest obligation 'tis possible for me to do; that is, to give you a fair occasion of being rid of me.

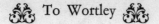 To Wortley

London, *26 February 1711*

I intended to make no answer to your letter. It was something very ungrateful, and I resolved to give over all thoughts of you. I could easily have performed that resolve some time ago, but then you took pains to please me. Now you have brought me to esteem you, you make use of that esteem to give me uneasiness, and I have the displeasure of seeing I esteem a man that dislikes me. Farewell then, since you will have it so. I renounce all the ideas I have so long flattered myself with, and will entertain my fancy no longer with the imaginary pleasure of pleasing you. How much wiser are all them women I have despised than myself! In placing their happiness in trifles they have placed it in what is attainable. I fondly thought fine clothes and gilt coaches, balls, operas and public adoration rather the fatigues of life, and that true happiness was justly defined by Mr Dryden (pardon the romantic air of repeating verses) when he says,

> Whom heaven would bless it does from pomps remove,
> And makes their wealth in privacy and love.[1]

These notions had corrupted my judgement as much as Mrs Biddy Tipkin's.[2] According to this scheme, I proposed to pass my life with you. I yet do you the justice to believe if any man could have been contented with this manner of living, it would have been you. Your indifference to me does not hinder me from thinking you capable of tenderness and the happinesses of friendship. But I find 'tis not to me you'll ever have them. You think me all that is detestable. You accuse me of want of sincerity and generosity. To convince you of your mistake I'll show you the last extremes of both.

While I foolishly fancied you loved me (which I confess I had never any great reason for, more than that I wished it) there is no condition of life I could not have been happy in with you, so very much I liked you. I may say loved, since 'tis the last thing I'll ever say to you. This is telling you sincerely my greatest weakness, and now I will oblige you with a new proof of generosity – I'll never see you more. I shall avoid all public places, and this is the last letter I shall send. If you write, be not displeased if I send it back unopened. I shall force my inclinations to oblige yours, and remember that you have told me I could not oblige you more than by refusing you. Had I intended ever to see you again I durst not have sent this letter. Adieu.

[1] The closing lines (slightly altered) of John Dryden's *Aureng-zebe* (1676), Act III.

[2] The heroine of Steele's *The Tender Husband* (1703); her reading filled her head with high-flown notions of romantic love.

I thought to return no answer to your letter, but I find I am not so wise as I thought myself. I cannot forbear fixing my mind a little on that expression, though perhaps the only insincere one in your whole letter. – I would die to be secure of your heart though but for a moment. – Were this but true, what is there I would not do to secure you?

I will state the case to you as plainly as I can, and then ask yourself if you use me well. I have showed in every action of my life an esteem for you that at least challenges a grateful regard. I have trusted my reputation in your hands. I have made no scruple of giving you under my own hand an assurance of my friendship. After all this I exact nothing from you. If you find it inconvenient for your affairs to take so small a fortune I desire you to sacrifice nothing to me. I pretend no tie upon your honour; but in recompense for so clear and so disinterested a proceeding, must I ever receive injuries and ill usage?

I have not the usual pride of my sex. I can bear being told I am in the wrong, but tell it me gently. Perhaps I have been indiscreet; I came young into the hurry of the world. A great innocence and an undesigning gaiety may possibly have been construed coquetry and a desire of being followed, though never meant by me. I cannot answer for the [reflections] that may be made on me – all the malicious attack the careless and defenceless. I own myself to be both. I know not anything I can say more to show my perfect desire of pleasing you and making you easy than to proffer to be confined with you in what manner you pleased. Would any woman but me renounce all the world for one, or would any man but you be insensible of such a proof of sincerity?

❧ To Miss Philippa Mundy ❧

I begin to discover that I am cursed proud, which amongst my other innumerable faults I never found out before. Nothing else, dear Phil, could hinder me from answering your letters the minute I receive them, but I find I must have many ejaculations for the grace of humility before I can bring down my proud stomach to convince you, in reality, I am very dull and stupid, which I am now forced to do, if I write at all. At length I am content to show my infirmities, especially being bribed by the agreeableness of your letter. The hopes of such another shall prevail, though at the same time 'tis mortifying enough to see you so capable of diverting me, while the greatest power I can have over you is to lull you to sleep. Such is my indolent state, I am hardly to be waked by animating hopes and fears, the ideas of things past grow faint and languid, and my imagination grows so dull I cannot form to myself one pleasing castle, my reason not being able to furnish me with one probable foundation. Thus are all my faculties so stupefied that I don't think it at all proper, in speaking of myself, to say me, but that which once was me, being dead to almost all intents and purposes.

My dear Phil, if your star carries you to London, the first step to Paradise,[1] remember your friends in distress, and once sisters in affliction, and write often to me, in spite of interruptions and temptations to the contrary. Wherever you are, continue to me your remembrance and correspondence, as I shall ever my friendship and desire (if I am denied other ways) to serve you. So may [you prove] an image of the first design of our creation (as the parsons say) and live in Paradise till you remove to heaven.

---

[1] In the private language used by the two young ladies, Paradise meant being married to a man one loved, Hell to a man one detested, and Limbo or Purgatory to a man one merely tolerated.

To Miss Philippa Mundy

I am glad, dear Phil, that you begin to find peace in this world. I despair of it, God knows; the Devil to pull, and a father to drive, and yet – I don't believe I shall go to Hell for all that, though I have no more hope of Paradise than if I was dead and buried a 1,000 fathom. To say truth, I have been this ten days in debate whether I should hang or marry, in which time I have cried some two hours every day and knocked my head against the wall some fifteen times. 'Tis yet doubtful which way my resolution will finally carry me.

So much for my own affairs; as to my advice concerning yours, you know it already. Scruples and demurs are as fatal to some young women as the flesh and Devil to others, and there are some proverbs written for our edification, as faint heart, etc., nothing venture nothing have, and more of the same nature. You know where you may have a faithful messenger – I say no more, you understand me.

Dear Phil, infuse into me notions of moderate happiness. I am yet so miserable to be incapable of Limbo, and such an infidel I cannot persuade myself there is any such place in the Creation. I rave of nothing but fire and brimstone, God help me. For you, if you do abandon hopes of the pretty Paradise you once placed your heaven in, however, may you find another flowing with milk and honey, as charming, as enchanting, and every way worthy of such a lovely Eve.

To Miss Philippa Mundy

Your obliging interesting letters, dear Phil, are some consolation to a poor distracted wretch of wretches. My head and my heart are both very full at this instant. I shall stay in the country all winter. I have only such dark and dismal prospects of futurity, I cannot raise my spirits to build one dear castle. My will is still good to serve you, but fortune never fails to put it out of my power to do anything I propose a pleasure in doing.

'Tis yet dubious whether I go to Hell or no, but while I delay between doubting and choosing, here I stay spending the irretrievable days of youth in looking upon withered trees and stone walls. I have generosity enough, dear Phil, to wish you in London, though I have no hopes of meeting you there; but when you are in the playhouse, I don't question one powerful glance can recall any heart

> – if it can be
> That any Lover can be false to thee –[1]

and fix it ever yours.

If predestination carries me to Hell (nothing else can), it will be a sort of comfort even there to look up and see you in Heaven, and I shall taste of happiness by reflection. The consideration you mention goes a great way in tempting me to prefer common Hell to the uncommon joined to my despair of Paradise. I'm afraid I jog on to the Devil. – Mercy on me!

Dear Phil, if your good fortune brings you to happy London town, don't forget your quondam sister in affliction. Write often, long and comforting letters, to your poor, distressed yet ever faithful friend,

M.P.

[1] Adapted from verse by Lord Lansdown.

To Miss Philippa Mundy

Thoresby, 12 December 1711

I am glad, dear Phil, you still retain hopes of seeing London. I begin to think of it as I have done of Salisbury steeple when I took the air upon the downs at four year old, that it runs away from me.

You penetrate to the very bottom of my heart, my dear. I have a mortal aversion to be an old maid; and a decayed oak before my window leafless, half rotten, and shaking its withered top, puts me in mind every morning of an antiquated virgin, bald, with rotten teeth, and shaking of the palsy. Since therefore Hell must be, why not now? These cruel reflections have nothing to do with your fortune. Paradise is in your view, fresh, young and blooming. Write but to him with half the spirit, life, and agreeableness you do to me, and 'tis impossible but you must attain it, at least if he has the good taste I don't doubt him master of.

Neither have you any reason to repeat that dismal poesie you do – rather remember:

> Ill grounded passions quickly wear away,
> What's built upon esteem can ne'er decay.

I prophesy nothing but happiness if he either sees or hears from you. He can neither resist your eyes or pen, but absence and silence are capable of wearing out the strongest impressions. My dear, I heartily thank you for your good wishes to serve me; a little rats' bane is all the remedy can be given me. For want of that I go to Hell – fire, brimstone, frosts and burnings, favours, a parson and wedding clothes. – Adieu, my head turns with these mixtures, but always fixed in being faithfully yours.

To Mrs Frances Hewet

Arlington Street, c. *8 March 1712*

I do not doubt but that before this time my dear Mrs Hewet has a thousand times called me ungrateful, and as often repented of the many kindnesses she has done me in the country. *Les apparences sont trompeuses* – I am as much your servant as ever, and think of you with the friendship and acknowledgment I owe you. A train of disagreeable events have hindered my having one leisure moment, and at this very time my poor head is distracted with such a variety of *galimatias* that I cannot tell you one bit of news. The fire I suppose you have had a long and true account of, though not perhaps that we were raised at three o'clock and kept waking 'till five by the most dreadful sight I ever saw in my life. It was near enough to fright all our servants half out of their senses; however, we escaped better than some of our neighbours.[1] Mrs Braithwayte, a Yorkshire beauty, who had been but two days married to a Mr Coleman, ran out of bed *en chemise*, and her husband followed her in his, in which pleasant dress they ran as far as St James's Street, where they met with a chair and prudently crammed themselves both into it, observing the rule of dividing the good and bad fortune of this life, resolved to run all hazards together, and ordered the chairmen to carry them both away, perfectly representing both in love and nakedness and want of eyes to see that they were naked, our first happy parents. Sunday last I had the pleasure of hearing the whole history from the lady's own mouth.

The next most extraordinary adventure is the famous quarrel between

[1] The house of Sir William Wyndham in Albemarle Street burned down 2 March 1712. In the confusion two maids who jumped from a window were killed.

her Grace of Hamilton with Captain Hero; but I suppose you cannot be ignorant of so surprising an event.[2]

Deaths nor marriages I know of none, but Sir Stephen Evance,[3] that hanged himself, and my sister Evelyn, who will be married next week.[4] The post bell rings; my next shall be longer, with some account of your fair family.

[2] The wife of the Duke of Hamilton quarrelled with James O'Hara 'at the playhouse ... so loud, that everybody heard it, with such language as is seldom used but at Billingsgate, and he taking it in the best manner that could be laughing extremely at her' (*Wentworth Papers*).

[3] Well-known goldsmith and jeweller who went bankrupt at the beginning of 1712. According to another contemporary source, he shot himself.

[4] Lady Evelyn Pierrepont married John Leveson-Gower, Baron Gower.

To Miss Philippa Mundy

London, April 1712

If your Paradise (dear Phil) could see your last letter, so much softness and good sense would certainly show him the folly he has committed, so plainly as to make him hang himself.

My reflections on the general inconstancy and ingratitude of men proceed from no experience in my own affairs. I should be happier than I am if I had not too much reason to think too well of one of them. I see no probable prospect of my ever entering charming Paradise, but since I cannot convince him of the necessity of what I do I rack myself in giving him pain. This is the real state of my heart, which is now so much perplexed and divided I change resolves every three minutes. The apparent impossibility of dear Paradise often makes me resolve to plunge to Hell and lose the thought forever. Sometimes I am on the point of determining to lead apes,[1] though I have much reason to fear the consequence of that will be a settlement in the country, and then perhaps after that mighty sacrifice I may find myself at one time withered and forgotten. These alternate thoughts fight battles in my breast; meantime I see daily preparations for my journey to Hell.[2] Something I must resolve on suddenly. – My head is so perplexed I forgot to tell you I have made inquiries concerning your murderess. Nobody says she is an agreeable woman. I suppose you know she was a great fortune, and married him for love.

[1] That is, to remain a spinster.

[2] Her father had engaged her to Clotworthy Skeffington, M.P., son and heir of Viscount Massereene.

❧❧ To Wortley ❧❧

I was never more surprised in my life than at seeing a letter from you.[1] I am willing to believe only curiosity made me weak enough to receive it.

In the whole course of your commerce with me I do not think you have always done right to me, but I do not think you have ever deceived me. Whatever you have to ask me I shall answer you with the greatest sincerity. Nothing can be more hazardous than meeting you, but I am willing to remove some mistakes of your letter. Indian houses[2] are too public, nor at all proper for a long conversation. I will go Tuesday between six and seven to Sir Godfrey Kneller's.[3] I set a real value on your friendship, and hope I shall never lose it.

[1] Apparently the first in over a year.
[2] Shops where Indian goods were sold.
[3] The most fashionable portrait painter of the day, Kneller painted several portraits of Lady Mary, the first in 1710.

❧❧ To Wortley ❧❧

London, 11 June 1712

I was at Sir Godfrey Kneller's yesterday a quarter after seven. It was so long after the time I had named I went almost without expecting you, but I was unavoidably hindered coming sooner. I cannot go there again soon without giving suspicion to my companion. If I should meet you in a private house I must trust the mistress of it, and I know nobody I dare trust. A formal visit will not permit us to talk. I cannot speak to you but before witnesses, and I choose rather to tell you in this way that your letter seems founded on a mistake. I did not ask you to write, nor desire to see you. As my circumstances are, I know no use it can be to me. I am very far from a thought of what you seem to hint at the end of your letter. My family is resolved to dispose of me where I hate. I have made all the opposition in my power; perhaps I have carried that opposition too far. However it is, things were carried to that height, I have been assured of never having a shilling except I comply. Since the time of Mandane's we have heard of no ladies ran away with, without fortunes.[1] That threat would not have obliged me to consent if it had

[1] Mandane was the heroine of Madeleine de Scudéry's romance *Artamène ou le Grand Cyrus* (1649–53), who in the course of the long tale is abducted several times before being won by Cyrus.

not been joined with an assurance of making my maiden life as miserable as lay in their power; that is so much in their power I am compelled to submit. – I was born to be unhappy, and I must fulfill the course of my destiny.

You see, Sir, the esteem I have for you. I have ventured to tell you the whole secret of my heart. 'Tis for the last time I indulge myself in complaints that in a little while will become indecent. By this real and sincere account of my affairs you may see I have no design of any engagement beyond friendship with you, since should we agree, 'tis now impossible, my fortune only following my obedience.

'Tis utterly inconvenient for you to write to me; I know no safe way of conveying a letter to me. After this long account, I don't suppose you have any farther inquiries to make, nor in my wretched circumstances is there room for advice. If you have anything to say (though I cannot imagine what it should be) I will be at Coleman's Friday between four and five. I cannot be more exact; it may be very soon after four, or very near five. If you have nothing to say, or that now you know the true state of my affairs you find advice can be of no importance, do not come. I shall ever think you my friend, and never give you occasion to be otherwise. My business is now to behave myself with my fortune in a manner to show I do not deserve it.

To Miss Philippa Mundy

London, 15 July 1712

You are, however, tolerably happy, my dear Phil, since Limbo is like to be your fate, and Paradise not obstructing your passage since he has rendered himself unworthy of that name.

> But I th'unhappiest of womankind
> No help can hope, no remedy can find,
> But doomed to drag a restless life in care,
> And all my pleasures poisoned with despair.

This quotation suits me too justly. I confess to you the supplications of Paradise and the pain I saw him in at length raised my spirit to oppose vigorously my progress to Hell, but all my opposition was vain, and all the difference I could obtain was making it yet worse. Instead of going I shall be dragged to the lowest of Hells, without the pleasure of satisfying Paradise, who would persuade me to continue resisting.[1] 'Tis

---

[1] On 19 July her friend Mrs Hewet wrote to the Duchess of Newcastle: 'Lady Mary Pierrepont is not yet married but is to be very soon . . .'.

certain the worst could befall me would be eternal confinement. But you that have some degree of knowledge of that kind of life can judge what a terrible thing it must be forever since I can see no kind of probability of my entering Paradise except miracles happen; but if miracles should happen – distraction and despair! – I shall curse myself for not preferring every suffering to what I am now going to do.

This is a long account of my affairs; I hope you will be as free in communicating yours. Be assured, my dear Phil, you cannot do it to a friend more entirely yours than

M.P.

🎀 To Wortley 🎀

London, c. 26 July 1712

I am going to write you a plain long letter. What I have already told you is nothing but the truth. I have no reason to believe I am going to be otherwise confined than by my duty, but I, that know my own mind, know that is enough to make me miserable. I see all the misfortune of marrying where it is impossible to love. I am going to confess a weakness that may perhaps add to your contempt of me. I wanted courage to resist at first the will of my relations, but as every day added to my fears, those at last grew strong enough to make me venture the disobliging them. A harsh word damps my spirits to a degree of silencing all I have to say. I knew the folly of my own temper, and took the method of writing to the disposer of me. I said everything in this letter I thought proper to move him, and proffered in atonement for not marrying whom he would, never to marry at all. He did not think fit to answer this letter, but sent for me to him. He told me he was very much surprised that I did not depend on his judgement for my future happiness, that he knew nothing I had to complain of etc., that he did not doubt I had some other fancy in my head which encouraged me to this disobedience, but he assured me if I refused a settlement he has provided for me, he gave me his word, whatever proposals were made to him, he would never so much as enter into a treaty with any other; that if I founded any hopes upon his death, I should find myself mistaken – he never intended to leave me anything but an annuity of £400;[1] that though another would proceed in this manner, after I had given so just a pretence for it, yet he had goodness to leave my destiny yet in my own choice; – and at the same time commanded me to communicate my design to my relations and ask their advice.

---

[1] As a girl living at home, she received from her father an allowance of £200 a year.

As hard as this may sound, it did not shock my resolution. I was pleased to think at any price I had it in my power to be free from a man I hated. I told my intention to all my nearest relations. I was surprised at their blaming it to the greatest degree. I was told they were sorry I would ruin myself, but if I was so unreasonable they could not blame my father whatever he inflicted on me. I objected I did not love him. They made answer they found no necessity of loving; if I lived well with him, that was all was required of me, and that if I considered this town I should find very few women in love with their husbands and yet a many happy. It was in vain to dispute with such prudent people; they looked upon me as a little romantic, and I found it impossible to persuade them that living in London at liberty was not the height of happiness. However, they could not change my thoughts, though I found I was to expect no protection from them. When I was to give my final answer to my father I told him that I preferred a single life to any other, and if he pleased to permit me I would take that resolution. He replied, he could not hinder my resolutions, but I should not pretend after that to please him, since pleasing him was only to be done by obedience; that if I would disobey, I knew the consequences – he would not fail to confine me where I might repent at leisure; that he had also consulted my relations and found them all agreeing in his sentiments.

He spoke this in a manner hindered my answering. I retired to my chamber, where I writ a letter to let him know my aversion to the man proposed was too great to be overcome, that I should be miserable beyond all things could be imagined, but I was in his hands, and he might dispose of me as he thought fit. He was perfectly satisfied with this answer, and proceeded as if I had given a willing consent. – I forgot to tell you he named you and said if I thought that way I was very much mistaken, that if he had no other engagements, yet he would never have agreed to your proposals, having no inclination to see his grandchildren beggars.

I do not speak this to endeavour to alter your opinion, but to show the improbability of his agreeing to it. I confess I am entirely of your mind. I reckon it among the absurdities of custom that a man must be obliged to settle his whole estate on an eldest son, beyond his power to recall, whatever he proves to be, and make himself unable to make happy a younger child that may deserve to be so. If I had an estate myself I should not make such ridiculous settlements, and I cannot blame you for being in the right.

I have told you all my affairs with a plain sincerity. I have avoided to move your compassion, and I have said nothing of what I suffer; and I have not persuaded you to a treaty which I am sure my family will never agree to. I can have no fortune without an entire obedience.

Whatever your business is, may it end to your satisfaction. I think of the public as you do. As little as that is a woman's care, it may be permitted into the number of a woman's fears. But wretched as I am, I have no more to fear for myself. I have still a concern for my friends, and I am in pain for your danger. I am far from taking ill what you say. I never valued myself as the daughter of ——, and ever despised those that esteemed me on that account. With pleasure I could barter all that, and change to be any country gentleman's daughter that would have reason enough to make happiness in privacy.

My letter is too long, I beg your pardon. You may see by the situation of my affairs 'tis without design.

✿ To Wortley ✿

London, 6 August 1712

You do me wrong in several parts of your letter. You seem not very well to know your own mind. You are unwilling to go back from your word, and yet you do the same thing as telling me you should think yourself more obliged to me for a refusal than a consent. Another woman would complain of this unsteadiness of resolution. I think in an affair of this nature, 'tis very natural to think one minute one thing and the next another, and I cannot blame you. I remember an expression in one of your letters to me which is certainly just. Should we not repent, we should both be happy beyond example; if we should, we should, I fear, be both wretched in as high a degree. I should not hesitate one moment was I not resolved to sacrifice everything to you. If I do it, I am determined to think as little of the rest of the world – men, women, acquaintance and relations – as if a deluge had swallowed them. I abandon all things that bear the name of pleasure but what is to be found in your company. I give up all my wishes, to be regulated by yours, and I resolve to have no other study but that of pleasing you.

These resolutions are absolutely necessary if we are to meet; and you need have no doubt but I will perform them. I know you too well to propose to myself any satisfaction in marrying you that must not be centred in yourself. A man that marries a woman without any advantages of fortune or alliance (as it will be the case) has a very good title to her future obedience. He has a right to be made easy every other way, and I will not impose on your generosity, which claims the sincerest proceeding on my side. I am as sensible as you yourself can be of the generosity of your proposal. Perhaps there is no other man that would take a woman under these disadvantages, and I am grateful to you with all the warmth gratitude can inspire. On the other side, consider a little whether there are many other women that would think as I do. The man my family would marry me to, is resolved to live in London. 'Tis my own fault if I do not (of the humour he is) make him always think whatever I please. If he dies I shall have £1,200 per annum rent charge; if he lives I shall enjoy every pleasure of life, those of love excepted. With you, I quit all things but yourself, as much as if we were to be placed alone together in an inaccessible island, and I hazard a possibility of being reduced to suffer all the evils of poverty. 'Tis true I had rather give my hand to the flames than to him, and cannot think of suffering him with common patience. To you – I could give it, without reluctance (it is to say more than I ought) but perhaps with pleasure.

This last consideration determines me. – I will venture all things for you. For our mutual good, 'tis necessary for us to consider the method the most likely to hinder either of us from repenting; on that point our whole repose seems to depend. If we retire into the country both your fortune and inclination require a degree of privacy. The greatest part of my family (as the greatest part of all families) are fools; they know no happiness but equipage and furniture, and they judge of everybody's by the proportion they enjoy of it. They will talk of me as one that has ruined herself, and there will be perpetual inquiries made of my manner of living. I do not speak this in regard of myself; I have always had a hearty contempt of those things, but on these and some other considerations I don't see why you should not pursue the plan that you say you began with your friend. I don't mean take him with you, but why may not I supply his place? At Naples we may live after our own fashion. For my part, as I design utterly to forget there is such a place as London, I shall leave no directions with nobody to write after me. People that enter upon a solitude are in the wrong if they do not make it as agreeable as they can. A fine country and beautiful prospects to people that are capable of tasting them are (at least) steps to promoting happiness. If I lived with you I should be sorry not to see you perfectly happy. I foresee the objection you will raise against this, but it is none. I have no acquaintance, nor I will make none, and 'tis your own fault if I ever see any creature but yourself. Your commands shall regulate that. If you please, I can take with me a lady you have heard me speak of, whom I am sure will follow me over all the world if I please, and I don't care if I never see anybody else but her and you. If you agree to this, there is but one point farther to be considered, whether you can make me any assurance of a provision if I should be so unhappy to lose you. You may think this an odd thing for me to name, when I bring you no fortune. My brother would keep me, but there is something very severe to submit to a dependence of that nature, not to mention a possibility of his death, and then, what am I to expect from the guardians of his son? I am sure I have nothing to expect from my father. By assurance I only mean your word, which I dare entirely depend on.

I know no faults that you are ignorant of; on the contrary, I believe you forgive more than you have occasion to forgive. I do not, however, look upon you as so far engaged that you cannot retreat. You are at liberty to raise what objections you please. I will answer them, or freely confess any that are unanswerable. I make no reply to the accusation of having no value for you; I think it needs none when I proffer to leave the whole world for you. I say nothing of pin money etc. I don't understand the meaning of any divided interest from a man I willingly give myself to. You speak of my father as if 'twere in my power to marry you with his consent. I know it is not. All is concluded with this other and he will not put it off. If you are not of my opinion (which, however, I am sure is right) you may do what you please in it, without naming me, which will only serve to expose me to a great deal of ill usage, and force me to what he will.

Adieu. I say nothing of time and place because I know not whether you will agree to what I speak of. We have now time enough, and I think we are in the wrong if we do not settle everything before we meet. I will not [*last page missing*]

🙦 To Miss Philippa Mundy 🙦

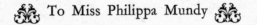

Acton, August 1712

My dear Phil,

I am very sorry that your affairs are not in a posture to expect Paradise, but I think you much in the right to accept of Limbo; there is nothing that is not preferable to the state you are now in,

> For when the mind so cool is grown
> As neither love, nor hate to own,
> Then life but dully lingers on.[1]

For my part, I know not what I shall do; perhaps at last I shall do something to surprise everybody. Wherever I am, and whatever becomes of me, I am ever yours. Limbo is better than Hell. My adventures are very odd; I may go into Limbo if I please, but 'tis accompanied with such circumstances, my courage will hardly come up to it, yet perhaps it may. In short I know not what will become of me. You'll think me mad, but I know nothing certain but that I shall not die an old maid; that's positive.[2]

Dear Phil, let me know if you go to Nottingham race, and what new conquests you make there. I wish you all the happiness you are capable of tasting, which is all that is most exquisite and delicate.

[1] Quoted from Aphra Behn.

[2] Lady Mary told Joseph Spence (in 1741) that 'she had a vast number of offers . . . and the thing that kept her awake was, who to fix upon. Most part of the month she was determined but as to two points, which were: to be married to somebody, and not to be married to the man her father . . . advised her to.' In the opinion of her granddaughter Lady Louisa Stuart this account 'appears to have been mere rattle; yet it is likely enough that she more than once wavered between Mr Wortley and others though unwilling ever to lose her hold of him entirely. It is pretty plain that he suspected this.'

❧ To Wortley ❧

Acton, 11 August 1712

Monday

My father has been here today. He bid me prepare to go to Dean this day sennight. I am not to come from thence but to give myself to all that I hate. I shall never see you more. These considerations fright me to death. Tell me what you intend to do. If you can think of me for your companion at Naples, come next Sunday under this garden wall, on the road, some little distance from the summer house, at ten o'clock. It will be dark, and it is necessary it should be so. I could wish you would begin our journey immediately; I have no fancy to stay in London or near it. I will not pretend to justify my proceeding. Everybody will object to me, why I did not do this sooner, before I put a man to the charges of equipage etc.? I shall not care to tell them, you did not ask me sooner. In short, as things have been managed I shall never care to hear any more on't. 'Tis an odd step, but something must be ventured when the happiness of a whole life is depending. I intend to be happy with you, and I am sure 'tis impossible with him.

If on the account of your health or for any other reason you had rather delay this till I return from Dean, 'tis certain I shall come hither, from thence, and 'twill be then in our power to do the same thing. But as the time of my return is uncertain, you must not be far off if you intend to do it, for I own I cannot, nor dare not, resist my father, and I know he has power over me to make me do whatever he pleases.

I shall not be surprised if you have changed your mind, or even if you should change your mind after you have consented to this. I would have no tie upon you but inclination; I have nothing to do with your word or your honour etc.

The scheme I propose to myself is living in an agreeable country with a man that I like, that likes me, and forgetting the rest of the world as much as if there was no other people in the world, and that Naples were the Garden of Eden. If there is any part of this scheme that does not agree either with your affairs or inclinations do not do it. I own I know not how to disoblige all my relations and live in the midst of them. If you will leave England immediately I am ready to wait on you, either next Sunday at ten or I'll wait till I come back and leave you all the time of my stay at Dean to consider. I shall be sorry if you resolve against me, but I should be doubly sorry to have you take me without your own inclination being entirely for it.

If you come Sunday 'tis indifferent to me whether 'tis with a coach and six or a pair. For my part, I could wish to make our first stage that night. Do what you please for that matter.

I say nothing of jointure. I begin to think myself in the wrong to imagine a man so generous to take me without a fortune would not be also generous enough to make me easy every other way. Consult your own heart, and let that determine you. Make no scruple of going back from your word, if you cannot resolve upon it. Should I go to the garden door and not find you there the disappointment would not be so hard as seeing you uneasy afterwards. On my side, if I find I cannot live with you at Naples without another wish, if I cannot answer for my own renouncing the pomps and vanities of this world, you shall not be troubled with me, and Saturday receive a letter that I cannot bring myself to it. In the opinion I am in this minute I think I can abandon the whole world for you.

Do not be apprehensive I shall take it for a mark of indifference if you delay till my return. Perhaps your health may require it, or the situation of your affairs, which may not be in order to travel before. I will think of it what you please, and will not reproach you if you do not do it then. Let us both be at liberty till the parson puts an end to it.

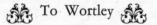

To Wortley

Acton, 15 August 1712

Friday, 7 o'clock

If I think till tomorrow after the same manner I have thought ever since I saw you, the wisest thing I can do is to do whatever you please. 'Tis an odd thing to confess, but I fear nothing so much as a change in my mind when there can be none in my condition. My thoughts of you are capable of improvement both ways. I am more susceptible of gratitude than anybody living. You may manage in a manner to make me passionately fond of you. Should you use me ill, can I answer that I should be able to hinder myself from reflecting back on the sacrifice I had made? An engagement for my whole life is no trifle, and should we both be so happy as to find we liked one another, yet even years of exquisite happiness, when they are past, could not pay me for a whole life of misery to come.

I think perhaps farther than I have occasion to think, but in an affair like this, all possible as well as all probable events are to be foreseen, since a mistake is not to be retrieved. In my present opinion, I think that if I was yours and you used me well nothing could be added to my misfortune should I lose you. But when I suffer my reason to speak, it tells me that in any circumstance of life (wretched or happy) there is a certain proportion of money, as the world is made, absolutely necessary to the living in it. I have never yet found myself in any straits of fortune, and am hardly able to imagine the misery arising from it. Should I find myself twenty year hence your widow, without a competency to maintain me in a manner suitable in some degree to my education, I shall not then be so old I may not possibly live twenty year longer, without what is requisite to make life easy. Happiness is what I should not think of.

After all these prudent considerations, the bias of my heart is in your favour. I hate the man they propose to me. If I did not hate him my reason would tell me he is not capable of either being my friend or my companion. I have an esteem for you, with a mixture of more kindness than I imagined. That kindness would persuade me to abandon all things for you – my fame, my family, the settlement they have provided for me – and rather embark with you through all the hazards of perhaps finding myself reduced to the last extremes of want (which would be heavier on me than any other body) than enjoy the certainty of a plentiful fortune with another. I can think with pleasure of giving you with my first declaration of love the sincerest proof of it. I read over some of your first letters, and I form romantic scenes to myself of love and solitude. I did not believe I was capable of thinking this way, but I find 'tis in your power to make me think what you please.

One would think this letter were determined; yet I know not what I shall do. – I know if I do not venture all things to have you, I shall repent it.

❧ To Wortley ❧

Acton 15 August 1712

Friday night

I tremble for what we are doing. Are you sure you will love me forever? Shall we never repent? I fear, and I hope. I foresee all that will happen on this occasion. I shall incense my family to the highest degree. The generality of the world will blame my conduct, and the relations and friends of —— will invent a thousand stories of me, yet – 'tis possible you may recompense everything to me. In this letter (which I am fond of) you promise me all that I wish. – Since I writ so far, I received your Friday letter. I will be only yours, and I will do what you please.

[*Postscript*] You shall hear from me again tomorrow, not to contradict but to give some directions. My resolution is taken – love me and use me well.

❧ To Wortley ❧

I would not give myself the pain of thinking you have suffered as much by this misfortune as I have done. The pain of my mind has very much affected my body. I have been sick ever since, yet though overcome by fatigue and misfortune I write to you from the first inn.

I blame myself for my cowardice and folly. I know not how my father received his intelligence but out of my fright. When I reflect, I don't believe he knew of the taking out the licence since he did not name it particularly,[1] but in general terms spoke of my keeping a correspondence, etc. I was so frighted and looked so guilty, I believe it was the worse for me. I had perhaps better have denied it, but instead of that I foolishly made what promises he would.

I lament my folly, but would remedy it if possible, though I cannot blame you if after so much trouble about it you resolve never to think more of so unlucky a creature as I am. But if like me you are still determined, if possible I will write to you every post, and what I can do I will.

I suppose I shall not be removed from hence till the night before my intended ———. If that should happen sooner than is convenient for you, perhaps sickness may serve for a pretence to delay it two or three days. I am afraid your affairs may suffer if you stay from your father. If so, do what is right for yourself in the first place. Neglect nothing upon my account. Go to him, if you can be back in ten days, to be sure I shall not be persecuted sooner. But do no harm to your health by fatigue or vexation; rather forget what becomes of me than any way injure yourself. I am distracted when I think how much trouble I have already given to the man on earth I have most reason to esteem, and for whose happiness I would do everything. If on my account your health or your fortune should ever be impaired I should wish I had never been born.

Write to me soon, to West Dean, near Salisbury, Wiltshire, by my own name. Did you write Sunday? I had no letter.

[*Postscript*] I made shift to get into the balcony at six and stayed till seven this morning. But heaven was not so kind to bring you. You once called my kindness a cordial to you. I wish it was so, for it runs in my head you are ill. Whatever is ordained for me, if my wishes were heard you should never feel any.

Adieu. I could say a great deal more.[2]

---

[1] To avoid publishing banns, Wortley applied twice on 16 August for a special marriage licence – the first time to be married in the Church of St Dunstan in the West (London), the second 'at any convenient time and place'.

[2] This letter was delivered the next day – when they were both staying at the same inn.

19 August 1712

Why did you not bring a coach etc., to be set up at another inn? I would fain come but fear being stopped. If you could carry me with you I would not care who saw me. Or if you had been lodged on the same floor with me I might have been married, perhaps, and returned unsuspected.

West Dean, c. 20 August 1712

We have more ill luck than any other people. Had you writ in your first letter where you intended to be etc. I could have ris up by myself at four o'clock and come to your chamber, perhaps undiscovered. At worst you could but have done what you resolved on at first if it had been known, which could not have been till after it was over, all our people being in bed. After my woman was up she watched me so much it was impossible; she apprehended you was in the house, but I believe has now lost that thought. Had I not been sick and gone to bed sooner than usual I should have seen your gentleman, and then he would have told me where you was.

All things conspire against the unfortunate, but if you are still determined I still hope it may be possible one way or other. Write to me always what contrivance you think on; I know best what is practicable for me. I have since asked my brother what he could have done if I had been married in that way. He made answer, he durst not have taken me with him; we must have stayed in the inn, and how odd that would have been!

If there had been any robbery lately committed, you had been taken up. They suspected you in the house for highwaymen. I hope some time of our lives we may laugh together at this adventure, though at this minute 'tis vexatious enough.

Do what is most convenient for your own affairs, but if you intend to go to the Spa, we are very near a seaport here, though if possible I would delay my flight till the night I come to Acton, or I must come quite alone. I should not much care to have this said, but if you judge it most convenient I will drop that scruple, and in everything prefer you to the world. I am [aware] of what you do for me, and my thoughts [of] it are all you would have them.

Pray write. If possible I would do what you desire, and say no, though they brought a parson, but I hope we shall not be put to that hard necessity, for I fear my own woman's weakness.

Adieu. I am entirely yours if you please.[1]

[1] The most authoritative account of Lady Mary's elopement is that in a letter from her sister Lady Frances to Philippa Mundy on 15 October [1712]: 'A week after her arrival to this place [Dean, *c.* 27 August] she went off with Mr Wortley Montagu and was married at Salisbury. My father is not yet reconciled to her. She writes everybody word she's perfectly happy, and it seems has found Paradise (as she terms it herself) when she expected but Limbo.'

PART II

❧

Domesticities and Politics
1712–1716

❧

After their marriage Wortley and his bride remained in England. His father gave them his blessing when they visited him in Yorkshire but Lady Mary's father was not yet ready to forgive. They then separated so that Wortley could attend to his business affairs, while Lady Mary stayed first with friends in Nottinghamshire and then at the house of Wortley's cousin in Huntingdon. To help dissipate her loneliness and spleen Wortley sent her a manuscript draft of his friend Joseph Addison's verse tragedy *Cato*, which she dutifully read and modestly criticized. (The play, slightly altered to conform to her suggestions, was staged in London the following year with spectacular success.) In May 1713 their son was born, and named for his father. Lady Mary then began to seek a house to rent in Yorkshire, finally choosing one at Middlethorpe, near York. There she was joined by Wortley, who along with other Whigs had been defeated for re-election to Parliament.

But with the death of Queen Anne in August 1714 the Whigs could expect their reward for supporting the Hanoverian Succession. Although distant from London, where Wortley stayed, Lady Mary plied him with advice on choosing a constituency and on advancing himself. Before long he won an appointment in the Treasury. Clearly his family would have to live in London; and so, guided by Lady Mary's solicitous advice and fears, he searched for a house.

When she arrived in London in January 1715 she was ready to take a prominent place at the Court of George I as wife of an M.P. who was also heir-presumptive to an earldom (Sandwich) and as the daughter of the newly elevated Duke of Kingston, who had finally forgiven her. Beyond these advantages she relied on her own ambition and energy. She cultivated the King's two mistresses, and tried to win favour with the Prince and Princess of Wales. She also found an outlet for her literary and intellectual interests in the cosmopolitan circle at Court, who included the Abbé Conti, savant and philosopher, William Congreve, the dramatist retired to play the gentleman, and the poets Alexander Pope and John Gay.

At the end of 1715 she was struck down with smallpox, and although she survived, her beauty was marred; henceforth she would have to depend on her wit. In April 1716 Wortley received the lucrative appointment of Ambassador to Turkey, and Lady Mary decided to accompany him on the arduous and dangerous journey to Constantinople.

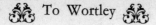

Wallingwells, Nottinghamshire, 22 October 1712

Wallingwells, October 22, which is the first post I could write, Monday night being so fatigued and sick I went straight to bed from the coach.

I don't know very well how to begin; I am perfectly unacquainted with a proper matrimonial style. After all, I think 'tis best to write as if we were not married at all. I lament your absence as if you was still my lover, and I am impatient to hear you are got safe to Durham and that you have fixed a time for your return.

I have not been very long in this family,[1] and I fancy myself in that described in the *Spectator*.[2] The good people here look upon their children with a fondness that more than recompenses their care of them. I don't perceive much distinction in regard to their merits, and when they speak sense or nonsense it affects the parents with almost the same pleasure. My friendship for the mother and kindness for Miss Biddy makes me endure the squalling of Miss Nanny and Miss Mary with abundance of patience, and my foretelling the future conquests of the eldest daughter makes me very well with the family.

I don't know whether you will presently find out that this seeming impertinent account is the tenderest expressions of my love to you, but it furnishes my imagination with agreeable pictures of our future life, and I flatter myself with the hope of one day enjoying with you the same satisfactions, and that after as many years together I may see you retain the same fondness for me as I shall certainly mine for you; and the noise of a nursery may have more charms for us than the music of an opera. [?] as these are the sure effect of my sincere love, since 'tis the nature of that passion to entertain the mind with pleasures in prospect, and I check myself when I grieve for your absence by remembering how much reason I have to rejoice in the hope of passing my whole life with you, a good fortune not to be valued. I am afraid of telling you that I return thanks for it to Heaven, because you will charge me with hypocrisy, but you are mistaken. I assist every day at public prayers in this family and never forget in my private ejaculations how much I owe to Heaven for making me yours.

'Tis candlelight, or I should not conclude so soon.

Pray, my dear, begin at the top and read till you come to the bottom.[3]

---

[1] Lady Mary was staying with a distant relation, Thomas White M.P.

[2] In the issue of 3 October 1712, Addison contributed a letter from Philogamus about the pleasures of a large family.

[3] A wide space separates the first two paragraphs of the letter.

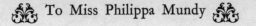

Wortley, Yorkshire, October 1712

Dear Phil,

With much justice you may accuse me of ingratitude or stupidity, and I am afraid have by this time entirely banished me your thoughts as unworthy of a place there, but upon my word you have always the same share in mine, though the various hurries of my life these many weeks past have been such as not to afford me leisure to express my thoughts, which have been full of you.

At this minute I am in Yorkshire,[1] but shall be in a few days not many miles from Newark. I think you are sometimes with a relation there. If there was any possibility of having you with me for a week or longer I would send my coach with pleasure.

Knowing me for such a coward as you do, I don't doubt but you were very much surprised to hear I had plucked up a spirit and entered upon rebellion with so much courage. It was certainly my good genius that inspired me, and I am more than ever persuaded

> An unseen hand makes all our moves,
> And some are great, and some are small . . .
> Figures alas! of speech, for Destiny plays us all.[2]

I have no longer reason to complain of mine; I hope to hear you say the same of yours.

My dear Phil, let me have a quick answer; I am ever and entirely yours,

M.W.M.

Direct your answer to Scofton, near Worksop, Nottinghamshire, by way of London.

[1] Probably visiting her husband's family at Wortley, about ten miles north of Sheffield.
[2] Quoted from Abraham Cowley's *Pindarique Odes* (1668).

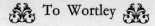

Wallingwells, October 1712

I am at present in so much uneasiness my letter is not likely to be intelligible if it all resembles the confusion in my head. I sometimes imagine you not well, and sometimes that you think it of small importance to write, or that greater matters have taken up your thoughts. This last imagination is too cruel for me; I will rather fancy your letter has miscarried, though I find little probability to think so. I know not what to think, and am very near being distracted amongst my variety of dismal apprehensions. I am very ill company to the good people of the house, who all bid me make you their compliments. Mr White begins your health twice every day. You don't deserve all this if you can be so entirely forgetful of all this part of the world. I am peevish with you by fits, and divide my time between anger and sorrow, which are equally troublesome to me. 'Tis the most cruel thing in the world to think one has reason to complain of what one loves. How can you be so careless? Is it because you don't love writing? You should remember I want to know you are safe at Durham.[1] I shall imagine you have had some fall from your horse or ill accident by the way, without regard to probabilities; there is nothing too extravagant for a woman's and a lover's fears. Did you receive my last letter? If you did not, the direction is wrong; you won't receive this and my question is in vain. I find I begin to talk nonsense and 'tis time to leave off. Pray, my dear, write, or I shall be very mad.

[1] Where he had gone to look after his family's business interests.

Huntingdon, c. 4 December 1712[1]

I don't believe you expect to hear from me so soon. If I remember, you did not so much as desire it, but I will not be so nice to quarrel with you on that point. Perhaps you would laugh at that delicacy which is however an attendant of a tender friendship.

I opened the closet where I expected to find so many books. To my great disappointment there were only some few pieces of the law and folios of mathematics, my Lord Hinchingbrooke and Mr Twyman[2] having disposed of the rest, but as there is no affliction no more than no happiness without allay, I discovered an old trunk of papers, which to my great diversion I found to be the letters of the first Earl of Sandwich, and am in hopes that those from his lady will tend much to my edification, being the most extraordinary lessons of economy that ever I read in my life. To the glory of your father, I find that his looked upon him as destined to be the honour of the family.

I walked yesterday two hours on the terrace. These are the most considerable events that have happened in your absence, excepting that a good-natured robin redbreast kept me company almost all the afternoon with so much good humour and humanity as gives me faith for the piece of charity ascribed to them little creatures in the *Children in the Wood*, which I have hitherto thought only a poetical ornament to that history.[3]

I expect a letter next post to tell me you are well in London, and that your business will not detain you long from her that cannot be happy without you.

[1] Lady Mary was staying at the house of Wortley's cousin, the 3rd Earl of Sandwich.

[2] Tutor to Lord Hinchingbrooke, Sandwich's son and heir.

[3] A popular ballad in which a robin covers with leaves the bodies of two murdered children.

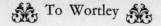

To Wortley

Huntingdon, c. 6 December 1712

I am not at all surprised at my Aunt Cheyne's conduct.[1] People are seldom very much grieved (and never ought to be) at misfortunes they expect. When I gave myself to you, I gave up the very desire of pleasing the rest of the world and am pretty indifferent about it.

I think you are very much in the right for designing to visit Lord Pierrepont.[2] As much as you say I love the town, if you think it necessary for your interest to stay some time here, I would not advise you to neglect a certainty for an uncertainty. But I believe if you pass the Christmas here, great matters will be expected from your hospitality; however, you are a better judge than I am.

I continue indifferently well, and endeavour as much as I can to preserve myself from spleen and melancholy, not for my own sake – I think that of little importance – but in the condition I am I believe it may be of very ill consequence;[3] yet passing whole days alone, as I do, I do not always find it possible, and my constitution will sometimes get the better of my reason. Human nature itself, without any additional misfortunes, furnishes disagreeable meditations enough. Life itself, to make it supportable, should not be considered too near. My reason represents to me in vain the inutility of serious reflections. The idle mind will sometimes fall into contemplations that serve for nothing but to ruin the health, destroy good humour, hasten old age and wrinkles, and bring on an habitual melancholy. 'Tis a maxim with me to be young as long as one can. There is nothing can pay one for that invaluable ignorance which is the companion of youth, those sanguine groundless hopes, and that lively vanity which makes all the happiness of life. To my extreme mortification I grow wiser every day than other. I don't believe Solomon was more convinced of the vanity of temporal affairs than I am. I lose all taste of this world, and I suffer myself to be bewitched by the charms of the spleen, though I know and foresee all the irremediable mischiefs arising from it.

I am insensibly fallen into the writing you a melancholy letter, after all my resolutions to the contrary, but I do not enjoin you to read it. Make no scruple of flinging it into the fire at the first dull line. Forgive the ill effects of my solitude, and think me (as I am) ever yours.

[1] Gertrude Pierrepont, sister to Lady Mary's father, was the wife of Viscount Cheyne; she disapproved of her niece's marriage.

[2] Gervase Pierrepont, 1st Baron, uncle to Lady Mary's father, was wealthy, childless and nearly sixty.

[3] Her son was born the following spring.

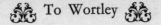

Huntingdon, 8 December 1712

Your short letter came to me this morning, but I won't quarrel with it since it brought the good news of your health. I wait with impatience for that of your return. The Bishop of Salisbury[1] writes me word that he hears my Lord Pierrepont declares very much for us. As the Bishop is no infallible prelate I should not depend much on that intelligence, but my sister Frances tells me the same thing. Since it is so, I believe you'll think it very proper to pay him a visit if he is in town, and give him thanks for the good offices you hear he has endeavoured to do me unasked. If his kindness is sincere 'tis too valuable to be neglected; however, the very appearance of it must be of use to us. If I know him, his desire of making my father appear in the wrong will make him zealous for us. I think I ought to write him a letter of acknowledgement for what I hear he has already done. The Bishop tells me he has seen Lord Halifax, who says besides his great esteem for you he has particular respects for me and will take pains to reconcile my father etc.[2]

I think this is near the words of my letter, which contains all the news I know except that of this place, which is that an unfortunate burgess of the town of Huntingdon was justly disgraced yesterday in the face of the congregation for being false to his first love, who with an audible voice forbid the banns published between him and a greater fortune. This accident causes as many disputes here as the duel could do where you are.[3] Public actions, you know, always make two parties. The great prudes say the young woman should have suffered in silence, and the pretenders to spirit and fire would have all false men so served, and hope it will be an example for the terror of infidelity throughout the whole country. For my part, I never rejoiced at anything more in my life. You'll wonder what private interest I could have in this affair. You must know, it furnished discourse all this afternoon, which was no little service when I was visited by the young ladies of Huntingdon.

This long letter I know must be particularly impertinent to a man of business, but idleness is the root of all evil. I write and read till I can't see, and then I walk; sleep succeeds; and thus my whole time is divided. If I was as well qualified all other ways as I am by idleness, I would publish a daily paper called the *Meditator*. The terrace is my place consecrated to meditation, which I observe to be gay or grave, as the sun shows or hides his face. Till today I have had no occasion of opening my mouth to speak since I wished you a good journey. I see nothing, but I think of everything, and indulge my imagination, which is chiefly employed on you.

[1] Gilbert Burnet, theologian and prominent Whig.
[2] Charles Montagu, 1st Baron Halifax, was a distant relation of Wortley's.
[3] The duel between the Duke of Hamilton and Lord Mohun in Hyde Park on 15 November resulted in the death of both.

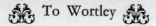

London, 22 June 1713

Y ou have not been gone three hours, I have called at two people's doors, and without knowing it myself, I find I am come home only to write to you. The late rain has drawn everybody to the park. I shall pass the whole evening in my chamber, alone, without any business but thinking of you, in a manner you would call affectation if I should repeat to you. That reflection brings me back to remember I should not write my thoughts to you. You will accuse me of deceit when I am opening my heart to you, and the plainness of expressing it will appear artificial. I am sorry to remember this, and check the inclination that I have to give a loose to my tenderness, and tell you how melancholy all things seem to me in your absence, how impatient I am for the end of this week, and how little possible I find it would be for me to live without you. – My eyes are so weak I can go no farther. 'Tis almost dusk. I dare not write by candlelight; I will finish my letter tomorrow.

Tuesday. My first news this morning is what I am very sorry to hear. My brother has the smallpox. I hope he will do well; I am sure we lose a friend if he does not.[1]

I expect tomorrow impatiently. If you break your word with me and I have no letter you do a very cruel thing and will make me more unhappy than you imagine. – The length of this letter will tire you. – adieu. May everything go as you would have it. Your little boy is very well and would present his duty to you if he could speak.[2]

[1] Lord Kingston died ten days later at the age of twenty-one, leaving a widow and two children.
[2] Edward Wortley Montagu, junior, was four weeks old.

London, 17 April 1714

Such agreeable friends as you (dear Phil) are so seldom met with, that 'tis impossible to forget them, or not to endeavour to preserve so great a treasure. Without affectation, I feel a concern for you that I am not often sensible of, and I cannot hear of your entering on so important an action as a settlement for life, without a degree of doubt and fear inseparable from a real concern. I wish I had been so fortunate to have met with Mr Massingberd, and conversed with him; but whatever he is, if he has a good understanding, so much virtue and so many charms as you have must engage him to be whatever you wish him.[1]

I saw the other gentleman's bride some time ago, the most disagreeable old woman I ever saw, but money can gild everything, and perhaps that way of thinking is not quite ridiculous, except the world could be altered from what it is.

When I come down, which I hope will be very soon, I will let you know it, and expect the pleasure of seeing you at Leicester. 'Tis so common a thing to see our sex unhappy that choose husbands without any guide but fancy, which is every hour changeable, I form better views for you that are so reasonable, and lay your happiness on a more lasting foundation.

Dear Phil, I wish Mr M. may be sensible how happy he is in that uncommon thing (so rare that like the phoenix its very existence is disputed), a woman of youth and beauty without coquetry. In this vile town, the [?] universal follies of the fair, the ugly – in short, the whole sex that way ought to make all husbands revere those wives that have sense enough not to be led by the crowd, and virtuous courage enough to stand the laugh that will infallibly insult them with the name of prudes.

Dear Phil, I am with an unalterable friendship, and a tender affection, yours,

M.W.M.

---

[1] On 8 July 1714 Philippa Mundy married Burrell Massingberd; he had been her suitor for more than three years.

c. *18 July 1714*

My dear Phil (for so I will still call you),

ʼTis impossible to have heard any news with more satisfaction than I did that of your happiness, and the obliging compliment you make me of having contributed to it. I do not doubt the continuation of it, as I know you have every quality to make a good husband as well as a passionate lover. I confess, contrary to the generality of my sex, I am of opinion that both good and ill husbands are their wives' making, for as folly is the root of all matrimonial quarrels, that distemper commonly runs highest of the woman's side. I have nothing to fear of that nature from you; your good humour and good sense will raise the esteem of Mr Massingberd every day, and as your beauty grows familiar to his eyes, your conduct and conversation will fix his love on a foundation that lasts for ever.

Whatever romances and heat of youth impose on the minds of young people, passion is soon sated; and a real friendship and mutual value [are] the only tie that makes life pass easily on, when two friends agree to lessen each other's care, and join in promoting one and the same interest.

I am extremely glad, my dear Phil, you are happy in a husband capable of this friendship. I do not doubt Mr Massingberd [is] sensible of the advantage he has above the rest of mankind, for 'tis a thing more uncommon, and a greater blessing, to marry a reasonable woman than a fortune of £40,000.[1]

I am, my dear Mrs Massingberd, with a sincere pleasure in your happiness, faithfully yours,

M.W.M.

[1] Philippa Mundy's dowry was £3,000.

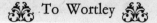

Middlethorpe, c. *3 August 1714*

I cannot forbear taking it something unkindly that you do not write to me when you may be assured I am in a great fright, and know not certainly what to expect upon this sudden change.[1] The Archbishop has been come to Bishopthorpe but three days. I went with my cousin today to see the King proclaimed, which was done, the Archbishop walking next the Lord Mayor, all the country gentry following with greater crowds of people than I believed to be in York, vast acclamations and the appearance of a general satisfaction, the Pretender afterwards dragged about the streets and burnt, ringing of bells, bonfires and illuminations, the mob crying liberty and property and long live King George.

This morning all the principal men of any figure took post for London, and we are alarmed with the fear of attempts from Scotland, though all Protestants here seem unanimous for the Hanover succession. The poor young ladies at Castle Howard are as much afraid as I am, being left all alone without any hopes of seeing their father again (though things should prove well) this eight or nine months.[2] They have sent to desire me very earnestly to come to them and bring my boy. 'Tis the same thing as pensioning in a nunnery, for no mortal man ever enters the doors in the absence of their father, who is gone post. During this uncertainty I think it will be a safe retreat, for Middlethorpe stands exposed to plunderers. If there be any at all, I dare say after the zeal the Archbishop has showed, they'll visit his house (and consequently this) in the first place. The Archbishop made me many compliments on our near neighbourhood and said he should be overjoyed at the happiness of improving his acquaintance with you.

I suppose you may now come in at Aldborough, and I heartily wish you was in Parliament.[3] I saw the Archbishop's list of the Lords Regents appointed and perceive Lord Wharton is not one of them, by which I guess the new scheme is not to make use of any man grossly infamous in either party;[4] consequently those that have been honest in regard to both will stand fairest for preferment.

You understand these things much better than me, but I hope you

---

[1] The death of Queen Anne on 1 August.

[2] Castle Howard, about fifteen miles north of York, was the seat of the Earl of Carlisle, whose three daughters were friends of Lady Mary. As one of the Lords Justices, Carlisle was in London awaiting the arrival of George I from Hanover.

[3] A new parliament had to be elected within six months of the death of the sovereign. Aldborough was a 'pocket borough' in Yorkshire controlled by Lord Pelham.

[4] The Archbishop of York was one of the Lords Justices, called Lords Regents by Lady Mary. Wharton's reward came six weeks later, after the King's arrival, when he was appointed Lord Privy Seal.

will be persuaded by me and your other friends (who I don't doubt will
be of my opinion) that 'tis necessary for the common good for an
honest man to endeavour to be powerful when he can be the one without losing the first more valuable title; and remember that money is the
source of power.

I hear the parliament sits but six months.[5] You know best whether
'tis worth any expense or bustle to be in for so short a time.

[5] This rumour proved unfounded.

❦ To Wortley ❦

Middlethorpe, 6 August 1714

You made me cry two hours last night. I cannot imagine why
you use me so ill, or for what reason you continue silent when
you know at any time that your silence cannot fail of giving me a great
deal of pain, and now to a higher degree because of the perplexity that
I am in, without knowing where you are, what you are doing, or what
to do with myself and my dear little boy. However, being persuaded
there can be no objection to it, I intend to go tomorrow to Castle
Howard and remain there locked up with the young ladies till I know
when I shall see you or what you would command.

The Archbishop and everybody else are gone to London. We are
alarmed with a story of a fleet being seen from the coasts of Scotland.
An express went from thence through York to the Earl of Mar.[1]

I beg you would write to me. Till you do, I shall not have any easy
minute. I am sure I do not deserve from you that you should make me
uneasy. – I find I am scolding. 'Tis better for me not to trouble you
with it, but I cannot help taking your silence very unkindly.

[1] Lady Mary's brother-in-law after his marriage to her sister Lady Frances on
20 July 1714. He was Secretary of State for Scotland.

Middlethorpe, c. *24 September 1714*

Though I am very impatient to see you I would not have you by
hastening to come down lose any part of your interest. I am
surprised you say nothing of where you stand. I had a letter from Mrs
Hewet last post who said she heard you stood at Newark and would be
chose without opposition, but I fear her intelligence is not at all to be
depended on. I am glad you think of serving your friends; I hope it will
put you in mind of serving yourself.

I need not enlarge upon the advantages of money. Everything we see
and everything we hear puts us in remembrance of it. If it was possible
to restore liberty to your country or limit the encroachments of the
prerogative by reducing yourself to a garret, I should be pleased to
share so glorious a poverty with you, but as the world is and will be,
'tis a sort of duty to be rich, that it may be in one's power to do good,
riches being another word for power, towards the obtaining of which
the first necessary qualification is impudence, and (as Demosthenes said
of pronunciation in oratory) the second is impudence, and the third,
still, impudence.[1] No modest man ever did or ever will make his fortune.
Your friend Lord Halifax, Robert Walpole and all other remarkable
instances of quick advancement have been remarkably impudent.[2] The
ministry is like a play at court. There's a little door to get in, and a great
crowd without, shoving and thrusting who shall be foremost; people
that knock others with their elbows, disregard a little kick of the shins,
and still thrust heartily forwards are sure of a good place. Your modest
man stands behind in the crowd, is shoved about by everybody, his
clothes tore, almost squeezed to death, and sees a thousand get in before
him that don't make so good a figure as himself. I don't say 'tis impossible for an impudent man not to rise in the world, but a moderate merit
with a large share of impudence is more probable to be advanced than
the greatest qualifications without it.

If this letter is impertinent it is founded upon an opinion of your
merit which if 'tis a mistake I would not be undeceived in. 'Tis my
interest to believe (as I do) that you deserve everything and are capable
of everything, but nobody else will believe it if they see you get
nothing.

---

[1] Lady Mary may be citing Francis Bacon's essay 'Of Boldness', where he
quotes Demosthenes as saying that Action, Action, and Action are the three
chief requisites in oratory.

[2] By this time the future prime minister had been secretary at war, treasurer of
the navy, and had been expelled from the House of Commons on charges of
bribery.

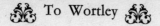

To Wortley

Middlethorpe, 9 October 1714

You do me wrong in imagining (as I perceive you do) that my reasons for being solicitous for your having this place was in view of spending more money than we do. You have no cause of fancying me capable of such a thought. I don't doubt but Lord Halifax will very soon have the staff,[1] and 'tis my belief you will not be at all the richer. But I think it looks well and may facilitate your election, and that is all the advantage I hope from it. When all your intimate acquaintance are preferred I think you would have an ill air in having nothing. Upon that account only I am sorry so many considerable places are disposed on. I suppose now you will certainly be chose somewhere or other, and I cannot see why you should not pretend to be Speaker.[2] I believe all the Whigs would be for you, and I fancy you have a considerable interest amongst the Tories, and for that reason would be very likely to carry it. 'Tis impossible for me to judge of this so well as you can do, but the reputation of being thoroughly of no party is (I think) of use in this affair, and I believe people generally esteem you impartial; and being chose by your country is more honourable than holding any place from any king.

---

[1] As Lord High Treasurer; but he was appointed instead First Lord of the Treasury.

[2] Of the House of Commons (after his election).

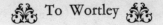

Middlethorpe c. *12 October 1714*

Your letter very much vexed me. I cannot imagine why you should doubt being the better for a place of that consideration which 'tis in your power to lay down whenever you dislike the measures that are taken.[1] Supposing the commission lasts but a short time, I believe those that have acted in it will have the offer of some other considerable thing.[2] I am perhaps the only woman in the world that would dissuade her husband (if he was inclined to't) from accepting the greatest place in England upon the condition of giving one vote disagreeing with his principle and the true interest of my country; but when 'tis possible to be of service to that country by going along with the ministry I know not any reason for declining an honourable post. The world never believes it possible for people to act out of the common tract, and whoever is not employed by the public may talk what they please of having refused or slighted great offers, but they are always looked upon either as neglected or discontented because their pretensions have failed, and whatever efforts they make against the Court are thought the effect of spleen and disappointment, or endeavours to get something they have set their heart on – as now Sir Thomas Hanmer is represented (and I believe truly) as aiming at being Secretary.[3] No man can make a better figure than when he enjoys a considerable place, being for the Place Bill; and if he finds the ministry in the wrong, withdrawing from them when 'tis visible that he might still keep his places if he did not choose to keep his integrity.[4]

I have sent you my thoughts of places in general, I solemnly protest, without any thought of any particular advantage to myself; and if I was your friend and not your wife I should speak in the same manner, which I really do without any consideration but that of your figure and reputation, which is a thousand times dearer to me than splendour, money, etc.

I suppose this long letter might have been spared, for your resolution I don't doubt is already taken.

---

[1] Wortley was appointed one of four junior Commissioners of the Treasury. Lady Mary later wrote that he was reluctant to accept any offer below that of Secretary of State.

[2] On his dismissal from the Treasury a year later, Wortley was granted the reversion of Auditorship of the Imprest, and in the spring of 1716 the Embassy to Turkey.

[3] Hanmer was offered the post of Chancellor of the Exchequer, but like most other prominent Tories refused, wishing to be free to serve his party.

[4] A place bill would forbid Members of Parliament from serving in the government. Such a bill was introduced (and defeated) in March 1714. Lady Mary argues that Wortley will not violate his conscience by accepting the Treasury post and standing for election.

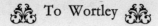

Middlethorpe, c. *25 October 1714*

I am told that you are very secure at Newark. If you are so in the West I cannot see why you should set up in three different places except it be to treble the expense.[1]

I am sorry you had not opportunity of paying Lord Pierrepont that compliment, though I hope that it will not weigh much with him in favour of another. I wish you would remember the common useful maxim – whatever is to be done at all ought to be done as soon as possible. I consider only your own interest when I speak, and I cannot help speaking warmly on that subject. I hope you will think of what I hinted in my last letters; and if you think of it at all, you cannot think of it too soon.

Adieu. I wish you would learn of Mr Steele to write to your wife.[2] Pray order me some money, for I'm in great want and must run in debt if you don't do it soon.

[1] Wortley finally stood for Westminster, a seat controlled by the Court, and was returned on 24 January 1715.
[2] Steele's letters to his 'Dear Prue' were frequent, even when they were living in the same place. Lady Mary, a visitor at their house during her courtship, must have witnessed his solicitude.

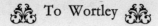 To Wortley

Middlethorpe, c. *24 November 1714*

I have taken up and laid down my pen several times, very much unresolved in what style I ought to write to you. For once I suffer my inclination to get the better of my reason. I have not oft opportunities of indulging myself, and I will do it in this one letter.

I know very well that nobody was ever teased into a liking, and 'tis perhaps harder to revive a past one than to overcome an aversion, but I cannot forbear any longer telling you I think you use me very unkindly. I don't say so much of your absence as I should do if you was in the country and I in London, because I would not have you believe I am impatient to be in town when I say I am impatient to be with you. But I am very sensible I parted with you in July, and 'tis now the middle of November. As if this was not hardship enough you do not tell me you are sorry for it. You write seldom and with so much indifference as shows you hardly think of me at all. I complain of ill health and you only say you hope 'tis not so bad as I make it. You never inquire after your child.

I would fain flatter myself you have more kindness for me and him than you express, but I reflect with grief – a man that is ashamed of passions that are natural and reasonable is generally proud of those that are shameful and silly.

You should consider solitude and spleen (the consequence of solitude) is apt to give the most melancholy ideas, and there needs at least tender letters and kind expressions to hinder uneasinesses almost inseparable from absence. I am very sensible how far I ought to be contented when your affairs oblige you to be without me. I would not have you do them any prejudice, but a little kindness will cost you nothing. I do not bid you lose anything by hasting to see me, but I would have you think it a misfortune when we are asunder. Instead of that, you seem perfectly pleased with our separation and indifferent how long it continues. When I reflect on all your behaviour I am ashamed of my own. I think I am playing the part of my Lady Winchester. At least to be as generous as my Lord; and as he made her an early confession of his aversion, own to me your inconstancy, and upon my word I will give you no more trouble about it.[1]

I have concealed as long as I can the uneasiness the nothingness of your letters has given me, under an affected indifference, but dissimulation always sits awkwardly upon me. I am weary of it and must beg you to write to me no more if you cannot bring yourself to write otherways. Multiplicity of business or diversions may have engaged you, but all people find time to do what they've a mind to. If your inclination is gone I had rather never receive a letter from you than one which in lieu of comfort for your absence gives me a pain even beyond it. For my part, as 'tis my first, this is my last complaint, and your next of that kind shall go back enclosed to you in blank paper.

[*Postscript*] I have received your money.

---

[1] Lord and Lady Winchester (afterwards Duke and Duchess of Bolton) separated soon after their marriage in July 1713. Her marital ill fortune was ascribed elsewhere by Lady Mary to an excess of virtue and lack of passion.

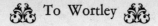
Middlethorpe, 20 December 1714

I am very well satisfied about the house,[1] and I think to hire horses here, but you say nothing to my question whether you have thoughts of returning soon, till which I know not what to resolve upon in relation to the boy, though I have a great inclination to bring him with me. I choose to stay till Monday after New Year's Day for the sake of the moon, which is absolutely necessary in so long a journey. I love travelling, and if I did not I should not think anything uneasy to come to you. I am only in care about your little child, who is now, I thank God, in perfect health.

[1] Wortley had rented a house for his family in Duke Street, Westminster.

PART III

❧

The Turkish Embassy
1716–1718

❧

As Ambassador to Turkey, Wortley's main diplomatic mission was to mediate the war then raging between the Austrians and the Turks. Hence his first destination was Vienna, where he could begin his negotiations. With Lady Mary and their son he crossed the Channel to Holland in August 1716; and after passing through the German States they sailed down the Danube to the Austrian capital. From the start Wortley's diplomatic strategy was misguided, for although the Turkish forces were steadily being beaten his peace terms favoured them. Lady Mary passed her time sight-seeing, attended the theatre and opera, and was entertained by Austrian grandees and at the elaborate Court festivities.

After two months in Vienna she accompanied Wortley on a swift journey to Hanover, where he procured additional credentials from the King, then visiting his beloved Electorate. They then returned to Vienna, and in January 1717 prepared for their journey into Turkish territory. After they reached Belgrade Lady Mary began her Oriental education in the house of a learned *effendi* where they lodged for three weeks. They then continued on to Sofia and then Adrianople, to see the Sultan and his army preparing to leave on a new campaign. Having submitted his mediation terms to both courts, Wortley set out with Lady Mary for Constantinople, and arrived there in June.

He rented a palace in Pera and settled his household. From this hill-top Lady Mary admired the wondrous views; she also adventured out to see the mosques and ancient monuments and to visit prominent ladies in their luxurious harems. She interested herself in the social life and customs of Islam, and studied the Turkish language and poetry. She did not neglect her English friends, who were delighted to receive her letters.

From September 1717 to May 1718 while Wortley was at the Turkish army camp near Sofia, Lady Mary remained in Constantinople. She bore a daughter in January, who was named after her. Then, Wortley having been replaced by another ambassador – who did succeed in ending the war – Lady Mary sadly prepared to leave. In June she sailed with Wortley and their children on a British man-of-war, and disembarked at Genoa. After a brief quarantine Wortley and Lady Mary travelled on through Turin, over the dangerous Mont Cénis to Lyons, and then to Paris, where they stayed for a fortnight. Unexpectedly she met her sister Lady Mar, who was visiting her attainted Jacobite husband. She arrived in London, finally, at the beginning of October.

❧ To Miss Jane Smith[1] ❧

Hague, 5 August 1716

I make haste to tell you, dear madam, that after all the dreadful fatigues you threatened me with, I am hitherto very well pleased with my journey. We take care to make such short stages every day, I rather fancy myself upon parties of pleasure than upon the road, and sure nothing can be more agreeable than travelling in Holland. The whole country appears a large garden, the roads all well paved, shaded on each side with rows of trees and bordered with large canals full of boats passing and repassing. Every twenty paces gives you the prospect of some villa and every four hours a large town, so surprisingly neat, I am sure you would be charmed with them. The place I am now at is certainly one of the finest villages in the world. Here are several squares finely built, and (what I think a particular beauty) set with thick large trees. The Voorhout is at the same time the Hyde Park and the Mall of the people of quality, for they take the air in it both on foot and in coaches. There are shops for wafers, cool liquors, etc. I have been to see several of the most celebrated gardens, but I will not tease you with their descriptions.

I dare swear you think my letter already long enough, but I must not conclude without begging your pardon for not obeying your commands in sending the lace you ordered me. Upon my word, I can yet find none that is not dearer than you may buy it in London. If you want any Indian goods, here are great variety of penn'orths, and I shall follow your orders with great pleasure and exactness, being, dear madam, etc.

---

[1] Almost certainly daughter of John Smith, former Speaker of the House of Commons; an early friend of Lady Mary's and since 1715 a Maid of Honour to the Princess of Wales.

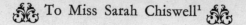 To Miss Sarah Chiswell[1]

Nijmegen, 13 August 1716

I am extremely sorry, my dear Sarah, that your fears of disobliging your relations and their fears for your health and safety has hindered me the happiness of your company, and you the pleasure of a diverting journey. I receive some degree of mortification from every agreeable novelty or pleasing prospect by the reflection of your having so unluckily missed the same pleasure, which I know it would have given you. If you were with me in this town you would be ready to expect to receive visits from your Nottingham friends. No two places were ever more resembling; one has but to give the Maese[2] the name of the Trent and there is no distinguishing the prospects: the houses, like those of Nottingham, built one above another and intermixed in the same manner with trees and gardens. The tower they call Julius Caesar's has the same situation with Nottingham Castle, and I can't help fancying I see from it the Trent field, Adboulton, etc., places so well known to us. 'Tis true the fortifications make a considerable difference. All the learned in the art of war bestow great commendations on them. For my part, that know nothing of the matter, I shall content myself with telling you 'tis a very pretty walk on the ramparts, on which there is a tower very deservedly called the Belvedere, where people go to drink coffee, tea, etc., and enjoy one of the finest prospects in the world. The public walks have no great beauty but the thick shade of the trees, but I must not forget to take notice of the bridge, which appeared very surprising to me. 'Tis large enough to hold hundreds of men with horses and carriages. They give the value of an English two pence to get upon it and then away they go, bridge and all, to the other side of the river, with so slow a motion one is hardly sensible of any at all.

I was yesterday at the French church and stared very much at their manner of service. The parson claps on a broad brimmed hat in the first place, which gave him entirely the air of what de'e call him, in *Bartholomew Fair*,[3] which he kept up by extraordinary antic gestures and talking much such stuff as t'other preached to the puppets. However, the congregation seemed to receive it with great devotion, and I was informed by some of his flock that he is a person of particular fame among 'em. I believe you are by this time as much tired of my account of him as I was with his sermon, but I'm sure your brother[4] will excuse a digression in favour of the Church of England. You know, speaking disrespectfully of Calvinists is the same thing as speaking honourably of the Church.

Adieu, my dear Sarah. Always remember me and be assured I can never forget you.

---

[1] A childhood friend from Nottingham.
[2] Actually the Waal.
[3] Zeal-of-the-Land Busy in Ben Jonson's play.
[4] Probably brother-in-law, Humphrey Perkins, Rector of Holme Pierrepont.

❧ To Lady Bristol[1] ❧

After five days travelling post I am sure I could sit down to write on no other occasion but to tell my dear Lady Bristol that I have not forgot her obliging command of sending her some account of my travels. I have already past a large part of Germany. I have seen all that is remarkable in Cologne, Frankfurt, Wurzburg, and this place, and 'tis impossible not to observe the difference between the free towns and those under the government of absolute princes (as all the little sovereigns of Germany are). In the first there appears an air of commerce and plenty. The streets are well built and full of people neatly and plainly dressed, the shops loaded with merchandise, and the commonalty clean and cheerful. In the other, a sort of shabby finery, a number of dirty people of quality tawdered out, narrow nasty streets out of repair, wretchedly thin of inhabitants, and above half of the common sort asking alms. I can't help fancying one under the figure of a handsome, clean, Dutch citizen's wife and the other like a poor town lady of pleasure, painted and ribboned out in her head-dress, with tarnished silver laced shoes, and a ragged under-petticoat, a miserable mixture of vice and poverty.

They have sumptuary laws in this town which distinguish their rank by their dress and prevent that excess which ruins so many other cities and has a more agreeable effect to the eye of a stranger than our fashions. I think after the Archbishop of Cambrai having declared for them, I need not be ashamed to own that I wish these laws were in force in other parts of the world.[2] When one considers impartially the merit of a rich suit of clothes in most places, the respect and the smiles of favour that it procures, not to speak of the envy and the sighs that it occasions (which is very often the principal charm to the wearer), one is forced to confess that there is need of an uncommon understanding to resist the temptation of pleasing friends and mortifying rivals, and that it is natural to young people to fall into a folly which betrays them to that want of money which is the source of a thousand basenesses. What numbers of men have begun the world with generous inclinations that have afterwards been the instruments of bringing misery on a whole people! led by a vain expense into debts that they could clear no other way but by the forfeit of their honour, and which they would never have contracted if the respect the many pay to habits was fixed by law only to a particular colour or cut of plain cloth! These reflections draw after them others that are too melancholy.

I will make haste to put 'em out of your head by the farce of relics with which I have been entertained in all the Romish churches. The Lutherans are not quite free from those follies. I have seen here in the

---

[1] Elizabeth, wife of John Hervey, first Earl of Bristol.

[2] The Archbishop, François Fénelon, had denounced luxury in two of his works: *Traité de l'éducation des filles* (1687) and *Télémaque* (1699).

principal church a large piece of the Cross set in jewels, and the point of a spear which they told me very gravely was the same that pierced the side of our Saviour. But I was particularly diverted in a little Roman Catholic church which is permitted here, where the professors of that religion are not very rich and consequently cannot adorn their images in so rich a manner as their neighbours, but not to be quite destitute of all finery they have dressed up an image of our Saviour over the altar in a fair full-bottomed wig, very well powdered.[3] I imagine I see your ladyship stare at this article, of which you very much doubt the veracity, but upon my word I have not yet made use of the privilege of a traveller, and my whole account is writ with the same plain sincerity of heart with which I assure you that I am, dear madam, your ladyship's etc.

[3] In 1687 another traveller, Maximilien Misson, had seen in Cologne a crucifix wearing a wig.

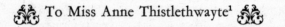 To Miss Anne Thistlethwayte[1]

Ratisbon, 30 August 1716

I had the pleasure of receiving yours but the day before I left London. I give you a thousand thanks for your good wishes, and have such an opinion of their efficacy I am persuaded that I owe (in part) to them the good luck of having proceeded so far in my long journey without any ill accident, for I do not reckon it any being stopped a few days in this town by a cold, since it has not only given me an opportunity of seeing all that is curious in it, but of making some acquaintance with the ladies, who have all been to see me with great civility, particularly Madame [von Wrisberg], the wife of our King's envoy from Hanover. She has carried me to all the assemblies and I have been magnificently entertained at her house, which is one of the finest here. You know that all the nobility of this place are envoys from different states. Here are a great number of them, and they might pass their time agreeably enough if they were less delicate on the point of ceremony. But instead of joining in the design of making the town as pleasant to one another as they can and improving their little societies, they amuse themselves no other way than with perpetual quarrels, which they take care to eternize by leaving them to their successors, and an envoy to Ratisbon receives regularly half a dozen quarrels amongst the perquisites of his employment.

You may be sure the ladies are not wanting on their side in cherishing and improving these important piques, which divides the town almost

[1] A friend who lived near West Dean, Wilts.

into as many parties as there are families, and they choose rather to suffer the mortification of sitting almost alone on their assembly nights than to recede one jot from their pretensions. I have not been here above a week and yet I have heard from almost every one of 'em the whole history of their wrongs and dreadful complaints of the injustice of their neighbours in hopes to draw me to their party, but I think it very prudent to remain neuter, though if I was to stay amongst them there would be no possibility of continuing so, their quarrels running so high they will not be civil to those that visit their adversaries. The foundation of these everlasting disputes turns entirely upon place and the title of Excellency, which they all pretend to, and what is very hard, will give it to nobody. For my part, I could not forbear advising them (for the public good) to give the title of Excellency to everybody, which would include the receiving it from everybody, but the very mention of such a dishonourable peace was received with as much indignation as Mrs Blackacre did the notion of a reference,[2] and I begun to think myself ill natured to offer to take from 'em, in a town where there is so few diversions, so entertaining an amusement. I know that my peaceable disposition already gives me a very ill figure, and that 'tis publicly whispered as a piece of impertinent pride in me that I have hitherto been saucily civil to everybody as if I thought nobody good enough to quarrel with. I should be obliged to change my behaviour if I did not intend to pursue my journey in a few days.

I have been to see the churches here and had the permission of touching the relics, which was never suffered in places where I was not known. I had by this privilege the opportunity of making an observation, which I don't doubt might have been made in all the other churches, that the emeralds and rubies that they show round their relics and images are most of them false, though they tell you that many of the crosses and Madonnas set round with them stones have been the gifts of the emperors and other great princes, and I don't doubt but they were at first jewels of value, but the good fathers have found it convenient to apply them to other uses and the people are just as well satisfied with bits of glass. Amongst these relics they showed me a prodigious claw set in gold, which they called the claw of a griffin, and I could not forbear asking the reverend priest that showed it, whether the griffin was a saint. This question almost put him beside his gravity, but he answered, they only kept it as a curiosity. But I was very much scandalized at a large silver image of the Trinity where the Father is represented under the figure of a decrepit old man with a beard down to his knees and a triple crown on his head, holding in his arms the Son fixed on the Cross, and the Holy Ghost in the shape of a dove hovering over him.

Madame [von Wrisberg] is come this minute to call me to the assembly and forces me to tell you very abruptly that I am ever yours.

---

[2] In William Wycherley's *The Plain Dealer* (1677), Act III, Mrs Blackacre scorns a 'reference' – that a dispute be settled by a Master in Chancery.

Vienna, 8 September 1716

I am now (my dear sister) safely arrived at Vienna and I thank God have not at all suffered in my health nor (what is dearer to me) in that of my child by all our fatigues. We travelled by water from Ratisbon, a journey perfectly agreeable, down the Danube in one of those little vessels that they very properly call wooden houses, having in them all the conveniencies of a palace; stoves in the chambers, kitchens, etc. They are rowed by twelve men each, and move with an incredible swiftness that in the same day you have the pleasure of a vast variety of prospects, and within a few hours' space of time one has the different diversion of seeing a populous city adorned with magnificent palaces, and the most romantic solitudes which appear distant from the commerce of mankind, the banks of the Danube being charmingly diversified with woods, rocks, mountains covered with vines, fields of corn, large cities, and ruins of ancient castles. I saw the great towns of Passau and Linz, famous for the retreat of the Imperial court when Vienna was besieged.[1]

This town, which has the honour of being the Emperor's residence, did not at all answer my ideas of it, being much less than I expected to find it. The streets are very close and so narrow one cannot observe the fine fronts of the palaces, though many of them very well deserve observation, being truly magnificent, all built of fine white stone and excessive high. The town being so much too little for the number of the people that desire to live in it, the builders seem to have projected to repair that misfortune by clapping one town on the top of another, most of the houses being of five and some of them of six stories. You may easily imagine that the streets being so narrow, the upper rooms are extreme dark, and what is an inconveniency much more intolerable in my opinion, there is no house that has so few as five or six families in it. The apartments of the greatest ladies and even of the ministers of state are divided but by a partition from that of a tailor or a shoe-maker, and I know nobody that has above two floors in any house, one for their own use and one higher for their servants. Those that have houses of their own let out the rest of them to whoever will take 'em; thus the great stairs (which are all of stone) are as common and as dirty as the street. 'Tis true when you have once travelled through them, nothing can be more surprisingly magnificent than the apartments. They are commonly a suite of eight or ten large rooms, all inlaid, the doors and windows richly carved and gilt, and the furniture such as is seldom seen in the palaces of sovereign princes in other countries: the hangings the finest tapestry of Brussels, prodigious large looking glasses in silver frames, fine Japan tables, the beds, chairs, canopies and window curtains

---

[1] In 1683, when the Turkish army reached the walls of Vienna, Emperor Leopold I and his court fled until the Turks were driven back by the King of Poland's army.

of the richest Genoa damask or velvet, almost covered with gold lace or embroidery – the whole made gay by pictures and vast jars of Japan china, and almost in every room large lustres of rock crystal.

I have already had the honour of being invited to dinner by several of the first people of quality, and I must do them the justice to say the good taste and magnificence of their tables very well answers to that of their furniture. I have been more than once entertained with fifty dishes of meat, all served in silver and well dressed, the dessert proportionable, served in the finest china; but the variety and richness of their wines is what appears the most surprising. The constant way is to lay a list of their names upon the plates of the guests along with the napkins, and I have counted several times to the number of eighteen different sorts, all exquisite in their kinds. I was yesterday at Count Schönborn's, the vice-chancellor's garden, where I was invited to dinner, and I must own that I never saw a place so perfectly delightful as the faubourgs of Vienna. It is very large and almost wholly composed of delicious palaces; and if the Emperor found it proper to permit the gates of the town to be laid open that the faubourgs might be joined to it, he would have one of the largest and best built cities of Europe. Count Schönborn's villa is one of the most magnificent, the furniture all rich brocades, so well fancied and fitted up, nothing can look more gay and splendid, not to speak of a gallery full of rarities of coral, mother of pearl, etc., and throughout the whole house a profusion of gilding, carving, fine paintings, the most beautiful porcelain, statues of alabaster and ivory, and vast orange and lemon trees in gilt pots. The dinner was perfectly fine and well ordered and made still more agreeable by the good humour of the Count.[2] I have not yet been at Court, being forced to stay for my gown, without which there is no waiting on the Empress, though I am not without a great impatience to see a beauty that has been the admiration of so many different nations. When I have had that honour I will not fail to let you know my real thoughts, always taking a particular pleasure in communicating them to my dear sister.

[2] Friedrich Karl, Count von Schönborn, had a reputation for affability and magnificence. His palace was the centre of Viennese social life and he himself the arbiter of its elegance.

Vienna, 14 September 1716

Perhaps you'll laugh at me for thanking you very gravely for all the obliging concern you express for me. 'Tis certain that I may, if I please, take the fine things you say to me for wit and raillery, and it may be it would be taking them right, but I never in my life was half so well disposed to believe you in earnest, and that distance which makes the continuation of your friendship improbable has very much increased my faith for it, and I find that I have (as well as the rest of my sex), whatever face I set on't, a strong disposition to believe in miracles. Don't fancy, however, that I am infected by the air of these popish countries, though I have so far wandered from the discipline of the Church of England to have been last Sunday at the opera, which was performed in the garden of the Favorita,[1] and I was so much pleased with it, I have not yet repented my seeing it. Nothing of that kind ever was more magnificent, and I can easily believe what I am told, that the decorations and habits cost the Emperor £30,000 sterling. The stage was built over a very large canal, and at the beginning of the second act divided into two parts, discovering the water, on which there immediately came from different parts two fleets of little gilded vessels that gave the representation of a naval fight. It is not easy to imagine the beauty of this scene, which I took particular notice of, but all the rest were perfectly fine in their kind. The story of the opera is the enchantments of Alcina,[2] which gives opportunity for a great variety of machines and changes of the scenes, which are performed with a surprising swiftness. The theatre is so large that 'tis hard to carry the eye to the end of it, and the habits in the utmost magnificence to the number of one hundred and eight. No house could hold such large decorations, but the ladies all sitting in the open air exposes them to great inconveniencies, for there is but one canopy for the Imperial family, and the first night it was represented, a shower of rain happening, the opera was broke off and the company crowded away in such confusion I was almost squeezed to death.

But if their operas are thus delightful, their comedies are in as high a degree ridiculous. They have but one playhouse, where I had the curiosity to go to a German comedy, and was very glad it happened to be the story of Amphitryon. That subject having been already handled by a Latin, French, and English poet, I was curious to see what an Austrian author would make of it.[3] I understood enough of the language to comprehend the greatest part of it, and besides I took with me a lady that had the goodness to explain to me every word. The way is to take a box which holds four for yourself and company. The fixed price is a gold

---

[1] The present day Theresianum.
[2] *Angelica Vincitrice di Alcina* by Johann Josef Fux.
[3] By Plautus, Molière, and Dryden; the German version seen by Lady Mary remains unidentified.

ducat. I thought the house very low and dark but I confess the comedy admirably recompensed that defect. I never laughed so much in my life. It begun with Jupiter's falling in love out of a peep hole in the clouds and ended with the birth of Hercules; but what was most pleasant was the use Jupiter made of his metamorphose, for you no sooner saw him under the figure of Amphitryon, but instead of flying to Alcmena with the raptures Mr Dryden puts into his mouth, he sends to Amphitryon's tailor and cheats him of a laced coat, and his banker of a bag of money, a Jew of a diamond ring, and bespeaks a great supper in his name; and the greatest part of the comedy turns upon poor Amphitryon's being tormented by these people for their debts, and Mercury uses Sosia in the same manner. But I could not easily pardon the liberty the poet has taken of larding his play with not only indecent expressions but such gross words as I don't think our mob would suffer from a mountebank, and the two Sosias very fairly let down their breeches in the direct view of the boxes, which were full of people of the first rank that seemed very well pleased with their entertainment, and they assured me this was a celebrated piece. I shall conclude my letter with this remarkable relation very well worthy the serious consideration of Mr Collier.[4] I won't trouble you with farewell compliments, which I think generally as impertinent as curtsies at leaving the room when the visit has been too long already.

[4] Jeremy Collier in his *Short View of the Immorality and Profaneness of the English Stage* (1698) attacked the Restoration playwrights, Dryden among them.

❧ To Lady Rich[1] ❧

Vienna, 20 September 1716

I am extremely pleased, but not at all surprised, at the long delightful letter you have had the goodness to send me. I know that you can think of an absent friend even in the midst of a Court, and that you love to oblige where you can have no view of a return, and I expect from you that you should love me and think of me when you don't see me.

I have compassion for the mortifications that you tell me befall our little friend, and I pity her much more since I know that they are only owing to the barbarous customs of our country. Upon my word, if she was here she would have no other fault but being something too young for the fashion, and she has nothing to do but to transplant hither about

[1] Elizabeth, wife of Sir Robert Rich; she was vain and frivolous.

seven years hence to be again a young and blooming beauty. I can assure you that wrinkles or a small stoop in the shoulders, nay, grey hair itself, is no objection to the making new conquests. I know you can't easily figure to yourself a young fellow of five and twenty ogling my Lady Suffolk with passion, or pressing to lead the Countess of Oxford from an opera, but such are the sights I see every day, and I don't perceive anybody surprised at 'em but myself. A woman till five and thirty is only looked upon as a raw girl and can possibly make no noise in the world till about forty. I don't know what your Ladyship may think of this matter, but 'tis a considerable comfort to me to know there is upon earth such a paradise for old women, and I am content to be insignificant at present in the design of returning when I am fit to appear nowhere else.

I cannot help lamenting upon this occasion the pitiful case of so many good English ladies long since retired to prudery and ratafia, whom, if their stars had luckily conducted them hither, would still shine in the first rank of beauties; and then that perplexing word reputation has quite another meaning here than what you give it at London, and getting a lover is so far from losing, that 'tis properly getting reputation, ladies being much more respected in regard to the rank of their lovers than that of their husbands. But what you'll think very odd, the two sects that divide our whole nation of petticoats are utterly unknown. Here are neither coquettes nor prudes. No woman dares appear coquette enough to encourage two lovers at a time, and I have not seen any such prudes as to pretend fidelity to their husbands, who are certainly the best natured set of people in the world, and they look upon their wives' gallants as favourably as men do upon their deputies that take the troublesome part of their business off of their hands, though they have not the less to do, for they are generally deputies in another place themselves. In one word, 'tis the established custom for every lady to have two husbands, one that bears the name, and another that performs the duties; and these engagements are so well known, that it would be a downright affront and publicly resented if you invited a woman of quality to dinner without at the same time inviting her two attendants of lover and husband, between whom she always sits in state with great gravity.

These sub-marriages generally last twenty year together, and the lady often commands the poor lover's estate even to the utter ruin of his family, though they are as seldom begun by any passion as other matches. But a man makes but an ill figure that is not in some commerce of this nature, and a woman looks out for a lover as soon as she's married as part of her equipage, without which she could not be genteel; and the first article of the treaty is establishing the pension, which remains to the lady though the gallant should prove inconstant, and this chargeable point of honour I look upon as the real foundation of so many wonderful instances of constancy. I really know several women of the first quality whose pensions are as well known as their annual rents, and yet nobody esteems them the less. On the contrary, their discretion would be called in question if they should be suspected to be mistresses for nothing, and a great part of their emulation consists in trying who shall get most; and having no intrigue at all is so far a disgrace that I'll assure you a lady who is very much my friend here told me but yesterday how much I was obliged to her for justifying my conduct in a conversation on my subject, where it was publicly asserted that I could not possibly have common sense that had been about town above a fortnight and had made no steps towards commencing an *amour*. My friend pleaded for me that my stay was uncertain and she believed that was the cause of my seeming stupidity, and this was all she could find to say in my justification.

But one of the pleasantest adventures I ever met in my life was last night and which will give you a just idea after what delicate manner the *belles passions* are managed in this country. I was at the assembly of the Countess of ——, and the young Count of —— led me down stairs, and he asked me how long I intended to stay here. I made answer that my stay depended on the Emperor and it was not in my power to determine it. 'Well, Madame,' said he, 'whether your time here is to be long or short, I think you ought to pass it agreeably, and to that end you must engage in a little affair of the heart.' – 'My heart,' answered I gravely enough, 'does not engage very easily, and I have no design of parting with it.' – 'I see, Madame,' said he, sighing, 'by the ill nature of that answer that I am not to hope for it, which is a great mortification to me that am charmed with you; but, however, I am still devoted to your service, and since I am not worthy of entertaining you myself, do me the honour of letting me know who you like best amongst us, and I'll engage to manage the affair entirely to your satisfaction.' – You may judge in what manner I should have received this compliment in my own country, but I was well enough acquainted with the way of this to know that he really intended me an obligation, and thanked him with a grave curtsy for his zeal to serve me and only assured him that I had no occasion to make use of it. Thus you see, my dear, gallantry and good breeding are as different in different climates as morality and religion. Who have the rightest notions of both we shall never know till the Day of Judgement, for which great day of *éclaircissement* I own there is very little impatience in your, etc.

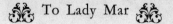

Leipzig, 21 November 1716

I believe (dear sister) you will easily forgive my not writing to you from Dresden as I promised, when I tell you that I never went out of my chaise from Prague to that place. You may imagine how heartily I was tired with twenty-four hours post travelling without sleep or refreshment (for I can never sleep in a coach however fatigued). We passed by moonshine the frightful precipices that divide Bohemia from Saxony, at the bottom of which runs the River Elbe, but I cannot say that I had reason to fear drowning in it, being perfectly convinced that in case of a tumble it was utterly impossible to come alive to the bottom. In many places the road is so narrow that I could not discern an inch of space between the wheels and the precipice; yet I was so good a wife not to wake Mr Wortley, who was fast asleep by my side, to make him share in my fears, since the danger was unavoidable, till I perceived, by the bright light of the moon, our postilions nodding on horseback while the horses were on a full gallop, and I thought it very convenient to call out to desire 'em to look where they were going. My calling waked Mr Wortley and he was much more surprised than myself at the situation we were in, and assured me that he had passed the Alps five times in different places without ever having done a road so dangerous.[1] I have been told since, 'tis common to find the bodies of travellers in the Elbe, but thank God that was not our destiny and we came safe to Dresden, so much tired with fear and fatigue it was not possible for me to compose myself to write. After passing these dreadful rocks, Dresden appeared to me a wonderful agreeable situation in a fine large plain on the banks of the Elbe. I was very glad to stay there a day to rest myself.[2]

The town is the neatest I have seen in Germany. Most of the houses are new built, the Elector's palace very handsome, and his repository full of curiosities of different kinds with a collection of medals very much esteemed. Sir [Richard Vernon], our King's envoy, came to see me here, and Madame de L[orme], whom I knew in London when her husband was minister to the King of Poland there. She offered me all things in her power to entertain me and brought some ladies with her whom she presented to me. The Saxon ladies resemble the Austrian no more than the Chinese those of London. They are very genteelly dressed after the French and English modes, and have generally pretty faces, but the most determined *minaudières* in the whole world. They would think it a mortal sin against good breeding if they either spoke or moved in a natural manner. They all affect a little soft lisp and a

---

[1] Wortley had made the Grand Tour from 1700 to 1703.

[2] After Nathaniel Wraxall travelled the same road in 1777 he wrote: 'I . . . crossed the mountains which divide Saxony from Bohemia with the greatest difficulty, among precipices which overhang the Elbe, and through continual snows. I found Lady Wortley Montagu's description, though written sixty years ago, literally verified.'

pretty pitty-pat step, which female frailties ought, however, to be forgiven 'em in favour of their civility and good nature to strangers, which I have a great deal of reason to praise.

The Countess of Cosel is kept prisoner in a melancholy castle some leagues from hence, and I cannot forbear telling you what I have heard of her, because it seems to me very extraordinary, though I foresee I shall swell my letter to the size of a packet. She was mistress to the King of Poland (Elector of Saxony) with so absolute a dominion over him that never any lady had had so much power in that Court. They tell a pleasant story of His Majesty's first declaration of love, which he made in a visit to her, bringing in one hand a bag of 100,000 crowns, and in the other a horseshoe, which he snapped in sunder before her face, leaving her to draw consequences from such remarkable proofs of strength and liberality. I know not which charmed her, but she consented to leave her husband to give herself up to him entirely, being divorced publicly in such a manner as (by their law) permits either party to marry again. God knows whether it was at this time or in some other fond fit, but 'tis certain the King had the weakness to make her a formal contract of marriage, which though it could signify nothing during the life of the Queen, pleased her so well that she could not be contented without telling all people she saw of it and giving herself the airs of a queen.

Men endure everything while they are in love, but when the excess of passion was cooled by long possession, His Majesty begun to reflect on the ill consequences of leaving such a paper in her hands, and desired to have it restored to him. She rather chose to endure all the most violent effects of his anger than give it up; and though she is one of the richest and most avaricious ladies of her country she has refused the offer of the continuation of a large pension and the security of a vast sum of money she has amassed, and has at last provoked the King to confine her person where she endures all the terrors of a strait imprisonment and remains still inflexible either to threats or promises, though her violent passion has brought her into fits, which 'tis supposed will soon put an end to her life.[3] I cannot forbear having some compassion for a woman that suffers for a point of honour, however mistaken, especially in a country where points of honour are not over scrupulously observed amongst ladies.

I could have wished Mr Wortley's business had permitted a longer stay at Dresden. Perhaps I am partial to a town where they profess the Protestant religion, but everything seemed to me with quite another air of politeness than I have found in other places. Leipzig, where I am at present, is a town very considerable for its trade, and I take this opportunity of buying pages' liveries, gold stuffs for myself, etc., all things of

---

[3] Except for the detail of the King's bending a horseshoe, Lady Mary's narrative is confirmed by other sources. In 1700 Anna Constanze von Brockdorf, who was Countess von Hoym, became mistress to Augustus the Strong, who created her Countess von Cosel in 1706. She died in 1765, aged eighty-five.

that kind being at least double the price at Vienna, partly because of the excessive customs and partly the want of genius and industry in the people, who make no one sort of thing there, and the ladies are obliged to send even for their shoes out of Saxony. The fair here is one of the most considerable in Germany, and the resort of all the people of quality as well as the merchants. This is a fortified town, but I avoid ever mentioning fortifications, being sensible that I know not how to speak of 'em. I am the more easy under my ignorance when I reflect that I am sure you'll willingly forgive the omission, for if I made you the most exact description of all the ravelins and bastions I see in my travels, I dare swear you would ask me – what is a ravelin? and what is a bastion?

Adieu, my dear sister.

To Lady Mar

Blankenburg, 17 December 1716

I received yours (dear sister) the very day I left Hanover. You may easily imagine I was then in too great a hurry to answer it, but you see I take the first opportunity of doing myself that pleasure. I came here the fifteenth very late at night, after a terrible journey in the worst roads and weather that ever poor travellers suffered. I have taken this little fatigue merely to oblige the reigning Empress and carry a message from Her Imperial Majesty to the Duchess of Blankenburg, her mother, who is a princess of great address and good breeding, and may be still called a fine woman. It was so late when I came to this town, I did not think it proper to disturb the Duke and Duchess with the news of my arrival and took up my quarters in a miserable inn; but as soon as I had sent my compliment to their Highnesses, they immediately sent me their own coach and six horses, which had, however, enough to do to draw us up the very high hill on which the castle is situated. The Duchess is extremely obliging to me and this little Court is not without its diversions. The Duke tallies at basset[1] every night; and the Duchess tells me that she is so well pleased with my company, I should find it very difficult to steal time to write if she was not now at church, where I cannot wait on her, not understanding the language enough to pay my devotions in it.

You will not forgive me if I do not say something of Hanover. I cannot tell you that the town is either large or magnificent. The opera

[1] Plays cards.

house, which was built by the late Elector,[2] is much finer than that of Vienna. I was very sorry the ill weather did not permit me to see Herrenhausen in all its beauty, but in spite of the snow I thought the gardens very fine. I was particularly surprised at the vast number of orange trees, much larger than any I have ever seen in England, though this climate is certainly colder. But I had more reason to wonder that night at the King's table. There was brought to him from a gentleman of this country two large baskets full of ripe oranges and lemons of different sorts, many of which were quite new to me, and what I thought worth all the rest, two ripe ananas, which to my taste are a fruit perfectly delicious. You know they are naturally the growth of Brazil, and I could not imagine how they could come there but by enchantment. Upon inquiry I learnt that they have brought their stoves to such perfection, they lengthen the summer as long as they please, giving to every plant the degree of heat it would receive from the sun in its native soil. The effect is very near the same. I am surprised we do not practise in England so useful an invention. This reflection naturally leads me to consider our obstinacy in shaking with cold six months in the year rather than make use of stoves, which are certainly one of the greatest conveniencies of life; and so far from spoiling the form of a room, they add very much to the magnificence of it when they are painted and gilt as at Vienna, or at Dresden where they are often in the shapes of china jars, statues, or fine cabinets, so naturally represented they are not to be distinguished. If ever I return, in defiance to the fashion you shall certainly see one in the chamber of, dear sister, etc.

I will write often, since you desire it, but I must beg you to be a little more particular in yours. You fancy me at forty miles distance and forget that after so long an absence I can't understand hints.

---

[2] Built inside the palace, 1688–89, by Ernst August I, it was one of the largest and handsomest theatres of the time.

Adrianople, 1 April 1717

I am now got into a new world where everything I see appears to me a change of scene, and I write to your Ladyship with some content of mind, hoping at least that you will find the charm of novelty in my letters and no longer reproach me that I tell you nothing extraordinary. I won't trouble you with a relation of our tedious journey, but I must not omit what I saw remarkable at Sophia, one of the most beautiful towns in the Turkish Empire and famous for its hot baths that are resorted to both for diversion and health. I stopped here one day on purpose to see them. Designing to go incognito, I hired a Turkish coach. These *voitures* are not at all like ours, but much more convenient for the country, the heat being so great that glasses would be very troublesome. They are made a good deal in the manner of the Dutch coaches, having wooden lattices painted and gilded, the inside being painted with baskets and nosegays of flowers, intermixed commonly with little poetical mottoes. They are covered all over with scarlet cloth, lined with silk and very often richly embroidered and fringed. This covering entirely hides the persons in them, but may be thrown back at pleasure and the ladies peep through the lattices. They hold four people very conveniently, seated on cushions, but not raised.

In one of these covered wagons I went to the bagnio about ten o'clock. It was already full of women. It is built of stone in the shape of a dome with no windows but in the roof, which gives light enough. There was five of these domes joined together, the outmost being less than the rest and serving only as a hall where the porteress stood at the door. Ladies of quality generally give this woman the value of a crown or ten shillings, and I did not forget that ceremony. The next room is a very large one, paved with marble, and all round it raised two sofas of marble, one above another. There were four fountains of cold water in this room, falling first into marble basins and then running on the floor in little channels made for that purpose, which carried the streams into the next room, something less than this, with the same sort of marble sofas, but so hot with steams of sulphur proceeding from the baths joining to it, 'twas impossible to stay there with one's clothes on. The two other domes were the hot baths, one of which had cocks of cold water turning into it to temper it to what degree of warmth the bathers have a mind to.

I was in my travelling habit, which is a riding dress, and certainly appeared very extraordinary to them, yet there was not one of 'em that showed the least surprise or impertinent curiosity, but received me with all the obliging civility possible. I know no European court where the ladies would have behaved themselves in so polite a manner to a stranger. I believe in the whole there were two hundred women[1] and yet none of those disdainful smiles or satiric whispers that never fail in our assemblies when anybody appears that is not dressed exactly in fashion. They repeated over and over to me, 'Uzelle, pek uzelle', which is nothing but, 'Charming, very charming'. The first sofas were covered with cushions and rich carpets, on which sat the ladies, and on the second their slaves behind 'em, but without any distinction of rank by their dress, all being in the state of nature, that is, in plain English, stark naked, without any beauty or defect concealed, yet there was not the least wanton smile or immodest gesture amongst 'em. They walked and moved with the same majestic grace which Milton describes of our General Mother.[2] There were many amongst them as exactly proportioned as ever any goddess was drawn by the pencil of Guido or Titian, and most of their skins shiningly white, only adorned by their beautiful hair divided into many tresses hanging on their shoulders, braided either with pearl or riband, perfectly representing the figures of the Graces.

I was here convinced of the truth of a reflection that I had often made, that if 'twas the fashion to go naked the face would be hardly observed. I perceived that the ladies with the finest skins and most delicate shapes had the greatest share of my admiration, though their faces were sometimes less beautiful than those of their companions. To tell you the truth, I had wickedness enough to wish secretly that Mr Jervas[3] could have been there invisible. I fancy it would have very much improved his art to see so many fine women naked in different postures, some in conversation, some working, others drinking coffee or sherbet, and many negligently lying on their cushions while their slaves (generally pretty girls of seventeen or eighteen) were employed in braiding their hair in several pretty manners. In short, 'tis the women's coffeehouse, where all the news of the town is told, scandal invented, etc. They generally take this diversion once a week, and stay there at least four or five hours without getting cold by immediate coming out of the hot bath into the cool room, which was very surprising to me. The lady that seemed the most considerable amongst them entreated me to sit by her and would fain have undressed me for the bath. I excused myself with some difficulty, they being all so earnest in persuading me. I was at last forced to open my skirt and show them my stays, which satisfied 'em very well, for I saw they believed I was so locked up in that machine that it was not in my own power to open it, which contrivance they attributed to my husband. I was charmed with their civility and beauty and should have been very glad to pass more time with them, but Mr Wortley resolving to pursue his journey the next morning early I was in haste to see the ruins of Justinian's church, which did not afford me

---

[1] Ingres copied into a notebook several passages from this letter, beginning here, using a French translation of the 1805 edition. His famous painting '*Le Bain Turc*' (1862), now in the Louvre, shows the influence of Lady Mary's sensuous descriptions.

[2] *Paradise Lost*, iv. 304–18.

[3] Charles Jervas, portrait painter and friend of the London wits.

so agreeable a prospect as I had left, being little more than a heap of stones.

Adieu, madam. I am sure I have now entertained you with an account of such a sight as you never saw in your life and what no book of travels could inform you of. 'Tis no less than death for a man to be found in one of these places.

🙖 To Lady Bristol 🙖

Adrianople, 1 April 1717

As I never can forget the smallest of your Ladyship's commands, my first business here has been to inquire after the stuffs you ordered me to look for, without being able to find what you would like. The difference of the dress here and at London is so great, the same sort of things are not proper for caftans and *manteaux*. However, I will not give over my search, but renew it again at Constantinople, though I have reason to believe there is nothing finer than what is to be found here, being the present residence of the Court.[1]

The Grand Signior's eldest daughter was married some few days before I came, and upon that occasion the Turkish ladies display all their magnificence. The bride was conducted to her husband's house in very great splendour. She is widow of the late Vizier who was killed at Peterwaradin, though that ought rather to be called a contract than a marriage, not having ever lived with him. However, the greatest part of his wealth is hers. He had the permission of visiting her in the Seraglio and, being one of the handsomest men in the Empire, had very much engaged her affections. When she saw this second husband, who is at least fifty, she could not forbear bursting into tears. He is a man of merit and the declared favourite of the Sultan, which they call Mosaip, but that is not enough to make him pleasing in the eyes of a girl of thirteen.[2]

The government here is entirely in the hands of the army, and the Grand Signior with all his absolute power as much a slave as any of his

---

[1] After two centuries of seclusion within the Grand Seraglio in Constantinople, the Sultans preferred the freer life of Adrianople, where they enjoyed game preserves and immense gardens.

[2] Princess Fatima married Ibrahim Pasha on 20 February 1717, more than a month before Lady Mary's arrival. He was in fact about the same age as her first husband, Ali Pasha, killed the previous year.

subjects, and trembles at a janissary's frown. Here is, indeed, a much
greater appearance of subjection than amongst us. A minister of state
is not spoke to but upon the knee. Should a reflection on his conduct be
dropped in a coffee-house (for they have spies everywhere) the house
would be razed to the ground and perhaps the whole company put to
the torture. No huzzaing mobs, senseless pamphlets and tavern disputes
about politics:

> A consequential ill that freedom draws,
> A bad effect but from a noble cause,

none of our harmless calling names; but when a minister here displeases
the people, in three hours' time he is dragged even from his master's
arms. They cut off his hands, head and feet, and throw them before the
palace gate with all the respect in the world, while that Sultan (to whom
they all profess an unlimited adoration) sits trembling in his apartment,
and dare neither defend nor revenge his favourite. This is the blessed
condition of the most absolute monarch upon earth, who owns no law
but his will. I cannot help wishing (in the loyalty of my heart) that the
Parliament would send hither a shipload of your passive obedient men
that they might see arbitrary government in its clearest strongest light,[3]
where 'tis hard to judge whether the prince, people or ministers are
most miserable. I could make many reflections on this subject, but I
know, madam, your own good sense has already furnished you with
better than I am capable of.

I went yesterday with the French Ambassadress[4] to see the Grand
Signior in his passage to the Mosque. He was preceded by a numerous
guard of janissaries with vast white feathers on their heads; *spahis* and
bostangées, these are the foot and horse guard; and the royal gardeners,
which are a very considerable body of men, dressed in different habits
of fine, lively colours that at a distance they appeared like a parterre of
tulips; after them, the Aga of the janissaries in a robe of purple velvet
lined with silver tissue, his horse led by two slaves richly dressed; next
him the Kuzlir Aga (your ladyship knows this is the chief guardian of
the Seraglio ladies) in a deep yellow cloth (which suited very well to his
black face) lined with sables; and last His Sublimity himself in green
lined with the fur of a black Muscovite fox, which is supposed worth
£1,000 sterling, mounted on a fine horse with furniture embroidered
with jewels. Six more horses richly furnished were led after him, and
two of his principal courtiers bore, one his gold and the other his silver
coffee pot, on a staff. Another carried a silver stool on his head for him
to sit on. It would be too tedious to tell your ladyship the various
dresses and turbans (by which their rank is distinguished) but they were
all extreme rich and gay to the number of some thousands, that perhaps

[3] The High Anglican Tories believed in passive obedience to authority.
[4] A daughter of the Duc de Biron, she had married the Marquis de Bonnac in
1715, and arrived in Adrianople in January 1717.

there cannot be seen a more beautiful procession. The Sultan appeared to us a handsome man of about forty, with a very graceful air but something severe in his countenance, his eyes very full and black.[5] He happened to stop under the window where we stood and (I suppose being told who we were) looked upon us very attentively that we had full leisure to consider him, and the French Ambassadress agreed with me as to his good mien.

I see that lady very often. She is young and her conversation would be a great relief to me if I could persuade her to live without those forms and ceremonies that make life formal and tiresome, but she is so delighted with her guards, her twenty-four footmen, gentleman ushers, etc., that she would rather die than make me a visit without 'em, not to reckon a coach full of attending damsels yclep'd maids of honour. What vexes me is that as long as she will visit with this troublesome equipage I am obliged to do the same. However, our mutual interest makes us much together. I went with her t'other day all round the town in an open gilt chariot with our joint train of attendants, preceded by our guards, who might have summoned the people to see what they never had seen, nor ever would see again, two young Christian Ambassadresses never yet having been in this country at the same time nor, I believe, ever will again. Your ladyship may easily imagine that we drew a vast crowd of spectators, but all silent as death. If any of them had taken the liberties of our mob upon any strange sight, our janissaries had made no scruple of falling on 'em with their scimitars without danger of so doing, being above law. Yet these people have some good qualities. They are very zealous and faithful where they serve, and look upon it as their business to fight for you upon all occasions, of which I had a very pleasant instance in a village on this side Philippopolis, where we were met by our domestic guard. I happened to bespeak pigeons for my supper, upon which one of my janissaries went immediately to the cadi (the chief civil officer of the town) and ordered him to send in some dozens. The poor man answered that he had already sent about but could get none. My janissary, in the height of his zeal for my service, immediately locked him up prisoner in his room, telling him he deserved death for his impudence in offering to excuse his not obeying my command, but out of respect to me he would not punish him but by my order, and accordingly came very gravely to me to ask what should be done to him, adding by way of compliment that, if I pleased, he would bring me his head. This may give some idea of the unlimited power of these fellows, who are all sworn brothers and bound to revenge the injuries done to one another, whether at Cairo, Aleppo, or any part of the world; and this inviolable league makes them so powerful, the greatest man at the Court never speaks to them but in a flattering

---

[5] Wortley's predecessor as ambassador had described him as 'exceedingly covetous, haughty, and ambitious . . . hasty, violent, and cruel, but variable and unsteady'.

tone, and in Asia any man that is rich is forced to enroll himself a janissary to secure his estate. – But I have already said enough and I dare swear, dear madam, that by this time 'tis a very comfortable reflection to you that there is no possibility of your receiving such a tedious letter but once in six months. 'Tis that consideration has given me the assurance to entertain you so long and will, I hope, plead the excuse of, dear madam, etc.

To Lady Mar

Adrianople, 1 April 1717

I wish to God (dear sister) that you was as regular in letting me have the pleasure of knowing what passes on your side of the globe as I am careful in endeavouring to amuse you by the account of all I see that I think you care to hear of. You content yourself with telling me over and over that the town is very dull. It may possibly be dull to you when everyday does not present you with something new, but for me that am in arrear at least two months' news, all that seems very stale with you would be fresh and sweet here; pray let me into more particulars. I will try to awaken your gratitude by giving you a full and true relation of the novelties of this place, none of which would surprise you more than a sight of my person as I am now in my Turkish habit, though I believe you would be of my opinion that 'tis admirably becoming. I intend to send you my picture; in the meantime accept of it here.

The first piece of my dress is a pair of drawers, very full, that reach to my shoes and conceal the legs more modestly than your petticoats. They are of a thin, rose-colour damask brocaded with silver flowers, my shoes of white kid leather embroidered with gold. Over this hangs my smock of a fine white silk gauze edged with embroidery. This smock has wide sleeves hanging half-way down the arm and is closed at the neck with a diamond button, but the shape and colour of the bosom very well to be distinguished through it. The *antery* is a waistcoat made close to the shape, of white and gold damask, with very long sleeves falling back and fringed with deep gold fringe, and should have diamond or pearl buttons. My caftan of the same stuff with my drawers is a robe exactly fitted to my shape and reaching to my feet, with very long strait falling sleeves. Over this is the girdle of about four fingers broad, which all that can afford have entirely of diamonds or other precious stones. Those that will not be at that expense have it of exquisite embroidery on satin, but it must be fastened before with a clasp of diamonds. The *curdée* is a loose robe they throw off or put on according to the weather, being of a rich brocade (mine is green and gold) either lined with ermine or sables; the sleeves reach very little below the shoulders.

The head-dress is composed of a cap called *talpack*, which is in winter of fine velvet embroidered with pearls or diamonds and in summer of a light, shining silver stuff. This is fixed on one side of the head, hanging a little way down with a gold tassel and bound on either with a circle of diamonds (as I have seen several) or a rich embroidered handkerchief. On the other side of the head the hair is laid flat, and here the ladies are at liberty to show their fancies, some putting flowers, others a plume of heron's feathers, and, in short, what they please, but the most general fashion is a large bouquet of jewels made like natural flowers, that is, the buds of pearl, the roses of different coloured rubies, the jasmines of diamonds, jonquils of topazes, etc., so well set and enamelled 'tis hard to imagine anything of that kind so beautiful. The hair hangs at its full length behind, divided into tresses braided with pearl or riband, which is always in great quantity.

I never saw in my life so many fine heads of hair. I have counted one hundred and ten of these tresses of one lady's, all natural; but it must be owned that every beauty is more common here than with us. 'Tis surprising to see a young woman that is not very handsome. They have naturally the most beautiful complexions in the world and generally large black eyes. I can assure you with great truth that the Court of England (though I believe it the fairest in Christendom) cannot show so many beauties as are under our protection here. They generally shape their eyebrows, and the Greeks and Turks have a custom of putting round their eyes on the inside a black tincture that, at a distance or by candlelight, adds very much to the blackness of them. I fancy many of our ladies would be overjoyed to know this secret, but 'tis too visible by day. They dye their nails rose colour; I own I cannot enough accustom myself to this fashion to find any beauty in it.

As to their morality or good conduct, I can say like Harlequin, ''Tis just as 'tis with you'; and the Turkish ladies don't commit one sin the less for not being Christians. Now I am a little acquainted with their ways, I cannot forbear admiring either the exemplary discretion or extreme stupidity of all the writers that have given accounts of 'em. 'Tis very easy to see they have more liberty than we have, no woman of what rank soever being permitted to go in the streets without two muslins, one that covers her face all but her eyes and another that hides the whole dress of her head and hangs half-way down her back; and their shapes are wholly concealed by a thing they call a *ferigée*, which no woman of any sort appears without. This has strait sleeves that reach to their fingers' ends and it laps all round 'em, not unlike a riding hood. In winter 'tis of cloth, and in summer, plain stuff or silk. You may guess how effectually this disguises them, that there is no distinguishing the great lady from her slave, and 'tis impossible for the most jealous husband to know his wife when he meets her, and no man dare either touch or follow a woman in the street.

This perpetual masquerade gives them entire liberty of following their inclinations without danger of discovery. The most usual method of intrigue is to send an appointment to the lover to meet the lady at a Jew's shop, which are as notoriously convenient as our Indian houses, and yet even those that don't make that use of 'em do not scruple to go to buy penn'orths and tumble over rich goods, which are chiefly to be found amongst that sort of people. The great ladies seldom let their gallants know who they are, and 'tis so difficult to find it out that they can very seldom guess at her name they have corresponded with above half a year together.

You may easily imagine the number of faithful wives very small in a country where they have nothing to fear from their lovers' indiscretion, since we see so many that have the courage to expose themselves to that in this world and all the threatened punishment of the next, which is never preached to the Turkish damsels. Neither have they much to apprehend from the resentment of their husbands, those ladies that are rich having all their money in their own hands, which they take with 'em upon a divorce with an addition which he is obliged to give 'em. Upon the whole, I look upon the Turkish women as the only free people in the empire. The very Divan pays a respect to 'em, and the Grand Signior himself, when a pasha is executed, never violates the privileges of the harem (or women's apartment) which remains unsearched entire to the widow. They are queens of their slaves, which the husband has no permission so much as to look upon, except it be an old woman or two that his lady chooses. 'Tis true their law permits them four wives, but there is no instance of a man of quality that makes use of this liberty, or of a woman of rank that would suffer it. When a husband happens to be inconstant (as those things will happen) he keeps his mistress in a house apart and visits her as privately as he can, just as 'tis with you. Amongst all the great men here I only know the *tefterdar* (*i.e.* treasurer) that keeps a number of she slaves for his own use (that is, on his own side of the house, for a slave once given to serve a lady is entirely at her disposal), and he is spoke of as a libertine, or what we should call a rake, and his wife won't see him, though she continues to live in his house.

Thus you see, dear sister, the manners of mankind do not differ so widely as our voyage writers would make us believe. Perhaps it would be more entertaining to add a few surprising customs of my own invention, but nothing seems to me so agreeable as truth, and I believe nothing so acceptable to you. I conclude with repeating the great truth of my being, dear sister, etc.

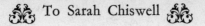

Adrianople, 1 April 1717

In my opinion, dear Sarah, I ought rather to quarrel with you for not answering my Nijmegen letter of August till December, than to excuse my not writing again till now. I am sure there is on my side a very good excuse for silence, having gone such tiresome land journeys, though I don't find the conclusion of 'em so bad as you seem to imagine. I am very easy here and not in the solitude you fancy me; the great quantity of Greek, French, English and Italians that are under our protection make their court to me from morning till night, and I'll assure you are many of 'em very fine ladies, for there is no possibility for a Christian to live easily under this government but by the protection of an ambassador, and the richer they are the greater their danger.

Those dreadful stories you have heard of the plague have very little foundation in truth. I own I have much ado to reconcile myself to the sound of a word which has always given me such terrible ideas, though I am convinced there is little more in it than a fever, as a proof of which we passed through two or three towns most violently infected. In the very next house where we lay, in one of 'em, two persons died of it. Luckily for me I was so well deceived that I knew nothing of the matter, and I was made believe that our second cook who fell ill there had only a great cold. However, we left our doctor to take care of him, and yesterday they both arrived here in good health and I am now let into the secret that he has had the plague. There are many that 'scape of it, neither is the air ever infected. I am persuaded it would be as easy to root it out here as out of Italy and France, but it does so little mischief, they are not very solicitous about it and are content to suffer this distemper instead of our variety, which they are utterly unacquainted with.

Apropos of distempers, I am going to tell you a thing that I am sure will make you wish yourself here. The smallpox, so fatal and so general amongst us, is here entirely harmless by the invention of engrafting (which is the term they give it). There is a set of old women who make it their business to perform the operation. Every autumn, in the month of September, when the great heat is abated, people send to one another to know if any of their family has a mind to have the smallpox. They make parties for this purpose, and when they are met (commonly fifteen or sixteen together) the old woman comes with a nutshell full of the matter of the best sort of smallpox and asks what veins you please to have opened. She immediately rips open that you offer to her with a large needle (which gives you no more pain than a common scratch) and puts into the vein as much venom as can lie upon the head of her needle, and after binds up the little wound with a hollow bit of shell, and in this manner opens four or five veins. The Grecians have commonly the superstition of opening one in the middle of the forehead, in each arm, and on the breast to mark the sign of the cross, but this has a very ill effect, all these wounds leaving little scars, and is not done by those that are not superstitious, who choose to have them in the legs or that part of the arm that is concealed. The children or young patients play together all the rest of the day and are in perfect health till the eighth. Then the fever begins to seize 'em and they keep their beds two days, very seldom three. They have very rarely above twenty or thirty in their faces, which never mark, and in eight days' time they are as well as before their illness. Where they are wounded there remains running sores during the distemper, which I don't doubt is a great relief to it. Every year thousands undergo this operation, and the French ambassador says pleasantly that they take the smallpox here by way of diversion as they take the waters in other countries. There is no example of anyone that has died in it, and you may believe I am very well satisfied of the safety of the experiment since I intend to try it on my dear little son.[1] I am patriot enough to take pains to bring this useful invention into fashion in England, and I should not fail to write to some of our doctors very particularly about it if I knew any one of 'em that I thought had virtue enough to destroy such a considerable branch of their revenue for the good of mankind, but that distemper is too beneficial to them not to expose to all their resentment the hardy wight that should undertake to put an end to it. Perhaps if I live to return I may, however, have courage to war with 'em. Upon this occasion, admire the heroism in the heart of your friend, etc.

[1] She did so a year later.

🍀 To the Abbé Conti[1] 🍀

Constantinople, 29 May 1717

I have had the advantage of very fine weather all my journey, and the summer being now in its beauty I enjoyed the pleasure of fine prospects; and the meadows being full of all sorts of garden flowers and sweet herbs, my berlin perfumed the air as it pressed 'em. The Grand Signior furnished us with thirty covered wagons for our baggage and five coaches of the country for my women. We found the road full of the great *spahis* and their equipages, coming out of Asia to the war. They always travel with tents, but I chose to lie in houses all the way. I will not trouble you with the names of the villages we passed in which there was nothing remarkable, but at Çorlu we were lodged in a *conac*, or little seraglio, built for the use of the Grand Signior when he goes this

[1] The Abbé Antonio Conti (1677–1749) was an Italian philosopher, savant, and poet. He had visited London in 1715.

road. I had the curiosity to view all the apartments destined for the ladies of his court. They were in the midst of a thick grove of trees, made fresh by fountains, but I was surprised to see the walls almost covered with little distiches of Turkish verse writ with pencils. I made my interpreter explain them to me and I found several of them very well turned, though I easily believed him that they lost much of their beauty in the translation. One runs literally thus in English:

> We come into this world, we lodge, and we depart;
> He never goes that's lodged within my heart.

The rest of our journey was through fine painted meadows by the side of the Sea of Marmara, the ancient Propontis. We lay the next night at Selivria, anciently a noble town. It is now a very good seaport, and neatly built enough, and has a bridge of thirty-two arches. Here is a famous ancient Greek church. I had given one of my coaches to a Greek lady who desired the conveniency of travelling with me. She designed to pay her devotions and I was glad of the opportunity of going with her. I found it an ill built place, set out with the same sort of ornaments but less rich than the Roman Catholic churches. They showed me a saint's body, where I threw a piece of money, and a picture of the Virgin Mary drawn by the hand of St Luke, very little to the credit of his painting, but, however, the finest Madonna of Italy is not more famous for her miracles. The Greeks have the most monstrous taste in their pictures, which for more finery are always drawn upon a gold ground. You may imagine what a good air this has, but they have no notion either of shade or proportion. They have a Bishop here, who officiated in his purple robe, and sent me a candle almost as big as myself for a present when I was at my lodging.

We lay the next night at a town called Büjük Cekmege or Great Bridge, and the night following at Küjük Cekmege, Little Bridge, in a very pleasant lodging, formerly a monastery of dervishes, having before it a large court encompassed with marble cloisters with a good fountain in the middle. The prospect from this place and the gardens round it are the most agreeable I have seen, and shows that monks of all religions know how to choose their retirements. 'Tis now belonging to a *hogia* or schoolmaster, who teaches boys here; and asking him to show me his own apartment I was surprised to see him point to a tall cypress tree in the garden, on the top of which was a place for a bed for himself, and a little lower, one for his wife and two children, who slept there every night. I was so much diverted with the fancy I resolved to examine his nest nearer, but after going up fifty steps I found I had still fifty to go and then I must climb from branch to branch with some hazard of my neck. I thought it the best way to come down again.

We arrived the next evening at Constantinople, but I can yet tell you very little of it, all my time having been taken up with receiving visits, which are at least a very good entertainment to the eyes, the young women being all beauties and their beauty highly improved by the good taste of their dress. Our palace is in Pera, which is no more a suburb of Constantinople than Westminster is a suburb to London. All the Ambassadors are lodged very near each other. One part of our house shows us the port, the city and the seraglio, and the distant hills of Asia, perhaps altogether the most beautiful prospect in the world. A certain French author says that Constantinople is twice as large as Paris.[2] Mr Wortley is unwilling to own 'tis bigger than London, though I confess it appears to me to be so, but I don't believe 'tis so populous. The burying fields about it are certainly much larger than the whole city. 'Tis surprising what a vast deal of land is lost this way in Turkey. Sometimes I have seen burying places of several miles belonging to very inconsiderable villages which were formerly great towns and retain no other mark of their ancient grandeur. On no occasion they remove a stone that serves for a monument. Some of them are costly enough, being of very fine marble. They set up a pillar with a carved turban on the top of it to the memory of a man, and as the turbans by their different shapes show the quality or profession, 'tis in a manner putting up the arms of the deceased; besides, the pillar commonly bears a large inscription in gold letters. The ladies have a simple pillar without other ornament, except those that die unmarried, who have a rose on the top of it. The sepulchres of particular families are railed in and planted round with trees. Those of the Sultans and some great men have lamps constantly burning in them.

When I spoke of their religion I forgot to mention two particularities, one of which I had read of, but it seemed so odd to me I could not believe it. Yet 'tis certainly true that when a man has divorced his wife in the most solemn manner, he can take her again upon no other terms than permitting another man to pass a night with her, and there are some examples of those that have submitted to this law rather than not have back their beloved.[3] The other point of doctrine is very extraordinary: any woman that dies unmarried is looked upon to die in a state of reprobation. To confirm this belief, they reason that the end of the creation of woman is to increase and multiply, and she is only properly employed in the works of her calling when she is bringing children or taking care of 'em, which are all the virtues that God expects from her; and indeed their way of life, which shuts them out of all public commerce, does not permit them any other. Our vulgar notion that they do not own women to have any souls is a mistake. 'Tis true they say they are not of so elevated a kind and therefore must not hope to be admitted into the paradise appointed for the men, who are to be entertained by celestial beauties; but there is a place of happiness destined for souls of the inferior order, where all good women are to be in eternal bliss. Many

[2] Jean Dumont, *Nouveau Voyage du Levant* (1694).
[3] Although this was true, other travellers remarked that the husband usually chose a friend whose tactful continence he could rely on.

of 'em are very superstitious and will not remain widows ten days for fear of dying in the reprobate state of a useless creature.[4] But those that like their liberty and are not slaves to their religion content themselves with marrying when they are afraid of dying. This is a piece of theology very different from that which teaches nothing to be more acceptable to God than a vow of perpetual virginity. Which divinity is most rational I leave you to determine.

I have already made some progress in a collection of Greek medals. Here are several professed antiquaries who are ready to serve anybody that desires them, but you can't imagine how they stare in my face when I inquire about 'em, as if nobody was permitted to seek after medals till they were grown a piece of antiquity themselves. I have got some very valuable of the Macedonian kings, particularly one of Perseus, so lively I fancy I can see all his ill qualities in his face.[5] I have a porphyry head finely cut of the true Greek sculpture, but who it represents is to be guessed at by the learned when I return, for you are not to suppose these antiquaries (who are all Greeks) know anything. Their trade is only to sell. They have correspondents at Aleppo, Grand Cairo, in Arabia, and Palestine, who send them all they can find, and very often great heaps that are only fit to melt into pans and kettles. They get the best price they can for any of 'em, without knowing those that are valuable from those that are not. Those that pretend to skill generally find out the image of some saint in the medals of the Greek cities. One of them, showing me the figure of a Pallas with a victory in her hand on a reverse, assured me it was the Virgin holding a crucifix. The same man offered me the head of a Socrates on a sardonyx, and to enhance the value gave him the title of St Augustine. I have bespoke a mummy, which I hope will come safe to my hands, notwithstanding the misfortune that befell a very fine one designed for the King of Sweden.[6] He gave a great price for it, and the Turks took it into their heads that he must certainly have some considerable project depending upon't. They fancied it the body of God knows who, and that the fate of their Empire mystically depended on the conservation of it. Some old prophecies were remembered upon this occasion, and the mummy committed prisoner to the Seven Towers, where it has remained under close confinement ever since. I dare not try my interest in so considerable a point as the release of it, but I hope mine will pass without examination. – I can tell you nothing more at present of this famous city. When I have looked a little about me you shall hear from me again. I am, sir, etc.

---

[4] But according to Muslim doctrine matrimony does not affect the spiritual fate of women; and a widow is forbidden to remarry for a period of four months and ten days.

[5] Perseus, last king of the Macedonians, had his brother murdered.

[6] Charles XII, after being defeated in 1709, remained near Adrianople until 1714 as a 'guest' of the Turks.

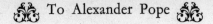

To Alexander Pope

Belgrade Village,[1] 17 June 1717

I hope before this time you have received two or three of my letters. I had yours but yesterday, though dated the third of February, in which you suppose me to be dead and buried. I have already let you know that I am still alive, but to say truth I look upon my present circumstances to be exactly the same with those of departed spirits. The heats of Constantinople have driven me to this place which perfectly answers the description of the Elysian fields. I am in the middle of a wood consisting chiefly of fruit trees, watered by a vast number of fountains famous for the excellency of their water, and divided into many shady walks upon short grass, that seems to me artificial but I am assured is the pure work of nature, within view of the Black Sea, from whence we perpetually enjoy the refreshment of cool breezes that makes us insensible of the heat of the summer. The village is wholly inhabited by the richest amongst the Christians, who meet every night at a fountain forty paces from my house to sing and dance, the beauty and dress of the women exactly resembling the ideas of the ancient nymphs as they are given us by the representations of the poets and painters. But what persuades me more fully of my decease is the situation of my own mind, the profound ignorance I am in of what passes amongst the living, which only comes to me by chance, and the great calmness with which I receive it. Yet I have still a hankering after my friends and acquaintance left in the world, according to the authority of that admirable author,

> That spirits departed are wondrous kind
> To friends and relations left behind,
> Which nobody can deny,

of which solemn truth I am a dead instance. I think Virgil is of the same opinion, that in human souls there will still be some remains of human passions.

> – Curae non ipsa in morte relinquunt;[2]

and 'tis very necessary to make a perfect Elysium that there should be a river Lethe, which I am not so happy to find. To say truth, I am sometimes very weary of this singing and dancing and sunshine, and wish for the smoke and impertinencies in which you toil, though I endeavour to persuade myself that I live in a more agreeable variety than you do, and that Monday setting of partridges, Tuesday reading English, Wednesday studying the Turkish language (in which, by the way, I am

---

[1] Some ten miles from Constantinople.
[2] 'Even in death the pangs leave them not' (*Aeneid*).

already very learned), Thursday classical authors, Friday spent in writing, Saturday at my needle, and Sunday admitting of visits and hearing music, is a better way of disposing the week than Monday at the Drawing Room,[3] Tuesday Lady Mohun's, Wednesday the opera, Thursday the play, Friday Mrs Chetwynd's,[4] etc.: a perpetual round of hearing the same scandal and seeing the same follies acted over and over, which here affect me no more than they do other dead people. I can now hear of displeasing things with pity and without indignation. The reflection on the great gulf between you and me cools all news that comes hither. I can neither be sensibly touched with joy or grief when I consider that possibly the cause of either is removed before the letter comes to my hands; but (as I said before) this indolence does not extend to my few friendships. I am still warmly sensible of yours and Mr Congreve's[5] and desire to live in your remembrances, though dead to all the world beside.

[3] At St James's Palace.

[4] Mary Chetwynd was the wife of an M.P. Her house was well known as a gossip centre.

[5] Lady Mary had known William Congreve, the dramatist, since her girlhood.

To Miss Anne Thistlethwayte

Pera of Constantinople, 4 January 1718

I am infinitely obliged to you, dear Mrs Thistlethwayte, for your entertaining letter. You are the only one of my correspondents that have judged right enough to think I would gladly be informed of the news amongst you. All the rest of 'em tell me (almost in the same words) that they suppose I know everything. Why they are pleased to suppose in this manner, I can guess no reason except they are persuaded that the breed of Mohammed's pigeon still subsists in this country and that I receive supernatural intelligence.[1] I wish I could return your goodness with some diverting accounts from hence, but I know not what part of the scenes here would gratify your curiosity or whether you have any curiosity at all for things so far distant. To say the truth, I am at this present writing not very much turned for the recollection of what is diverting, my head being wholly filled with the preparations necessary for the increase of my family, which I expect every day.[2] You

[1] A pigeon was said to have been taught by Mohammed to pick corn out of his ear, which the vulgar took to be the whispering of the Holy Ghost.

[2] A daughter, the future Countess of Bute, was born on 19 January and christened Mary.

may easily guess at my uneasy situation; but I am, however, in some degree comforted by the glory that accrues to me from it, and a reflection on the contempt I should otherwise fall under.

You won't know what to make of this speech, but in this country 'tis more despicable to be married and not fruitful than 'tis with us to be fruitful before marriage. They have a notion that whenever a woman leaves off bringing children, 'tis because she is too old for that business, whatever her face says to the contrary, and this opinion makes the ladies here so ready to make proofs of their youth (which is as necessary in order to be a received beauty as it is to show the proofs of nobility to be admitted Knight of Malta) that they do not content themselves with using the natural means, but fly to all sort of quackeries to avoid the scandal of being past child-bearing and often kill themselves by 'em. Without any exaggeration, all the women of my acquaintance that have been married ten year have twelve or thirteen children, and the old ones boast of having had five-and-twenty or thirty a piece and are respected according to the number they have produced. When they are with child, 'tis their common expression to say they hope God will be so merciful to 'em to send two this time, and when I have asked them sometimes how they expected to provide for such a flock as they desire, they answer that the plague will certainly kill half of 'em; which, indeed, generally happens without much concern to the parents, who are satisfied with the vanity of having brought forth so plentifully. The French Ambassadress is forced to comply with this fashion as well as myself. She has not been here much above a year and has lain in once and is big again. What is most wonderful is the exemption they seem to enjoy from the curse entailed on the sex. They see all company the day of their delivery and at the fortnight's end return visits, set out in their jewels and new clothes.

I wish I may find the influence of the climate in this particular, but I fear I shall continue an English woman in that affair as well as I do in my dread of fire and plague, which are two things very little feared here, most families having had their houses burnt down once or twice, occasioned by their extraordinary way of warming themselves, which is neither by chimneys nor stoves, but a certain machine called a *tendour*, the height of two foot, in the form of a table, covered with a fine carpet or embroidery. This is made only of wood, and they put into it a small quantity of hot ashes and sit with their legs under the carpet. At this table they work, read, and very often sleep; and if they chance to dream, kick down the *tendour* and the hot ashes commonly sets the house on fire. There was five hundred houses burnt in this manner about a fortnight ago, and I have seen several of the owners since who seem not at all moved at so common a misfortune. They put their goods into a bark and see their houses burn with great philosophy, their persons being very seldom endangered, having no stairs to descend.

But having entertained you with things I don't like, 'tis but just I should tell you something that pleases me. The climate is delightful in the extremest degree. I am now sitting, this present fourth of January, with the windows open, enjoying the warm shine of the sun, while you are freezing over a sad sea-coal fire; and my chamber is set out with carnations, roses and jonquils, fresh from my garden. I am also charmed with many points of the Turkish law, to our shame be it spoken, better designed and better executed than ours, particularly the punishment of convicted liars (triumphant criminals in our country, God knows). They are burnt in the forehead with a hot iron, being proved the authors of any notorious falsehood. How many white foreheads should we see disfigured? How many fine gentlemen would be forced to wear their wigs as low as their eyebrows were this law in practice with us? I should go on to tell you many other parts of justice, but I must send for my midwife.

To Lady Mar

Pera of Constantinople, 10 March 1718

I have not writ to you (dear sister) these many months, a great piece of self-denial, but I knew not where to direct or what part of the world you were in. I have received no letter from you since your short note of April last in which you tell me that you are on the point of leaving England and promise me a direction for the place you stay in, but I have in vain expected it till now, and now I only learn from the *Gazette* that you are returned, which induces me to venture this letter to your house at London. I had rather ten of my letters should be lost than you imagine I don't write, and I think 'tis hard fortune if one in ten don't reach you. However, I am resolved to keep the copies as testimonies of my inclination to give you (to the utmost of my power) all the diverting part of my travels while you are exempt from all the fatigues and inconveniencies.

In the first place I wish you joy of your niece, for I was brought to bed of a daughter five weeks ago. I don't mention this as one of my diverting adventures, though I must own that it is not half so mortifying here as in England, there being as much difference as there is between a little cold in the head, which sometimes happens here, and the consumptive coughs so common in London. Nobody keeps their house a month for lying-in, and I am not so fond of any of our customs to retain them when they are not necessary. I returned my visits at three weeks' end, and about four days ago crossed the sea which divides this place from Constantinople to make a new one, where I had the good fortune to pick up many curiosities.

I went to see the Sultana Hafise, favourite of the last Emperor Mustafa, who, you know (or perhaps you don't know), was deposed by his brother, the reigning Sultan, and died a few weeks after, being poisoned, as it was generally believed.[1] This lady was immediately after his death saluted with an absolute order to leave the Seraglio and choose herself a husband from the great men at the Porte. I suppose you imagine her overjoyed at this proposal. Quite contrary; these women, who are called and esteem themselves queens, look upon this liberty as the greatest disgrace and affront that can happen to them. She threw herself at the Sultan's feet and begged him to poniard her rather than use his brother's widow with that contempt. She represented to him in agonies of sorrow that she was privileged from this misfortune by having brought five princes into the Ottoman family, but all the boys being dead and only one girl surviving, this excuse was not received and she compelled to make her choice. She chose Ebubekir Efendi, then secretary of state, and above fourscore year old, to convince the world that she firmly intended to keep the vow she had made of never suffering a second husband to approach her bed, and since she must honour some subject so far as to be called his wife she would choose him as a mark of her gratitude, since it was he that had presented her at the age of ten year old to her lost lord. But she has never permitted him to pay her one visit, though it is now fifteen year she has been in his house, where she passes her time in uninterrupted mourning with a constancy very little known in Christendom, especially in a widow of twenty-one, for she is now but thirty-six. She has no black eunuchs for her guard, her husband being obliged to respect her as a queen and not enquire at all into what is done in her apartment, where I was led into a large room, with a sofa the whole length of it, adorned with white marble pillars like a *ruelle*, covered with pale *bleu* figured velvet on a silver ground, with cushions of the same, where I was desired to repose till the Sultana appeared, who had contrived this manner of reception to avoid rising up at my entrance, though she made me an inclination of her head when I ris up to her. I was very glad to observe a lady that had been distinguished by the favour of an Emperor to whom beauties were every day presented from all parts of the world. But she did not seem to me to have ever been half so beautiful as the fair Fatima I saw at Adrianople, though she had the remains of a fine face more decayed by sorrow than time.

But her dress was something so surprisingly rich I cannot forbear describing it to you. She wore a vest called *dolaman*, and which differs from a caftan by longer sleeves, and folding over at the bottom. It was of purple cloth strait to her shape and thick set, on each side down to her feet and round the sleeves, with pearls of the best water, of the same

---

[1] Mustafa II, deposed in August 1703, died four months later – of dropsy.

size as their buttons commonly are. You must not suppose I mean as large as those of my Lord — but about the bigness of a pea; and to these buttons, large loops of diamonds in the form of those gold loops so common upon birthday coats. This habit was tied at the waist with two large tassels of smaller pearl, and round the arms embroidered with large diamonds; her shift fastened at the bosom with a great diamond shaped like a lozenge; her girdle as broad as the broadest English riband entirely covered with diamonds. Round her neck she wore three chains which reached to her knees, one of large pearl at the bottom of which hung a fine coloured emerald as big as a turkey egg, another consisting of two-hundred emeralds close joined together, of the most lively green, perfectly matched, every one as large as a half-crown piece and as thick as three crown pieces, and another of small emeralds perfectly round. But her earrings eclipsed all the rest; they were two diamonds shaped exactly like pears, as large as a big hazel nut. Round her *talpack* she had four strings of pearl, the whitest and most perfect in the world, at least enough to make four necklaces every one as large as the Duchess of Marlborough's, and of the same size, fastened with two roses consisting of a large ruby for the middle stone, and round them twenty drops of clean diamonds to each. Besides this, her headdress was covered with bodkins of emeralds and diamonds. She wore large diamond bracelets and had five rings on her fingers, all single diamonds, (except Mr Pitt's) the largest I ever saw in my life.[2] 'Tis for jewellers to compute the value of these things, but according to the common estimation of jewels in our part of the world, her whole dress must be worth above £100,000 sterling. This I am very sure of, that no European queen has half the quantity, and the Empress's jewels (though very fine) would look very mean near hers.

She gave me a dinner of fifty dishes of meat, which (after their fashion) was placed on the table but one at a time, and was extremely tedious, but the magnificence of her table answered very well to that of her dress. The knives were of gold, the hafts set with diamonds, but the piece of luxury that grieved my eyes was the table cloth and napkins, which were all tiffany embroidered with silks and gold in the finest manner in natural flowers. It was with the utmost regret that I made use of these costly napkins, as finely wrought as the finest handkerchiefs that ever came out of this country. You may be sure that they were entirely spoilt before dinner was over. The sherbet (which is the liquor they drink at meals) was served in china bowls, but the covers and salvers, massy gold. After dinner, water was brought in a gold basin and towels of the same kind of the napkins, which I very unwillingly wiped my hands upon, and coffee was served in china with gold *soucoupes*.

The Sultana seemed in very good humour, and talked to me with the utmost civility. I did not omit this opportunity of learning all that I

---

[2] Thomas Pitt, an East India merchant, owned an enormous diamond of almost 140 carats; in 1717 he sold it to the French Regent.

possibly could of the Seraglio, which is so entirely unknown amongst us. She assured me that the story of the Sultan's throwing a handkerchief is altogether fabulous, and the manner upon that occasion no other but that he sends the Kuslir Aga to signify to the lady the honour he intends her. She is immediately complimented upon it by the others, and led to the bath where she is perfumed and dressed in the most magnificent and becoming manner. The Emperor precedes his visit by a royal present and then comes into her apartment. Neither is there any such thing as her creeping in at the bed's feet. She said that the first he made choice of was always after the first in rank, and not the mother of the eldest son, as other writers would make us believe. Sometimes the Sultan diverts himself in the company of all his ladies, who stand in a circle round him, and she confessed that they were ready to die with jealousy and envy of the happy she that he distinguished by any appearance of preference. But this seemed to me neither better nor worse than the circles in most courts, where the glance of the monarch is watched and every smile waited for with impatience and envied by those that cannot obtain it.

She never mentioned the Sultan without tears in her eyes, yet she seemed very fond of the discourse. 'My past happiness,' said she, 'appears a dream to me, yet I cannot forget that I was beloved by the greatest and most lovely of mankind. I was chosen from all the rest to make all his campaigns with him. I would not survive him if I was not passionately fond of the Princess, my daughter, yet all my tenderness for her was hardly enough to make me preserve my life when I lost him. I passed a whole twelvemonth without seeing the light. Time has softened my despair, yet I now pass some days every week in tears devoted to the memory of my Sultan.' There was no affectation in these words. It was easy to see she was in a deep melancholy, though her good humour made her willing to divert me.

She asked me to walk in her garden, and one of her slaves immediately brought her a *pelisse* of rich brocade lined with sables. I waited on her into the garden, which had nothing in it remarkable but the fountains, and from thence she showed me all her apartments. In her bed chamber her toilet was displayed, consisting of two looking-glasses, the frames covered with pearls, and her night *talpack* set with bodkins of jewels, and near it three vests of fine sables, every one of which is at least worth 1,000 dollars, £200 English money. I don't doubt these rich habits were purposely placed in sight, but they seemed negligently thrown on the sofa. When I took my leave of her I was complimented with perfumes as at the Grand Vizier's, and presented with a very fine embroidered handkerchief. Her slaves were to the number of thirty, besides ten little ones, the eldest not above seven year old. These were the most beautiful girls I ever saw, all richly dressed; and I observed that the Sultana took a great deal of pleasure in these lovely children, which is a vast expense, for there is not a handsome girl of that age to be bought under £100 sterling. They wore little garlands of flowers, and their own hair braided, which was all their head-dress, but their habits all of gold stuffs. These served her coffee kneeling, brought water when she washed, etc. 'Tis a great part of the business of the older slaves to take care of these girls, to learn them to embroider and serve them as carefully as if they were children of the family.

Now do I fancy that you imagine I have entertained you all this while with a relation that has (at least) received many embellishments from my hand. This is but too like (says you) the Arabian tales; these embroidered napkins, and a jewel as large as a turkey's egg! – You forget, dear sister, those very tales were writ by an author of this country and (excepting the enchantments) are a real representation of the manners here. We travellers are in very hard circumstances. If we say nothing but what has been said before us, we are dull and we have observed nothing. If we tell anything new, we are laughed at as fabulous and romantic, not allowing for the difference of ranks, which afford difference of company, more curiosity, or the changes of customs that happen every twenty year in every country. But people judge of travellers exactly with the same candour, good nature, and impartiality they judge of their neighbours upon all occasions. For my part, if I live to return amongst you, I am so well acquainted with the morals of all my dear friends and acquaintance, that I am resolved to tell them nothing at all, to avoid the imputation (which their charity would certainly incline them to) of my telling too much. But I depend upon your knowing me enough to believe whatever I seriously assert for truth, though I give you leave to be surprised at an account so new to you.

But what would you say if I told you that I have been in a harem where the winter apartment was wainscoted with inlaid work of mother of pearl, ivory of different colours and olive wood, exactly like the little boxes you have seen brought out of this country; and those rooms designed for summer, the walls all crusted with Japan china, the roofs gilt, and the floors spread with the finest Persian carpets. Yet there is nothing more true; such is the palace of my lovely friend, the fair Fatima, who I was acquainted with at Adrianople. I went to visit her yesterday, and (if possible) she appeared to me handsomer than before. She met me at the door of her chamber, and, giving me her hand with the best grace in the world: 'You Christian ladies,' said she with a smile that made her as handsome as an angel, 'have the reputation of inconstancy, and I did not expect, whatever goodness you expressed for me at Adrianople, that I should ever see you again; but I am now convinced that I have really the happiness of pleasing you, and if you knew how I speak of you amongst our ladies, you would be assured that you do me justice if you think me your friend.' She placed me in the corner of the sofa, and I spent the afternoon in her conversation with the greatest pleasure in the world.

The Sultana Hafise is what one would naturally expect to find a Turkish lady, willing to oblige but not knowing how to go about it, and 'tis easy to see in her manner that she has lived excluded from the world. But Fatima has all the politeness and good breeding of a court, with an air that inspires at once respect and tenderness; and now I understand her language, I find her wit as engaging as her beauty. She is very curious after the manners of other countries and has not that partiality for her own so common to little minds. A Greek that I carried with me who had never seen her before (nor could have been admitted now if she had not been in my train) showed that surprise at her beauty and manner which is unavoidable at the first sight, and said to me in Italian: 'This is no Turkish lady; she is certainly some Christian.' Fatima guessed she spoke of her, and asked what she said. I would not have told, thinking she would have been no better pleased with the compliment than one of our court beauties to be told she had the air of a Turk. But the Greek lady told it her and she smiled, saying: 'It is not the first time I have heard so. My mother was a Poloneze taken at the siege of Camieniec,[3] and my father used to rally me, saying he believed his Christian wife had found some Christian gallant, for I had not the air of a Turkish girl.' I assured her that if all the Turkish ladies were like her, it was absolutely necessary to confine them from public view for the repose of mankind, and proceeded to tell her what a noise such a face as hers would make in London or Paris. 'I can't believe you,' replied she agreeably; 'if beauty was so much valued in your country as you say, they would never have suffered you to leave it.'

Perhaps (dear sister) you laugh at my vanity in repeating this compliment, but I only do it as I think it very well turned and give it you as an instance of the spirit of her conversation. Her house was magnificently furnished and very well fancied, her winter rooms being furnished with figured velvet on gold grounds, and those for summer with fine Indian quilting embroidered with gold. The houses of the great Turkish ladies are kept clean with as much nicety as those in Holland. This was situated in a high part of the town, and from the windows of her summer apartment we had the prospect of the sea and the islands and the Asian mountains.

My letter is insensibly grown so long, I am ashamed of it. This is a very bad symptom. 'Tis well if I don't degenerate in a downright storyteller. It may be, our proverb that knowledge is no burden, may be true as to one's self, but knowing too much is very apt to make us troublesome to other people.

[3] A Polish fortress captured by the Turks in 1672.

Genoa, 28 August 1718

I beg your pardon (my dear sister) that I did not write to you from
Tunis (the only opportunity I have had since I left Constantinople), but the heat there was so excessive and the light so bad for the
sight, I was half blind by writing one letter to the Abbot Conti and
durst not go on to write many others I had designed, nor, indeed, could
I have entertained you very well out of that barbarous country. I am
now surrounded with objects of pleasure, and so much charmed with
the beauties of Italy I should think it a kind of ingratitude not to offer
a little praise in return for the diversion I have had here. I am in the
house of Mrs Davenant at San Pietro d'Arena[1] and should be very unjust not to allow her a share of that praise I speak of, since her good
humour and good company has very much contributed to render this
place agreeable to me.

Genoa is situate in a very fine bay, and being built on a rising hill,
intermixed with gardens and beautified with the most excellent architecture, gives a very fine prospect off at sea, though it lost much of its
beauty in my eyes, having been accustomed to that of Constantinople.
The Genoese were once masters of several islands in the archipelago
and all that part of Constantinople which is now called Galata. Their
betraying the Christian cause, by facilitating the taking of Constantinople by the Turk, deserved what has since happened to them, the loss
of all their conquest on that side to those infidels.[2] They are at present
far from rich, and despised by the French since their Doge was forced
by the late King to go in person to Paris to ask pardon for such a trifle
as the Arms of France over the house of the envoy being spattered with
dung in the night (I suppose) by some of the Spanish faction, which
still makes up the majority here, though they dare not openly declare
it.[3]

The ladies affect the French habit and are more genteel than those
they imitate. I do not doubt but the custom of *tetis beys* [*cicisbeismo*] has
very much improved their airs. I know not whether you have ever heard
of those animals. Upon my word, nothing but my own eyes could have
convinced [me] there were any such upon earth. The fashion begun here
and is now received all over Italy, where the husbands are not such
terrible creatures as we represent them. There are none among them

---

[1] A fashionable suburb, where the British envoy, Henry Davenant, and his wife
   lived.
[2] When Mehmed II besieged Constantinople in 1453 the Genoese allowed him
   to carry his light boats across Galata and into the Golden Horn, thus evading
   the naval barrier.
[3] In 1684 the French bombarded Genoa in retaliation; and in May of the
   following year, the Doge and four Senators travelled to Versailles to apolo-
   gize to Louis XIV.

such brutes to pretend to find fault with a custom so well established and so politically founded, since I am assured here that it was an expedient first found out by the Senate to put an end to those family hatreds which tore their state to pieces, and to find employment for those young men who were forced to cut one another's throats *pour passer le temps*, and it has succeeded so well that since the institution of *tetis beys* there has been nothing but peace and good humour amongst them. These are gentlemen that devote themselves to the service of a particular lady (I mean a married one, for the virgins are all invisible, confined to convents). They are obliged to wait on her to all public places, the plays, operas, and assemblies (which are called here conversations), where they wait behind her chair, take care of her fan and gloves if she plays, have the privilege of whispers, etc. When she goes out they serve her instead of lackeys, gravely trotting by her chair. 'Tis their business to present against any day of public appearance, not forgetting that of her name. In short, they are to spend all their time and money in her service who rewards them according to her inclination (for opportunity they want none), but the husband is not to have the impudence to suppose 'tis any other than pure platonic friendship. 'Tis true they endeavour to give her a *tetis bey* of their own choosing, but when the lady happens not to be of the same taste (as that often happens) she never fails to bring it about to have one of her own fancy. In former times one beauty used to have eight or ten of these humble admirers, but those days of plenty and humility are no more; men grow more scarce and saucy, and every lady is forced to content herself with one at a time. You see the glorious liberty of a republic, or more properly an aristocracy, the common people being here as arrant slaves as the French but the old nobles pay little respect to the Doge, who is but two years in his office, and at that very time his wife assumes no rank above another noble lady. 'Tis true the family of Andrea Doria (that great man who restored them that liberty they enjoy) has some particular privileges; when the Senate found it necessary to put a stop to the luxury of dress, forbidding the wear of jewels and brocades, they left them at liberty to make what expense they pleased. I looked with great pleasure on the statue of that hero[4] which is in the court belonging to the house of Duke Doria.

This puts me in mind of their palaces, which I can never describe as I ought. Is it not enough that I say they are most of them of the design of Palladio? The street called Strada Nova here is perhaps the most beautiful line of building in the world. I must particularly mention the vast palace of Durazzo, those of two Balbi joined together by a magnificent [colonnade], that of the Imperiali at this village of San Pietro d'Arena, and another of the Doria. The perfection of architecture and the utmost profusion of rich furniture is to be seen here, disposed with most elegant taste and lavish magnificence, but I am charmed with

---

[4] A naval commander, Doria expelled the French from Genoa in 1528, and reestablished the republic.

nothing so much as the collection of pictures by the pencils of Raphael, Paulo Veronese, Titian, Carracci, Michelangelo, Guido, and Correggio, which two I mention last as my particular favourites. I own I can find no pleasure in objects of horror, and in my opinion the more naturally a crucifix is represented the more disagreeable it is. These, my beloved painters, show nature and show it in the most charming light. I was particularly pleased with a Lucretia in the House of Balbi. The expressive beauty of that face and bosom gives all the passion of pity and admiration that could be raised in the soul by the finest poem on that subject. A Cleopatra of the same hand deserves to be mentioned, and I should say more of her if Lucretia had not first engaged my eyes.

Here are also some inestimable ancient bustos. The Church of St Lawrence is all black and white marble, where is kept that famous plate of a single emerald, which is not now permitted to be handled since a plot which (they say) was discovered to throw it on the pavement and break it, a childish piece of malice which they ascribe to the King of Sicily, to be revenged for their refusing to sell it to him.[5] The Church of the Annunciata is finely lined with marble, the pillars of red and white marble, that of St Ambrose very much adorned by the Jesuits; but I confess all those churches appeared so mean to me after that of Saint Sophia, I can hardly do them the honour of writing down their names; but I hope you'll own I have made good use of my time in seeing so much, since 'tis not many days that we have been out of the quarantine from which nobody is exempt coming from the Levant; but ours was very much shortened and very agreeably passed in Mrs Davenant's company in the village of San Pietro d'Arena, about a mile from Genoa in a house built by Palladio, so well designed and so nobly proportioned 'twas a pleasure to walk in it. We were visited here only in the company of a noble Genoese commissioned to see we did not touch one another. I shall stay here some days longer and could almost wish it for all my life, but mine (I fear) is not destined to so much tranquillity.

[5] This emerald was said to be a present from the Queen of Sheba to Solomon. The scepticism of many travellers regarding it proved to be well founded when it was taken to Paris during the Napolenic wars and analysed as glass-paste.

❧ To Miss Anne Thistlethwayte ❧

I received at my arrival here both your obliging letters, and from many of my other friends, designed to Constantinople and sent me from Marseilles hither, our merchant there knowing we were upon our return.

I am surprised to hear my sister Mar has left England.[1] I suppose what I writ to her from Turin will be lost, and where to direct I know not, having no account of her affairs from her own hand. For my own part, I am confined to my chamber, having kept my bed till yesterday ever since the seventeenth that I came to this town, where I have had so terrible a fever I believed for some time that all my journeys were ended here, and I do not at all wonder that such fatigues as I have passed should have such an effect.

The first day's journey, from Turin to Novalese, is through a very fine country, beautifully planted, and enriched by art and nature. The next day we begun to ascend Mount Cenis, being carried in little seats of twisted osiers fixed upon poles, on men's shoulders, our chaises taken to pieces and laid upon mules. The prodigious prospect of mountains covered with eternal snow, clouds hanging far below our feet, and the vast cascades tumbling down the rocks with a confused roaring would have been solemnly entertaining to me if I had suffered less from the extreme cold that reigns here, but the misty rain, which falls perpetually, penetrated even the thick fur I was wrapped in, and I was half dead with cold before we got to the foot of the mountain, which was not till two hours after 'twas dark. This hill has a spacious plain on the top of it, and a fine lake there, but the descent is so steep and slippery, 'tis surprising to see these chairmen go so steadily as they do, yet I was not half so much afraid of breaking my neck as I was of falling sick, and the event has showed that I placed my fears in the right place.

The other mountains are now all passable for a chaise, and very fruitful in vines and pastures; amongst them is a breed of the finest goats in the world. Aiguebelette is the last, and soon after we entered Pont-de-Beauvoisin, the frontier town of France, whose bridge parts this kingdom and the dominion of Savoy. The same night we arrived late at this town, where I have had nothing to do but to take care of my health. I think myself already out of any danger, and am determined that the sore throat, which still remains, shall not confine me long. I am impatient to see the antiquities of this famous city and more impatient to continue my journey to Paris, from whence I hope to write you a more diverting letter than 'tis possible for me to do now, with a mind weakened by sickness, a head muddled with spleen, from a sorry inn, and a chamber crammed with the mortifying objects of apothecary's vials and bottles.

---

[1] She arrived in France on 12 September.

Paris, September 1718

I cannot give my dear Lady Rich a better proof of the pleasure I
have in writing to her than choosing to do it in this seat of
various amusements, where I am *accablé* with visits, and those so full of
vivacity and compliment that 'tis full employment to hearken whether
one answers or not. The French Ambassadress at Constantinople has a
very considerable and numerous family here, who all come to see me
and are never weary of making inquiries. The air of Paris has already
had a good effect on me, for I was never in better health, though I have
been extreme ill all the road from Lyons to this place. You may judge
how agreeable the journey has been to me, which did not need that
addition to make me dislike it. I think nothing so terrible as objects of
misery, except one had the God-like attribute of being capable to redress them, and all the country villages of France show nothing else.
While the post horses are changed, the whole town comes out to beg,
with such miserable starved faces and thin, tattered clothes, they need
no other eloquence to persuade [one of] the wretchedness of their
condition.

This is all the French magnificence till you come to Fontainebleau.
There you begin to think the kingdom rich when you are showed 1,500
rooms in the King's hunting palace. The apartments of the royal family
are very large and richly gilt, but I saw nothing in the architecture or
painting worth remembering, The Long Gallery, built by Henry the
Fourth, has prospects of all the King's houses on its walls, designed
after the taste of those times, but appears now very mean. The park is
indeed finely wooded and watered, the trees well grown and planted,
and in the fish ponds are kept tame carp, said to be some of them eighty
years of age. The late King passed some months every year at this seat;
and all the rocks round it, by the pious sentences inscribed on them,
show the devotion in fashion at his court, which I believe died with
him. At least I see no exterior marks of it at Paris, where all people's
thoughts seem to be on present diversion. The Fair of St Lawrence is
now in season. You may be sure I have been carried thither, and think
it much better disposed than ours of Bartholomew. The shops being all
set in rows so regularly well lighted, they made up a very agreeable
spectacle.But I was not at all satisfied with the *grossièreté* of their harlequin, no more than with their music at the opera, which was abominable
grating after being used to that of Italy. Their house is a booth compared to that of the Haymarket, and the playhouse not so neat as that in
Lincoln's Inn Fields; but then it must be owned to their praise, their
tragedians are much beyond any of ours. I should hardly allow Mrs
Oldfield[1] a better place than to be confidante to La [Desmares]. I have
seen the tragedy of *Bajazet* so well represented, I think our best actors

---

[1] Anne Oldfield was the leading actress at Drury Lane.

can be only said to speak, but these to feel;[2] and 'tis certainly infinitely more moving to see a man appear unhappy than to hear him say that he is so, with a jolly face and a stupid smirk in his countenance.

Apropos of countenances, I must tell you something of the French ladies. I have seen all the beauties, and such (I can't help making use of the coarse word) nauseous ——, so fantastically absurd in their dress! so monstrously unnatural in their paint! their hair cut short and curled round their faces, loaded with powder that makes it look like white wool, and on their cheeks to their chins, unmercifully laid on, a shining red japan that glistens in a most flaming manner, that they seem to have no resemblance to human faces, and I am apt to believe took the first hint of their dress from a fair sheep newly raddled. 'Tis with pleasure I recollect my dear pretty country women, and if I was writing to any-body else I should say that these grotesque daubers give me still a higher esteem of the natural charms of dear Lady Rich's auburn hair and the lively colours of her unsullied complexion.

I have met the Abbé Conti here, who desires me to make his compliments to you.

[2] Racine's *Bajazet* was performed at the *Comédie française* while Lady Mary was in Paris, with Charlotte Desmares as Roxane.

❧ To the Abbé Conti ❧

Dover, September 1718

I am willing to take your word for it that I shall really oblige you by letting you know as soon as possible my safe passage over the water. I arrived this morning at Dover after being tossed a whole night in the packet-boat in so violent a manner that the master, considering the weakness of his vessel, thought it prudent to remove the mail, and gave us notice of the danger. We called a little fisher boat, which could hardly make up to us, while all the people on board us were crying to heaven, and 'tis hard to imagine one's self in a scene of greater horror than on such an occasion; and yet, shall I own it to you? though I was not at all willing to be drowned, I could not forbear being entertained at the double distress of a fellow passenger. She was an English lady that I had met at Calais, who desired me to let her go over with me in my cabin. She had bought a fine point head[dress] which she was con-triving to conceal from the custom-house officers. When the wind grew high and our little vessel cracked, she fell very heartily to her prayers and thought wholly of her soul; when it seemed to abate, she returned to the worldly care of her head-dress, and addressed herself to me. 'Dear

Madame, will you take care of this point? if it should be lost – Ah Lord! we shall all be lost! Lord have mercy on my soul – pray, Madame, take care of this head-dress.' This easy transition from her soul to her head-dress, and the alternate agonies that both gave her, made it hard to determine which she thought of greatest value.

But, however, the scene was not so diverting but I was glad to get rid of it and be thrown into the little boat, though with some hazard of breaking my neck. It brought me safe hither, and I cannot help looking with partial eyes on my native land. That partiality was certainly given us by nature to prevent rambling, the effect of an ambitious thirst after knowledge which we are not formed to enjoy. All we get by it is a fruitless desire of mixing the different pleasures and conveniencies which are given to different parts of the world and cannot meet in any one of them. After having read all that is to be found in the languages I am mistress of, and having decayed my sight by midnight studies, I envy the easy peace of mind of a ruddy milkmaid who, undisturbed by doubt, hears the sermon with humility every Sunday, having not confused the sentiments of natural duty in her head by the vain inquiries of the schools, who may be more learned, yet after all must remain as ignorant. And after having seen part of Asia and Africa and almost made the tour of Europe I think the honest English squire more happy who verily believes the Greek wines less delicious than March beer, that the African fruits have not so fine a flavour as golden pippins, and the *beccafichi* of Italy are not so well tasted as a rump of beef, and that, in short, there is no perfect enjoyment of this life out of Old England. I pray God I may think so for the rest of my life, and since I must be contented with our scanty allowance of daylight, that I may forget the enlivening sun of Constantinople.

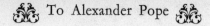

To Alexander Pope

Dover, September 1718

I have this minute received a letter of yours sent me from Paris. I believe and hope I shall very soon see both you and Mr Congreve, but as I am here in an inn where we stay to regulate our march to London, bag and baggage, I shall employ some of my leisure time in answering that part of yours that seems to require an answer.

I must applaud your good nature in supposing that your pastoral lovers (vulgarly called haymakers) would have lived in everlasting joy and harmony if the lightning had not interrupted their scheme of happiness.[1] I see no reason to imagine that John Hughes and Sarah Drew were either wiser or more virtuous than their neighbours. That a well-set man of twenty-five should have a fancy to marry a brown woman of eighteen is nothing marvellous, and I cannot help thinking that had they married, their lives would have passed in the common tract with their fellow parishioners. His endeavouring to shield her from the storm was a natural action and what he would have certainly done for his horse if he had been in the same situation. Neither am I of opinion that their sudden death was a reward of their mutual virtue. You know the Jews were reproved for thinking a village destroyed by fire more wicked than those that had escaped the thunder. Time and chance happen to all men. Since you desire me to try my skill in an epitaph, I think the following lines perhaps more just, though not so poetical as yours:

> Here lies John Hughes and Sarah Drew;
> Perhaps you'll say, what's that to you?
> Believe me, friend, much may be said
> On this poor couple that are dead.
> On Sunday next they should have married,
> But see how oddly things are carried.
> On Thursday last it rained and lightened;
> These tender lovers sadly frightened
> Sheltered beneath the cocking hay
> In hopes to pass the storm away.
> But the bold thunder found them out
> (Commissioned for that end no doubt)
> And seizing on their trembling breath,
> Consigned them to the shades of death.
> Who knows if 'twas not kindly done?
> For had they seen the next year's sun

[1] In his letter Pope had related a pathetic tale of two rustic lovers struck by lightning; evidently the man had tried to shield the woman. Pope's letter contained two epitaphs that treated the subject sentimentally.

A beaten wife and cuckold swain
Had jointly cursed the marriage chain.
Now they are happy in their doom,
For Pope has wrote upon their tomb.

I confess these sentiments are not altogether so heroic as yours, but I hope you will forgive them in favour of the two last lines. You see how much I esteem the honour you have done them, though I am not very impatient to have the same and had rather continue to be your stupid living humble servant than be celebrated by all the pens in Europe.

I would write to Mr Congreve but suppose you will read this to him if he inquires after me.

PART IV

❧

England Again

1721-1739

❧

After their return from Turkey in 1718 Wortley and Lady Mary rented a house in Covent Garden. He henceforth applied himself to business affairs, amassing a vast fortune, and to his career in Parliament, where he sat as an independent Whig for the rest of his life. On her side, besides carefully managing her household and rearing her two children Lady Mary enjoyed her reputation as a traveller and wit. Pope had recently moved to Twickenham, and Lady Mary and her husband soon took a house there as a retreat from London. Although the gallantry of Pope's epistolary friendship had abated, they still shared literary and neighbourly interests.

For Lady Mary the 1720s were a particularly difficult decade, filled with disappointments and fears. Her marriage had not been a success; Wortley was a cold, stolid man, unable to respond to her emotional warmth. The deaths of her father and sister Lady Gower increased her loneliness, and she fearfully entered 'old age' (when she was about thirty-five). Her son, whom she doted on, began his truant career; and her sister, Lady Mar, whose melancholy she tried to dispel with her brilliant letters, finally lost her sanity, and in 1728 was sent back to England and – in spite of opposition from Lord Mar's family – put in Lady Mary's custody.

During this decade her friendship with Pope cooled; and beginning with his 1728 *Dunciad* he exposed his resentment with a succession of personal and literary attacks in his satires. When she retaliated in 1733 with *Verses to the Imitator of Horace* (assisted by her friend Lord Hervey), she simply exacerbated Pope's resentment and provoked further attacks. Her daughter's disobedience in marrying the impoverished Earl of Bute in 1736 added still another entry to her ample catalogue of dissatisfactions.

As though a compensating gift from fate, in 1736 she met Francesco Algarotti, a young, handsome Italian writer, who engaged her emotions more profoundly than any other man in her life. By the time he left to return to Italy six months later he had conquered at least two hearts – Lord Hervey's and Lady Mary's. During his absence she busied herself with, among other activities, writing the essays for *The Nonsense of Common-Sense*. Unable to forget him, she proposed that they retire together to Italy, and he evidently agreed. They discussed the scheme in person when he returned to England in March 1739. He stayed only two months, and then sailed off to St Petersburg as the guest of Lord Baltimore. In July, Lady Mary herself left England. Although her husband and her friends (except Hervey) believed her motive was to regain her health, her main reason was to try to seize happiness through love.

c. 11 August 1721

Dear Sister,

I give you 10,000 thanks for the trouble you have given yourself. I hope you will continue to take some care of my affairs, because I do not hear they are finished and cannot yet get rid of my fears.[1] You have not told me that you have received what I sent you by Lady Lansdown, as also three guineas that she took for you, one of which I beg, you would lay out in the same narrow mignonette that you sent Mrs Murray,[2] and send it me by the first opportunity for the use of my daughter, who is very much your humble servant, and grows a little woman.

I suppose you know our sister Gower has lain in, in the country, of a son.[3] The Duchess of Kingston is preparing for the Bath.[4] I live in a sort of solitude that wants very little of being just what I would have it. Lady J. Wharton is to be married to Mr Holt,[5] which I am sorry for, to see a young woman that I really think one of the agreeablest girls upon earth so vilely misplaced; but where are people matched! I suppose we shall all come right in Heaven, as in a country dance; though hands are strangely given and taken while they are in motion, at last all meet their partners when the jig is done.

[1] Nicolas-François Rémond, an acquaintance by correspondence, had come to England in the summer of 1720. Although Lady Mary hardly saw him she advised him to invest his money in South Sea stock. After the bubble burst – he had in the meantime returned to Paris – he threatened to expose their correspondence to Wortley unless she reimbursed him for his losses. His blackmail threats embittered her life until the beginning of 1722, when a settlement of some sort was arranged.

[2] Lady Lansdown's husband, attainted as a Jacobite, lived in Paris, where she frequently visited. Mrs Griselda Murray, who was separated from her husband, lived in her father's London house.

[3] Lady Gower's son, later 1st Marquess of Stafford, was born at Trentham, Staffordshire.

[4] Lady Mary's stepmother; her father had become 1st Duke of Kingston in 1715.

[5] Lady Jane, daughter of Lord Wharton, did not marry John Holt until two years later.

April 1722

I have had no answer (dear sister) to a long letter that I writ to you a month ago, but however I shall continue letting you know (*de temps en temps*) what passes in this corner of the world till you tell me 'tis disagreeable. I shall say little of the death of our great minister because the newspapers say so much.[1] I suppose the same faithful historians give you regular accounts of the growth and spreading of the inoculation of the smallpox, which is become almost a general practice, attended with great success.[2] I pass my time in a small snug set of dear intimates, and go very little into the *grand monde*, which has always had my hearty contempt. I see sometimes Mr Congreve, and very seldom Mr Pope, who continues to embellish his house at Twickenham. He has made a subterranean grotto, which he has furnished with looking-glass, and they tell me it has a very good effect. I here send you some verses addressed to Mr Gay, who writ him a congratulatory letter on the finishing his house. I stifled them here, and I beg they may die the same death at Paris, and never go farther than your closet.

> Ah friend, 'tis true (this truth you lovers know),
> In vain my structures rise, my gardens grow,
> In vain fair Thames reflects the double scenes
> Of hanging mountains and of sloping greens;
> Joy lives not here; to happier seats it flies,
> And only dwells where W[ortley] casts her eyes.
> What is the gay parterre, the chequered shade,
> The morning bower, the evening colonnade,
> But soft recesses of uneasy minds,
> To sigh unheard in, to the passing winds?
> So the struck deer in some sequestered part
> Lies down to die, the arrow at his heart;
> There, stretched unseen in coverts hid from day,
> Bleeds drop by drop, and pants his life away.

My paper is done, and I will only put you in mind of my lutestring, which I beg you will send me plain, of what colour you please.

[1] Probably Lord Sunderland, who died suddenly on 19 April 1722; he had resigned a year before as First Lord of the Treasury.
[2] In April 1722 were inoculated the two younger daughters of the Prince of Wales, Lord Bathurst's six children, and the Duke of Dorset's eldest son.

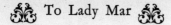

To Lady Mar

Dear Sister,

I have writ you so many letters which you say you have not received that I suppose you won't receive this; however, I will acquit myself to my own conscience as a good Christian ought to do. I am sure I can never be really wanting in any expression of affection to you, to whom I can never forget what I owe in many respects.

Our mutual acquaintance are exceedingly dispersed, and I am engaged in a new set, whose ways would not be entertaining to you since you know not the people. Mrs Murray is still at Castle Howard. I am at Twickenham, where there is (at this time) more company than at London. That poor soul Mrs Johnston[1] is returned into our neighbourhood, and sent to me to carry her to Richmond Court tomorrow, but I begged to be excused. She's still in sad pickle, I think. Mr and Madam Hervey are at Lord Bristol's.[2] Apropos of that family, the Countess is come out a new creature. She has left off the dull occupations of hazard and basset, and is grown young, blooming, coquette and gallant; and to show she is fully sensible of the errors of her past life, and resolved to make up for time misspent, she has two lovers at a time, and is equally, wickedly talked of for the genteel Colonel Cotton and the superfine Mr Braddock.[3] Now I think this the greatest compliment in nature to her own lord, since 'tis plain that when she will be false to him, she is forced to take two men in his stead, and that no one mortal has merit enough to make up for him.

Poor Lady Gage is parting from her discreet spouse[4] for a mere trifle. She had a mind to take the air this spring in a new yacht (which Lord Hillsborough[5] built for many good uses, and which has been the scene of much pleasure and pain). She went in company with his Lordship, Fabrice, Mr Coke, Lady Lichfield and her sister[6] as far as Greenwich,

---

[1] Catherine *née* Poulett, wife of James Johnston, a former Secretary of State for Scotland, lived at Twickenham. Horace Walpole thought her demented.

[2] John Hervey, who subsequently became one of Lady Mary's most intimate friends, had (in 1720) married the beautiful Molly Lepell, a Maid of Honour to the Princess of Wales. His father, Lord Bristol, had a house in St James's Square.

[3] Lady Bristol wrote to her husband of Colonel Cotton's kindness to her at Bath. Edward Braddock in later life was a well-known general in the British army.

[4] Viscount Gage, called by Hervey 'a petulant, silly, busy, meddling, profligate fellow'.

[5] Viscount Hillsborough was described by Thomas Hearne as very handsome, wanton, and immodest.

[6] Fabrice was George I's confidential secretary; Thomas Coke, later Earl of Leicester, had not allowed his marriage (in 1718) to interrupt his debaucheries for more than six months; and Hearne described Lady Lichfield as very virtuous, but his information came from her brother.

and from thence as far as the buoy of the Nore, when to the great surprise of all the good company, who thought it impossible the wind should not be as fair to bring them back as it was to carry 'em thither, they found there was no possibility of returning that night. Lady Gage, in all the concern of a good wife, desired her Lord might be informed of her safety, and that she was no way blameable in staying out all night. Fabrice writ a most gallant letter to Lord Gage, concluding that Mr Coke presented his humble service to him, and let him know (in case of necessity) Lady Margaret[7] was in town; but his lordship, not liking the charge, I suppose, carried the letter straight to the King's Majesty, who not being at leisure to give him audience, he sent it in open by Mahomet,[8] though 'tis hard to guess what sort of redress he intended to petition for, the nature of the thing being such that had he complained he was no cuckold his Majesty (at least) might have prevailed that some of his court might confer that dignity upon him, but if he was, neither King, Council, nor the two Houses of Parliament could make it null and of none effect. This public rupture is succeeded by a treaty of separation, and here is all the scandal that is uppermost in my head.

Dear sister, I should be glad to contribute any way to your entertainment, and am very sorry you seem to stand in so much need of it. I am ever yours.

I wish you would think of my lutestring, for I'm in terrible want of linings.

[7] Coke's wife.
[8] Lewis Maximilian Mahomet, *valet de chambre* to the King, who had captured him in 1685 in the war against the Turks.

To Lady Mar

London, May 1723

Dear Sister,

I have writ to you twice since I received yours in answer to that I sent by Mr de Caylus,[1] but I believe none that I send by the post ever come to your hands, nor ever will, while they are directed to Mr Waters, for reasons that you may easily guess.[2] I wish you would give me a safer direction. 'Tis very seldom I can have the opportunity of a private messenger, and 'tis very often that I have a mind to write to my dear sister. If you have not heard of the Duchess of Montagu's intended journey, you will be surprised at your manner of receiving this, since I send it by one of her servants. She does not design to see anybody or anything at Paris, and talks of going from Montpellier to Italy. I have

[1] Comte de Caylus, archaeologist and man of letters, had been in England since the previous autumn.
[2] George Waters, a banker at Paris, was closely connected with the Jacobites.

a tender esteem for her, and am heartily concerned to lose her conversation, yet I cannot condemn her resolution.[3]

I am yet in this wicked town but propose to leave it as soon as the Parliament rises. Mrs Murray and all her satellites have so seldom fallen in my way I can say little about 'em. Your old friend Mrs Lowther[4] is still fair and young and in pale pink every night in the parks; but after being highly in favour, poor I am in utter disgrace without my being able to guess wherefore, except she fancied me the author or abettor of two vile ballads written on her dying adventure, which I am so innocent of, I never saw.[5] Apropos of ballads, a most delightful one is said or sung in most houses about our dearly beloved plot, which has been laid firstly to Pope and secondly to me, when God knows we have neither of us wit enough to make it.[6]

Mrs Hervey lies in of a female child. Lady Rich is happy in dear Sir Robert's absence[7] and the polite Mr Holt's return to his allegiance, who though in a treaty of marriage with one of the prettiest girls in town (Lady Jane Wharton)[8] appears better with her than ever. Lady Betty Manners is on the brink of matrimony with a Yorkshire Mr Monckton of £3,000 per annum. 'Tis a match of the young Duchess's making and, as she thinks, matter of great triumph over the two coquette beauties, who can get nobody to have and to hold. They are decayed to a piteous degree and so neglected that they are grown constant and particular to the two ugliest fellows in London.[9] Mrs Pulteney condescends to be publicly kept by the noble Earl of Cadogan; whether Mr Pulteney has a pad nag deducted out of the profits for his share I can't tell, but he appears very well satisfied with it.[10] This is (I think) the whole state of love. As to that of wit, it splits itself into 10,000 branches. Poets increase

[3] Mary, wife of the Duke of Montagu, was one of the Duke of Marlborough's daughters.

[4] Jane Lowther, sister of Viscount Lonsdale.

[5] The title of one of the ballads, as printed many years later and attributed to Lady Mary, summarizes the adventure: 'On a Lady mistaking a Dyeing Trader for a Dying Lover'.

[6] This Jacobite plot was led by Francis Atterbury, Bishop of Rochester, imprisoned in August 1722 and impeached in March 1723. The ballad may have been Swift's 'Upon the Horrid Plot Discovered by Harlequin, the Bishop of Rochester's French Dog'.

[7] Sir Robert Rich had left for Ireland to join his regiment.

[8] Their engagement (see above, p. 123) finally ended in marriage on 3 July 1723.

[9] Lady Elizabeth Manners, daughter of the 2nd Duke of Rutland, was fourteen years old at this time; and the young Duchess was wife of the 3rd Duke. The 'two coquette beauties' were Lady Elizabeth's older sisters: Catherine, who married (1724) Henry Pelham, and Frances, who married (1732) Richard Arundel.

[10] Margaret, *née* Tichborne, was married to Daniel Pulteney, a Whig politician. A 'pad nag', or road-horse, was appropriate payment from Earl Cadogan, a cavalry officer.

and multiply to that stupendous degree, you see 'em at every turn, even in embroidered coats and pink coloured top knots. Making verses is almost as common as taking snuff, and God can tell what miserable stuff people carry about in their pockets and offer to all their acquaintance, and you know one can't refuse reading and taking a pinch. This is a very great grievance, and so particularly shocking to me, that I think our wise lawgivers should take it into consideration and appoint a fast-day to beseech Heaven to put a stop to this epidemical disease, as they did last year for the plague with great success.

Dear sister, adieu. I have been very free in this letter because I think I am sure of its going safe. I wish my night-gown may do the same. I only choose that as most convenient to you, but if it was equally so, I had rather the money was laid out in plain lutestring, if you could send me eight yards at a time of different colours, designing it for linings; but if this scheme is impracticable, send me a night-gown *à la mode*.

To Lady Mar

Twickenham, July 1723

Dear Sister,

I have received by Lady Lansdown the very pretty night-gown you sent me. I give you many thanks for it, but I should have thought it much more valuable if it had been accompanied with a letter. I can hardly persuade myself you have received all mine, and yet can never spare time from the pleasures of Paris to answer one of 'em.

I am sorry to inform you of the death of our nephew my sister Gower's son of the smallpox. I think she has a great deal of reason to regret it, in consideration of the offer I made her two year together of taking the child home to my house where I would have inoculated him with the same care and safety I did my own.[1] I know nobody that has hitherto repented the operation though it has been very troublesome to some fools who had rather be sick by the doctors' prescriptions than in health in rebellion to the college.[2]

I am at present at Twickenham, which is become so fashionable and the neighbourhood so much enlarged that 'tis more like Tunbridge or the Bath than a country retreat. Adieu, dear sister. I shall write you longer letters when I am sure you receive 'em, but it really takes off very much from the pleasure of correspondence when I have no assurance of their coming to your hands. Pray let me know if this does, and believe me ever affectionately yours.

[1] In April 1721 Lady Mary engaged Charles Maitland, who had been surgeon on the Turkish Embassy, to inoculate her daughter.

[2] Lady Mary wrote a vigorous essay, published in a newspaper in September 1722, advocating the operation and attacking physicians who opposed it.

✂ To Lady Mar ✂

Dear Sister,

I am heartily sorry to have the pleasure of hearing from you lessened by your complaints of uneasiness, which I wish with all my soul I was capable of relieving either by my letters or any other way. My life passes in a kind of indolence, which is now and then awakened by agreeable moments, but pleasures are transitory and the groundwork of everything in England stupidity, which is certainly owing to the coldness of this vile climate. I envy you the serene air of Paris, as well as many other conveniencies. Here, what between the things one can't do and the things one must not do, the time but dully lingers on, though I make as good a shift as any of my neighbours.

To my great grief some of my best friends have been extreme ill, and in general death and sickness have never been more frequent than now. You may imagine poor gallantry droops, and except in the Elysian shades of Richmond there is no such thing as love or pleasure. 'Tis said there is a fair lady retired for having taken too much on't.[1] For my part they are not at all cooked to my taste, and I have very little share in the diversions there, which except seasoned with wit or at least vivacity will not go down with me, who have not altogether so voracious an appetite as I once had. I intend, however, to shine and be fine on the Birth Night, and review the figures there. My poor friend the young Duchess of Marlborough I'm afraid has exposed herself to a most violent ridicule; she is as much embarrassed with the loss of her big belly, and as much ashamed of it, as ever dairymaid was with the getting one.[2]

I desire you would say something very pretty to your daughter in my name.[3] Notwithstanding the great gulf that is at present between us, I hope to wait on her to an opera one time or other.

[*Postscript*] I suppose you know our uncle Fielding is dead.[4] I regret him prodigiously.

---

[1] This may refer to Mrs Henrietta Howard, mistress of the Prince of Wales; she was at this time engaged in a passionate epistolary affair with Lord Peterborough.

[2] The Duke of Marlborough's daughter, wife of Lord Godolphin, had succeeded to her father's title in 1722. She gave birth to a daughter, whose father was William Congreve, her lover for many years.

[3] Lady Frances Erskine, about eight years old, lived with her parents in Paris.

[4] William Fielding, M.P. and Groom of the Bedchamber to George I.

London, 31 October 1723

I write to you at this time piping hot from the Birth Night,[1] my brain warmed with all the agreeable ideas that fine clothes, fine gentlemen, brisk tunes and lively dances can raise there. 'Tis to be hoped that my letter will entertain you; at least you will certainly have the freshest account of all passages on that glorious day. First, you must know that I led up the ball, which you will stare at; but what's more, I think in my conscience I made one of the best figures there. To say truth, people are grown so extravagantly ugly that we old beauties are forced to come out on show days to keep the Court in countenance. I saw Mrs Murray there, through whose hands this epistle is to be conveyed. I don't know whether she'll make the same complaint to you that I do. Mrs West was with her, who is a great prude, having but two lovers at a time; I think those are Lord Haddington and Mr Lindsay, the one for use, the one for show.

The world improves in one virtue to a violent degree – I mean plain dealing. Hypocrisy being (as the Scripture declares) a damnable sin, I hope our publicans and sinners will be saved by the open profession of the contrary virtue. I was told by a very good author, who is deep in the secret, that at this very minute there is a bill cooking up at a hunting seat in Norfolk to have *not* taken out of the Commandments and clapped into the Creed the ensuing session of Parliament. This bold attempt for the liberty of the subject is wholly projected by Mr Walpole, who proposed it to the secret committee in his parlour.[2] Will Yonge seconded it, and answered for all his acquaintance voting right to a man. Dodington very gravely objected that the obstinacy of human nature was such that he feared when they had positive commandments so to do, perhaps people would not commit adultery and bear false witness against their neighbours with the readiness and cheerfulness they do at present. This objection seemed to sink deep into the minds of the greatest politicians at the board; and I don't know whether the bill won't be dropped, though 'tis certain it might be carried with great ease, the world being entirely *revenue du bagatelle*, and honour, virtue, reputation etc., which we used to hear of in our nursery, is as much laid aside and forgotten as crumpled riband. To speak plainly, I am very sorry for the forlorn state of matrimony, which is as much ridiculed by our young ladies as it used to be by young fellows; in short, both sexes have found the inconveniencies of it, and the appellation of rake is as genteel in a woman as a man of quality. 'Tis no scandal to say, Miss ——, the Maid of Honour, looks very well now she's up again, and poor Biddy Noel has never been quite well since her last flux.[3] You may imagine we

---

[1] The Prince and Princess of Wales had returned to Leicester House from Richmond to celebrate his birthday with a splendid ball.

[2] Robert Walpole was entertaining a hunting party of his political cronies.

[3] The following year Bridget Noel married the son and heir of the Earl of Portmore.

married women look very silly; we have nothing to excuse ourselves but that 'twas done a great while ago and we were very young when we did it.

This is the general state of affairs; as to particulars, if you have any curiosity for things of that kind, you have nothing to do but to ask me questions and they shall be answered to the best of my understanding, my time never being passed more agreeably than when I am doing something obliging to you. This is truth in spite of all the beaux, wits, and witlings in Great Britain.

To Lady Mar

March 1724

I do verily believe (dear sister) that this is the twelfth, if not the thirteenth letter I have writ since I had the pleasure of hearing from you, and 'tis an uncomfortable thing to have precious time spent and one's wit neglected in this manner. Sometimes I think you are fallen into that utter indifference for all things on this side the water, that you have no more curiosity for the affairs of London than for those of Peking; and if that be the case 'tis downright impertinent to trouble you with news, but I cannot cast off the affectionate concern I have for my dear sister, and consequently must put you in mind of me whenever I have an opportunity.

The bearer of this epistle is our cousin,[1] and a consummate puppy as you'll perceive at first sight. His shoulder-knot last birthday made many a pretty gentleman's heart ache with envy, and his addresses have made Miss Howard the happiest of her Highness's honourable virgins, besides the glory of thrusting the Earl of Delorain from the post he held in her affections.[2] But his relations are so ill bred to be quite insensible of the honour arising from this conquest, and fearing that so much gallantry may conclude in captivity for life pack him off to you, where 'tis to be hoped there is no such killing fare as Miss Howard.

I made a sort of resolution at the beginning of my letter not to trouble with the mention of what passes here, since you receive it with so much coldness, but I find 'tis impossible to forbear telling the metamorphosis of some of your acquaintance, which appear as wondrous to me as any in Ovid. Could one believe that Lady Holdernesse is a beauty and in

[1] Henry Vane, a distant relation.
[2] Mary Howard, Maid of Honour to the Princess of Wales since 1721, married the Earl of Delorain two years later.

love? and that Mrs Robinson is at the same time a prude and a kept
mistress? and these things in spite of nature and fortune. The first of
these ladies is tenderly attached to the polite Mr Mildmay, and sunk in
all the joys of happy love notwithstanding she wants the use of her two
hands by a rheumatism, and he has an arm that he can't move. I wish I
could send you the particulars of this *amour*, which seems to me as
curious as that between two oysters, and as well worthy the serious
inquiry of the naturalists.[3] The second heroine has engaged half the
town in arms from the nicety of her virtue, which was not able to bear
the too near approach of Senesino in the opera,[4] and her condescension
in accepting of Lord Peterborough for a champion, who has signalized
both his love and courage upon this occasion in as many instances as
ever Don Quixote did for Dulcinea.[5] Poor Senesino like a vanquished
giant was forced to confess upon his knees that Anastasia was a *non
pareil* of virtue and of beauty. Lord Stanhope, as dwarf to the said giant,
joked of his side, and was challenged for his pains.[6] Lord De La Warr[7]
was Lord Peterborough's second; my lady miscarried. The whole town
divided into parties on this important point. Innumerable have been the
disorders between the two sexes on so great an account, besides half the
House of Peers being put under arrest. By the providence of Heaven
and the wise cares of his Majesty no bloodshed ensued. However,
things are now tolerably accommodated, and the fair lady rides through
the town in triumph in the shining berlin of her hero, not to reckon the
essential advantage of one hundred pounds per month which ('tis said)
he allows her.

In general, never was gallantry in so elevated a figure as it is at
present. Twenty very pretty fellows (the Duke of Wharton[8] being
president and chief director) have formed themselves into a committee
of gallantry. They call themselves Schemers, and meet regularly three
times a week to consult on gallant schemes for the advancement of that
branch of happiness which the vulgar call whoring. Viscount Hillsborough (who I verily believe compensates in the sight of God for his
indirect acquirement of riches by his public-spirited distribution of

---

[3] In June 1724 Lady Holdernesse, widow of the 3rd Earl (whom Lady Mary
admired), married Benjamin Mildmay. The bride was thirty-six and the
groom fifty-two years old.

[4] Anastasia Robinson, prima donna, and Francesco Bernardi (Senesino), famous
castrato, sang together frequently. At the end of the season in June she retired.

[5] Famous as a military hero, in 1723 Peterborough took a house for Miss Robinson and her sister near his own villa. Just before his death in 1735 he acknowledged her as his wife, stating that they had been secretly married for many
years.

[6] Philip Stanhope, later famous as Earl of Chesterfield, was notably short in
stature while Senesino had a majestic figure.

[7] A colonel in the Horse Guards; long, lank, and awkward in appearance.

[8] Philip Wharton, 1st Duke, notorious for his brilliance, instability, and pro-
fligacy.

them, as much as ever Cardinal Wolsey did by his foundation of colleges) has turned his house, one of the handsomest in Hanover Square, into an edifice appropriated to this use. He opened on Ash Wednesday by the best contrived entertainment in the world, and the only remedy against spleen and vapours occasioned by the formality of that day, which still subsists amongst other rags of popery not yet rooted out.

The Schemers were all sworn to several articles absolutely necessary for the promotion of public good and the conservation of peace in private families: first, that every member should come at the hour of six masked in a domino, leading in the then predominant lady of his affections masked likewise; secondly, that no member should presume, by peeping, squeaking, staring or any other impertinence, to discover his brother's incognita, who should remain wholly and solely his, without any molestation soever, to his use for that night being; thirdly, no member should dare to introduce any lady who did not appear sometimes barefaced at the Drawing-Room, Lord Strafford's,[9] etc.; fourthly and lastly, that if by accident or the lady's indiscretion her name should chance to be discovered by one or more of the Schemers, that name should remain sacred and as unspeakable as the name of the Deity amongst the Jews.

You may imagine such wholesome laws brought all the best company to this polite assembly; add to these the inducement of good music, fine liquors, a splendid supper, and the best punch you ever tasted. But you'll ask, how could they sup without showing their faces? You must know the very garrets were cleaned and lighted out at this solemnity. The whole company viewed the supper, which was large enough to suffer every fair one to point to what she thought most delightful to be conveyed to her respective apartment. Those who were yet in the state of probation, and scrupled too much happiness in this world for fear of its being deducted in the next, had screens set round little neat tables in the public rooms, which were as inviolate (but to the partners) as walls of adamant. You may imagine there were few of this latter class, and 'tis to be hoped that good examples and the indefatigable endeavours of the Schemers (who spare no pains in carrying on the good cause) will lessen them daily. These gallantries are continued every Wednesday during Lent, and I won't ask your pardon for this long account of 'em since I consider the duty of a true Englishwoman is to do what honour she can to her native country, and that it would be a sin against the pious love I bear the land of my nativity to confine the renown due to the Schemers within the small extent of this little island, which ought to be spread wherever men can sigh or women wish. 'Tis true they have the envy and curses of the old and ugly of both sexes, and a general persecution from all old women, but this is no more than all reformations must expect in their beginning, and what the Christian

---

[9] Thomas Wentworth, 1st Earl of Strafford, considered by Swift as 'infinitely proud, and wholly illiterate'.

Church suffered in a remarkable manner at its first blaze. You may easily believe, the whole generation of fathers, mothers, and husbands raise as great a clamour against this new institution as the pagan priests did of old against the light of the Gospel, and for the same reasons, since it strikes at the very foundation of their authority, which authority is built on gross impositions upon mankind.

To Lady Mar

London, December 1724

I am heartily sorry (dear sister), without any affectation, for any uneasiness that you suffer, let the cause be what it will, and wish it was in my power to give you some more essential mark of it than unavailing pity. But I am not so fortunate, and till a fit occasion of disposing of some superfluous diamonds, I shall remain in this sinful sea-coal town; and all that remains for me to do to show my willingness (at least) to divert you, is to send you faithful accounts of what passes amongst your acquaintance in this part of the world. Madam de Broglie makes a great noise, but 'tis only from the frequency and quantity of her pissing, which she does not fail to do at least ten times a day amongst a cloud of witnesses.[1]

> One would think her daughter of a river,
>   As I heard Mr Miremont tell,
> And the best commendation that he could give her
>   Was that she made water excellent well.
>   With a fa la la etc.

My Lord Clare attracts the eyes of all the ladies, and gains all the hearts of those who have no other way of disposing of them but through their eyes.[2] I have dined with him twice, and had he been dumb I believe I should have been in the number of his admirers, but he lessened his beauty every time he spoke, till he left himself as few charms as Mr Vane, though I confess his outside very like Mrs Duncombe, but that the lovely lines are softer there, with wit and spirit, and improved by learning.

---

[1] The Duchess de Broglie, wife of the French ambassador, had arrived in England in August 1724. She gave birth to a son on 25 November; hence her visitors.

[2] Charles O'Brien, Viscount Clare, raised in France by his attainted family, impressed others as a conceited and silly Adonis.

The Duke of Wharton has brought his Duchess to town, and is fond of her to distraction, in order to break the hearts of all the other women that have any claim upon his.[3] Besides the family duties that he pretends to perform o'nights, he has public devotions twice o'day and assists at them in person with exemplary devotion; and there is nothing pleasanter than the remarks of some pious ladies on the conversion of so great a sinner. For my own part, I have some coteries where wit and pleasure reign, and I should not fail to amuse myself tolerably enough but for the damned, damned quality of growing older and older every day, and my present joys are made imperfect by fears of the future.

[3] The Duke, estranged from his wife, had unexpectedly been reconciled to her.

🌸 To Lady Mar 🌸

London, January 1725

Dear Sister,

I am extremely sorry for your indisposition, and did not wait for a letter to write to you, but my Lord Clare has been going every day this three weeks, and I intended to charge him with a packet. Nobody ever had such ineffectual charms as his Lordship. Beauty and money are equally ill bestowed when a fool has the keeping of them; they are incapable of happiness and every blessing turns useless in their hands.

You advise a change of taste, which I confess I have no notion of. I may (with time) change my pursuit, for the same reason that I may feed upon butcher's meat when I am not able to purchase greater delicates, but I am sure I shall never forget the flavour of *gibier*. In the meantime I divert myself passably enough and take care to improve as much as possible that stock of vanity and credulity that Heaven in its mercy has furnished me with, being sensible that to those two qualities (simple as they appear) all the pleasures of life are owing.

My sister Gower is in town on the point of lying in. I see everybody but converse with nobody but *des amies choisies*. In the first rank of these are Lady Stafford and dear Molly Skerrett, both of which have now the additional merit of being old acquaintance and never having given me any reason to complain of either of 'em.[1] I pass some days with the

[1] Lady Stafford, widow of the Earl and daughter of the celebrated Comte de Grammont, was witty and outspoken; Maria Skerrett, daughter of a London merchant, was Robert Walpole's mistress and later became his second wife. Lady Mary had known both ladies since 1720.

Duchess of Montagu, who might be a reigning beauty if she pleased. I see the whole town every Sunday, and select a few that I retain to supper. In short, if life could be always what it is, I believe I have so much humility in my temper, I could be contented without anything better this two or three hundred year, but alas!

> Dullness and wrinkles and disease must come,
> And age and death's irrevocable doom.

To Lady Mar

London, February 1725

I believe you have by this time, dear sister, received my letter from the hand of that thing my Lord Clare. However, I love you well enough to write again in hopes you will answer my letters one time or other.

All our acquaintance are run mad; they do such things, such monstrous and stupendous things! Lady Hervey and Lady Bristol have quarrelled in such a polite manner that they have given one another all the titles so liberally bestowed amongst the ladies at Billingsgate.[1] Sophia and I have been quite reconciled and are now quite broke, and I believe not likely to piece up again.[2] Ned Thompson is as happy as the money and charms of Belle Dunch can make him, and a miserable dog for all that.[3] Public places flourish more than ever; we have assemblies for every day in the week besides Court, operas, and masquerades. With youth and money 'tis certainly possible to be very well diverted in spite of malice and ill nature, though they are more and more powerful every day. For my part, as it is my established opinion that this globe of ours is no better than a Holland cheese and the walkers about in it mites, I possess my mind in patience, let what will happen, and should feel tolerably easy though a great rat came and ate half of it up.

---

[1] Lady Bristol, who had an irascible temper, was occasionally on bad terms with her daughter-in-law.

[2] Lady Mary and her sister had evidently agreed on 'Sophia' as a cipher for the Duke of Wharton, whose Jacobite intrigues made mention of his name suspect in a letter sent by post.

[3] Edward Thompson, one of the Schemers, married Arabella Dunch on 6 February 1725, but his marital bliss did not last long. Mrs Thompson was seduced in 1727 by her brother-in-law Sir George Oxenden (also a Schemer), separated from her husband, and died in childbirth.

My sister Gower has got a sixth daughter by the grace of God, and is as merry as if nothing had happened. My poor love Mr Cooke has fought and been disarmed by J. Stapylton on a national quarrel; in short he was born to conquer nothing in England, that's certain, and has good luck neither with our ladies nor gentlemen.[4] B. Noel is come out Lady Milsington, to the encouragement and consolation of all the coquettes about town, and they make haste to be as infamous as possible in order to make their fortunes.

I have this moment received from Mrs Pelling a very pretty cap for my girl. I give you many thanks for the trouble you have had in sending it, and desire you would be so good to send the other things when you have opportunity. I have another favour to ask, that you would make my compliments to our English Ambassador when you see him.[5] I have a constancy in my nature that makes me always remember my old friends.

[4] Mr Cooke, a captain of dragoons attached to the French Embassy, was wounded in the duel.

[5] Horatio Walpole, Ambassador at Paris.

❦ To Lady Mar ❦

c. *20 March 1725*

Dear Sister,

Having a few momentary spirits, I take pen in hand, though 'tis impossible to have tenderness for you without having spleen upon reading your letter, which will I hope be received as a lawful excuse for the dullness of the following lines, and I plead (as I believe has been done upon other occasions) I should please you better if I loved you less.[1]

My Lord Carleton has left this transitory world, and disposed of his estate as he did of his time, between Lady Clarendon and the Duchess of Queensbury. Jewels to a great value he has given, as he did his affections, first to the mother and then to the daughter. He was taken ill in my company at a consort at the Duchess of Marlborough's, and died two days after, holding the fair Duchess [of Queensbury] by the hand and being fed at the same time with a fine fat chicken, thus dying, as he

[1] A line adapted from the epilogue of Dryden's *Conquest of Granada* (1672).

lived, indulging his pleasures.[2] Your friend Lady A. Bateman[3] (everybody being acquainted with her affair) is grown discreet, and nobody talks of it now but his family, who are violently piqued at his refusing a great fortune. Lady Gainsborough has stolen poor Lord Shaftesbury, aged fourteen, and chained him for life to her daughter upon pretence of having been in love with her for several years.[4] But Lady Hervey makes the top figure in town, and is so good as to show twice a week at the Drawing Room and twice more at the opera for the entertainment of the public. As for myself, having nothing to say I say nothing. I insensibly dwindle into a spectatress and lead a kind of – as it were –

I wish you here every day, and see in the meantime Lady Stafford, the Duchess of Montagu, and Miss Skerrett, and really speak to almost nobody else, though I walk about everywhere. Adieu, dear sister. If my letters could be any consolation to you I should think my time best spent in writing. When you buy the trifles that I desired of you, I fancy Mr Walpole will be so good to give you opportunity of sending them without trouble if you make it your request and tell him they are for me.

[2] Lady Clarendon had been Carleton's mistress, and one of their daughters was the famous beauty who married the Duke of Queensbury. Carleton, who never married, actually left the Duchess a life interest in some of his estates as well as £5,000, and to her mother all his diamond and ruby rings. The largest part of his estate, however, went to his nephew the Earl of Burlington.

[3] A granddaughter of the Duke of Marlborough, Lady Anne had been Viscount Bateman's wife since 1720.

[4] Both bride and groom were fourteen at the time; and shortly after the wedding Shaftesbury returned to his studies at Oxford.

🎕 To Lady Mar 🎕

May 1725

Dear Sister,

I take this occasion of writing to you though I have received no answer to my last, but 'tis always most agreeable to me to write when I have the conveniency of a private hand to convey my letter, though I have no dispositions to *politiquer*. But I have such a complication of things both in my head and heart that I do not very well know what I do; and if I can't settle my brains your next news of me will be that I am locked up by my relations. In the meantime I lock myself up and keep my distraction as private as possible. The most facetious part of the history is that my distemper is of such a nature, I know not whether to laugh or cry at it. I am glad and sorry, and smiling and sad – but this is too long an account of so whimsical a being. I give myself sometimes admirable advice but I am incapable of taking it.

Mr Baillie you know is dismissed the Treasury, and consoled with a pension of equal value.[1] Your acquaintance Don Rodrigo has had a small accident befallen him: Mr Annesley found him in bed with his wife, prosecuted, and brought a bill of divorce into Parliament.[2] Those things grow more fashionable every day, and in a little while won't be at all scandalous. The best expedient for the public and to prevent the expense of private families would be a general act of divorcing all the people of England. You know, those that pleased might marry over again, and it would save the reputations of several ladies that are now in peril of being exposed every day.

I saw Horace [Horatio Walpole] the other day, who is a good creature. He returns soon to France, and I will engage him to take care of any packet that you design for me.

[1] George Baillie had been a Lord of the Treasury since 1717. His pension was £1,500.

[2] When Francis Annesley sued for divorce he named as co-respondent Rodrigo, who was either the Chamberlain at the Court of Spain or perhaps his son.

To Lady Mar

c. *10 June 1725*

I can't help being very sorry for your sake to hear that you persist in your design of retiring, though as to my own part I have no view of conversing with you where you now are, and ninety leagues is but a small addition to the distance between us. London never was more gay than it is at present but – I don't know how – I would fain be ten years younger. I love flattery so well I could fain have some circumstances of probability added to it that I might swallow it with comfort. The reigning Duchess of Marlborough has entertained the town with consorts of Bononcini's composition very often,[1] but she and I are not in that degree of friendship to have me often invited. We continue to see one another like two people that are resolved to hate with civility.

Sophia is going to Aix-la-Chapelle and from thence to Paris.[2] I dare swear she'll endeavour to get acquainted with you. We are broke to an irremediable degree. Various are the persecutions I have endured from

[1] Henrietta, junior Duchess of Marlborough, who was fanatically fond of music, was a liberal patroness of Giovanni Bononcini, the opera-composer, resident in England since 1720.

[2] The Duke of Wharton, then at Aix-la-Chapelle to take the waters, never returned to England.

her this winter, in all which I remain neuter, and shall certainly go to Heaven from the passive meekness of my temper. Lady Lansdown is in that sort of figure here nobody cares to appear with her. Madame Villette has been the favourite of the town, and by a natural transition is become the aversion.[3] She has now nobody attached to her suite but the vivacious Lord Bathurst, with whom I have been well and ill ten times within this two months; we now hardly speak to one another.[4]

I wish you would lay out part of my money in a made-up mantua and petticoat of Rat de St Maur. It will be no trouble to you to send a thing of that nature by the first travelling lady.

I give you many thanks for the good offices you promise me with regard to Mrs Murray, and I shall think myself sincerely obliged to you, as I already am on many accounts. 'Tis very disagreeable in her to go about behaving and talking as she does, and very silly into the bargain.[5] I am ever affectionately yours.

[3] The widowed Marquise de Villette, married to the attainted Lord Bolingbroke in 1720, had been in England since May 1724.
[4] Bathurst was a friend of Pope and his circle.
[5] Mrs Griselda Murray's resentment had a complicated history. In November 1721 she had been the victim of an unfortunate scandal when a footman in her father's house tried to rape her. A witty ballad about the episode was then circulated, but Mrs Murray waited two years before accusing Lady Mary – who protested – of having written it; and she continued to harass her whenever they met.

To Lady Mar

Twickenham, July 1725

I am now at the same distance from London that you are from Paris, and could fall into solitary amusements with a good deal of taste, but I resist it as a temptation of Satan, and rather turn my endeavours to make the world as agreeable to me as I can, which is the true philosophy; that of despising it is of no use but to hasten wrinkles. I ride a good deal, and have got a horse superior to any two legged animal, he being without a fault. I work like an angel, I receive visits upon idle days, and shade my life as I do my tent-stitch, that is, make as easy transitions as I can from business to pleasure. The one would be too flaring and gaudy without some dark shades of t'other, and if I worked all together in the grave colours, you know 'twould be quite dismal. Miss Skerrett is in the house with me, and Lady Stafford has taken a lodging at Richmond. As their ages are different and both agreeable in their kind, I laugh with one or reason with t'other as I happen to be in a gay or serious humour, and I manage my friends with such a strong yet with a gentle hand that they are both willing to do whatever I've a mind to.

My daughter presents her duty to you, and service to Lady Frances, who is growing to womanhood apace. I long to see her and you, and am not destitute of wandering designs to that purpose.

🎀 To Lady Mar 🎀

Twickenham, August 1725

Dear Sister,

I think this is the first time of my life that a letter of yours has lain by me two posts unanswered. You'll wonder to hear that short silence is occasioned by not having a moment unemployed at Twickenham, but I pass many hours on horseback, and I'll assure you ride stag-hunting, which I know you stare to hear of. I have arrived to vast courage and skill that way, and am as well pleased with it as with the acquisition of a new sense. His Royal Highness hunts in Richmond Park, and I make one of the *beau monde* in his train. I desire you after this account not to name the word 'old woman' to me any more; I approach to fifteen nearer than I did ten year ago, and am in hopes to improve every year in health and vivacity. Lord Bolingbroke is returned to England,[1] and is to do the honours at an assembly at Lord Berkeley's the ensuing winter,[2] but the most surprising news is Lord Bathurst's assiduous court to their Royal Highnesses, which fills the coffee houses with profound speculations. But I, who smell a rat at a considerable distance, do believe in private that Mrs Howard and his Lordship have a friendship that borders upon the tender.

> And though in histories, learned ignorance
> Attributes all to cunning or to chance,
> Love in that grave disguise does often smile,
> Knowing the cause was kindness all the while.[3]

[1] Bolingbroke returned to England incognito in May 1725 after the House of Commons had passed a bill of conditional pardon.

[2] Berkeley was 1st Lord of the Admiralty, and a zealous supporter of Bolingbroke.

[3] On occasion Bathurst, unaccompanied by his wife, visited Mrs Howard at her house in Twickenham, but Horace Walpole commented later that their friendship was 'merely political'. The verse is from 'The Rapture' by John Sheffield, Duke of Buckingham.

I am in hopes your King of France behaves better[4] than our Duke of Bedford, who by the care of a pious mother certainly preserved his virginity to his marriage bed, where he was so much disappointed in his fair bride (who though his own inclination could not bestow on him those expressless raptures he had figured to himself) that he already pukes at the very name of her, and determines to let his estate go to his brother, rather than go through the filthy drudgery of getting an heir to it.[5] N.B., this is true history and I think the most extraordinary has happened in this last age. This comes of living till sixteen without a competent knowledge either of practical or speculative anatomy, and literally thinking fine ladies composed of lilies and roses. Apropos of the best red and white to be had for money, Lady Hervey is more delightful than ever, and such a politician that if people were not blind to merit she would govern the nation. Mrs Murray has got a new lover of the most accomplished, Mr Dodington. – So far for the progress of love. That of wit has taken a very odd course and is making the tour of Ireland, from whence we have packets of ballads, songs, petitions, panegyrics, etc. So powerful is the influence of Lord Carteret's wit and my Lady's beauty,[6] the Irish rhyme that never rhymed before.

Adieu, dear sister. I take a sincere part in all that relates to you, and am ever yours. I beg as the last favour that you would make some small inquiry and let me know the minute Lord Finch is at Paris.

[4] On 25 August, Louis XV married Marie Leszczynska, whose father was informed that 'during the night the husband gave his wife seven proofs of his affection'.

[5] Bedford, who was married in April 1725, had no children, and was succeeded by his brother seven years later.

[6] Carteret, Lord Lieutenant of Ireland from 1724 to 1730, was handsome, learned, and witty; his wife was musical, beautiful, and agreeable.

c. 3 February 1726

It is very true, dear sister, that if I writ to you a full account of all that passes, my letters would be both frequent and voluminous. This sinful town is very populous, and my own affairs very much in a hurry, but the same things that afford me much matter give me very little time, and I am hardly at leisure to make observations, much less to write them down. But the melancholy catastrophe of poor Lady Lechmere is too extraordinary not to attract the attention of everybody. After having played away her reputation and fortune, she has poisoned herself – this is the effect of prudence![1] All indiscreet people live and flourish. Mrs Murray has retrieved his Grace,[2] and being reconciled to the temporal, has renounced the spiritual. Her friend Lady Hervey by aiming too high has fallen very low, and is reduced to trying to persuade folks she has an intrigue, and gets nobody to believe her, the man in question taking a great deal of pains to clear himself of the scandal.[3] Her Chelsea Grace of Rutland is married to an attorney; there's prudence for you![4] 'Tis a strange thing that women can't converse with a lawyer, a parson, nor a man midwife without putting them all to the same use, as if one could not sign a deed, say one's prayers, or take physic without doing you know what after it. This instinct is so odd, I am sometimes apt to think we were made to no other end. If that's true, Lord ha' mercy upon me; to be sure, I shall broil in the next world for living in the neglect of a known duty in this.

[1] Lady Lechmere had piled up huge gambling debts that her husband refused to pay in full. Horace Walpole described her suicide attempt: 'She took laudanum, but told it immediately and was saved by a vomit.'

[2] Probably the Duke of Atholl.

[3] In the opinion of Charles Hanbury Williams, she was 'incapable of love . . . her total, real indifference to mankind has hindered her ever having a lover'.

[4] The widow of the 2nd Duke lived in Chelsea; and the attorney was Peter Walters, eminent for his wealth and usury. The rumoured marriage never took place.

❧ To Lady Mar ❧

Dear Sister,

I cannot positively fix a time for my waiting on you at Paris, but I do verily believe I shall make a trip thither sooner or later. This town improves in gaiety every day. The young people are younger than they used to be, and all the old are grown young. Nothing is talked of but entertainments of gallantry by land and water, and we insensibly begin to taste all the joys of arbitrary power. Politics are no more; nobody pretends to wince or kick under their burdens, but we go on cheerfully with our bells at our ears, ornamented with ribands and highly contented with our present condition.

So much for the general state of the nation. The last pleasure that fell in my way was Madame de Sévigné's letters; very pretty they are,[1] but I assert without the least vanity that mine will be full as entertaining forty years hence. I advise you therefore to put none of 'em to the use of waste paper. You say nothing to me of the change of your ministry.[2] I thank you for your silence on that subject; I don't remember myself ever child enough to be concerned who reigned in any part of the earth. I am more touched at the death of poor Miss Chiswell, who is carried off by the smallpox.[3] I am so oddly made that I never forget the tendernesses contracted in my infancy, and I think of my past playfellow with a concern that few people feel for their present favourites. After giving you melancholy by this tragedy, 'tis but reasonable I should conclude with a farce, that I may not leave you in ill humour. I have so good an opinion of your taste to believe Harlequin in person will never make you laugh so much as the Earl of Stair's furious passion for Lady Walpole, aged fourteen and some months.[4] Mrs Murray undertook to bring the business to bear, and provided the opportunity (a great ingredient you'll say), but the young lady proved skittish. She did not only turn this heroic flame into present ridicule, but exposed all his generous sentiments to divert her husband and father-in-law. His Lordship is gone to Scotland; and if there was anybody wicked enough to write upon it, here is a subject worthy the pen of the best ballad-maker in Grub Street.

---

[1] These letters were first published in 1726. But thirty years later Lady Mary maintained that Madame de Sévigné 'only gives us, in a lively manner and fashionable phrases, mean sentiments, vulgar prejudices, and endless repetitions! Sometimes the tittle tattle of a fine lady, sometimes that of an old nurse, always tittle tattle . . .'.

[2] The duc de Bourbon, dismissed on 31 May, was replaced by Louis XV's former tutor, the Abbé Fleury.

[3] Sarah Chiswell was Lady Mary's friend in Nottingham to whom she had addressed the Embassy letter on inoculation.

[4] Sir Robert Walpole's daughter-in-law was actually a little over seventeen years old, and Stair, a military man, about fifty-three.

🦢 To Lady Mar 🦢

November 1726

I am very sorry (dear sister) for your ill health, but hope it is so
entirely past that you have by this time forgot it. I never was
better in my life, nor ever passed my hours more agreeably. I ride between London and Twickenham perpetually and have little societies
quite to my taste, and that is saying everything. I leave the great world
to girls that know no better and do not think one bit the worse of myself
for having outlived a certain giddiness which is sometimes excusable
but never pleasing. Depend upon it, 'tis only the spleen that gives you
those ideas; you may have many delightful days to come, and there is
nothing more silly than to be too wise to be happy.

> If to be sad is to be wise,
> I do most heartily despise
> Whatever Socrates has said
> Or Tully writ or Montaigne read.[1]

So much for philosophy –

What do you say to Pelham's marriage? There's flame! There's
constancy![2] If I could not employ my time better I would write the
history of their loves in twelve tomes. Lord Hervey should die in her
arms like the poor King of Assyria; she should be sometimes carried
off by troops of masques and at other times blocked up in the strong
castles of the bagnio, but her honour should always remain inviolate
by the strength of her own virtue and the friendship of the enchantress
Mrs Murray, till her happy nuptials with her faithful Cyrus.[3] – 'Tis a
thousand pities I have not time for these vivacities. Here is a book come
out, that all our people of taste run mad about. 'Tis no less than the
united work of a dignified clergyman, an eminent physician, and the
first poet of the age, and very wonderful it is, God knows.[4] Great eloquence have they employed to prove themselves beasts, and show such
a veneration for horses that since the Essex Quaker nobody has
appeared so passionately devoted to that species;[5] and to say truth, they
talk of a stable with so much warmth and affection I can't help suspect-
ing some very powerful motive at the bottom of it.

[1] Verse adapted from Matthew Prior's *Alma* (1718).

[2] Henry Pelham married Lady Catherine Manners on 17 October 1726 after a
courtship of at least three years.

[3] This passage alludes to Mlle de Scudéry's romance *Artamène ou Le Grand
Cyrus* (in 10 vols.).

[4] *Gulliver's Travels* was published 28 October 1726. Other contemporaries assumed that Pope and Dr Arbuthnot had collaborated with Swift. As to its
popularity, John Gay wrote: 'From the highest to the lowest it is universally
read, from the Cabinet-council to the nursery.'

[5] Lady Mary refers to 'News from Colchester. Or, A Proper new Ballad of
certain Carnal Passages betwixt a Quaker and a Colt, at Horsly near Colchester, in Essex', by John Denham (1659).

London, April 1727

My Lady Stafford set out towards France this morning and has carried half the pleasures of my life along with her. I am more stupid than I can describe, and am as full of moral reflections as either Cambrai or Pascal.[1] I think of nothing but the nothingness of the good things of this world, the transitoriness of its joys, the pungency of its sorrows, and many discoveries that have been made this 3,000 years and committed to print ever since the first erecting of presses. I advise you as the best thing you can do that day, let it happen when it will, to visit Lady Stafford. She has the goodness to carry with her a true-born Englishwoman, who is neither good nor bad nor capable of being either, Lady Phil Pratt by name, of the Hamilton family, and who will be glad of your acquaintance, and you can never be sorry for hers.[2]

Peace or war, cross or pile, makes all the conversation.[3] The town never was fuller, and God be praised some people *brille* in it who *brille*d twenty years ago. My cousin Butler is of that number, who is just what she was in all respects when she inhabited Bond Street. The sprouts of this age are such green withered things, 'tis a great comfort to us grown-up people. I except my own daughter, who is to be the ornament of the ensuing Court. I beg you would exact from Lady Stafford a particular of her perfections, which would sound suspected from my hand. At the same time I must do justice to a little twig belonging to my sister Gower. Miss Jenny is like the Duchess of Queensbury both in face and spirit. Apropos of family affairs, I had almost forgot our dear and amiable cousin Lady Denbigh, who has blazed out all this winter.[4] She has brought with her from Paris cart-loads of riband, surprising fashions, and a complexion of the last edition, which naturally attracts all the she and he fools in London; and accordingly she is surrounded with a little court of both, and keeps a Sunday assembly to show she has learnt to play at cards on that day. Lady F. Fielding is really the prettiest woman in town and has sense enough to make one's heart ache to see her surrounded with such fools as her relations are.[5]

[1] Fénelon, Archbishop of Cambrai, and Blaise Pascal were philosophers.

[2] Lady Philippa *née* Hamilton was widow of an elderly clergyman. After they parted, Lady Stafford characterized her to Lady Mary as 'not only stupid, as you know, but deceitful and utterly unreasonable about everything'.

[3] Whether England would go to war with Spain. (Cross and pile means head and tail of a coin.)

[4] Isabella de Jonge, daughter of a Dutch burgomaster, married (about 1718) the 5th Earl of Denbigh, Lady Mary's cousin.

[5] Lady Frances was Denbigh's youngest sister. In 1729 she married Daniel Finch, later Earl of Winchilsea.

The man in England that gives the greatest pleasure and the greatest pain is a youth of Royal blood, with all his grandmother's beauty, wit, and good qualities; in short he is Nell Gwyn in person with the sex altered, and occasions such fracas amongst the ladies of gallantry that it passes belief.[6] You'll stare to hear of her Grace of Cleveland at the head of them.[7] If I was poetical I would tell you:

> The god of love, enraged to see
> The nymph despise his flame,
> At dice and cards misspend her nights
> And slight a nobler game:
>
> For the neglect of offers past
> And pride in days of yore,
> He kindles up a fire at last
> That burns her at threescore.
>
> A polished white is smoothly spread
> Where whilom wrinkles lay,
> And glowing with an artful red
> She ogles at the play.
>
> Along the Mall she softly sails
> In white and silver dressed,
> Her neck exposed to eastern gales,
> And jewels on her breast.
>
> Her children banished, age forgot,
> Lord Sidney is her care,
> And, what is much a happier lot,
> Has hopes to be her heir.

This is all true history though it is doggerel rhyme. In good earnest, she has turned Lady Grace and family out o'doors to make room for him,[8] and there he lies like leaf-gold upon a pill. There never was so violent and so indiscreet a passion. Lady Stafford says, nothing was ever like it since Phaedra and Hippolytus. – Lord ha' mercy upon us; see what we may all come to!

[6] Lord Sidney Beauclerk was a son of the 1st Duke of St Albans, Charles II's bastard son.
[7] The Duchess of Cleveland was the wife of another bastard son of Charles II (by Barbara Villiers). Since she was related by marriage to Lord Sidney, and their ages were 63 and 25, the comparison at the end of the letter to Phaedra (who fell in love with her stepson Hippolytus) is apt.
[8] Her daughter Lady Grace, wife of Henry Vane, had an infant son.

Twickenham, May 1727

Dear Sister,

I was very glad to hear from you, though there were some things in your letters very monstrous and shocking. I wonder with what conscience you can talk to me of your being an old woman; I beg I may hear no more on't. For my part I pretend to be as young as ever, and really am as young as needs to be, to all intents and purposes. I attribute all this to your living so long at Chatton, and fancy a week at Paris will correct such wild imaginations and set things in a better light. My cure for lowness of spirits is not drinking nasty water but galloping all day, and a moderate glass of champagne at night in good company; and I believe this regimen closely followed is one of the most wholesome that can be prescribed, and may save one a world of filthy doses and more filthy doctors' fees at the year's end.

I rid to Twickenham last night, and after so long a stay in town am not sorry to find myself in my garden. Our neighbourhood is something improved by the removal of some old maids, and the arrival of some fine gentlemen, amongst which are Lord Middleton and Sir J. Gifford, who are perhaps your acquaintance.[1] They live with their aunt Lady Westmorland,[2] and we endeavour to make the country agreeable to one another. Dr Swift[3] and Johny Gay are at Pope's, and their conjunction has produced a ballad which if nobody else has sent you I will, being never better pleased than when I am endeavouring to amuse my dear sister.

[1] Sir John Gifford was Lord Middleton's nephew; both were Jacobite sympathizers.
[2] Whose house adjoined Lady Mary's.
[3] Swift arrived in England at the end of April, and stayed with Pope at Twickenham then and in May. Their ballad is impossible to identify with any certainty.

23 June 1727

I am always pleased to hear from you (dear sister), particularly
when you tell me you are well. I believe you'll find upon the
whole my sense is right, that air, exercise and company are the best
medicines, and physic and retirement good for nothing but to break
hearts and spoil constitutions.

I was glad to hear Mr Rémond's history from you, though the newspaper had given it me *en gros* and my Lady Stafford in detail some time
before.[1] I will tell you in return, as well as I can, what happens amongst
our acquaintance here. To begin with family affairs: the Duchess of
Kingston grunts on as usual, and I fear will put us in black bombazine
soon, which is a real grief to me. My dear Aunt Cheyne makes all the
money she can of Lady Frances, and I fear will carry on those politics
to the last point, though the girl is such a fool, 'tis no great matter.[2] I
am going within this half-hour to call her to Court.

Our poor cousins the Fieldings are grown yet poorer by the loss of
all the little money they had, which in their infinite wisdom they put
into the hands of a roguish broker who has fairly walked off with it.

The most diverting story about town at present is in relation to
Edgcumbe,[3] though your not knowing the people concerned as well as
I do will, I fear, hinder you from being so much entertained by it. I
can't tell whether you know a tall, musical, silly, ugly thing, niece to
Lady Essex Roberts, who is called Miss Legh.[4] She went a few days ago
to visit Mrs Betty Tichborne, Lady Sunderland's sister, who lives in the
house with her, and was denied at the door; but with the true manners
of a great fool told the porter that if his Lady was at home she was
very positive she would be very glad to see her. Upon which she was
showed up stairs to Miss Tichborne, who was ready to drop down at
the sight of her, and could not help asking her in a grave way how she
got in, being denied to every mortal, intending to pass the evening in
devout preparations. Miss Legh said she had sent away her chair and
servants with intent of staying till nine o'clock. There was then no
remedy and she was asked to sit down, but had not been there a quarter
of an hour when she heard a violent rap at the door, and somebody
vehemently run up stairs. Miss Tichborne seemed much surprised and
said she believed it was Mr Edgcumbe, and was quite amazed how he

---

[1] Rémond's 'history' was probably that of his engagement to be married to the
daughter of a jeweller.

[2] Lady Frances Pierrepont, fourteen-year-old daughter of Lady Mary's brother,
was orphaned. She had lived with her grandfather the Duke of Kingston, and
after his death (in March 1726) she lived with his sister Lady Cheyne.

[3] Richard Edgcumbe, later 1st Baron, politician.

[4] Elizabeth Legh was described by Horace Walpole as 'a virtuosa, a musician,
a madwoman', who was in love with Handel and wore his picture, along with
the Pretender's, on her breast.

took it into his head to visit her. During these excuses, enter Edgcumbe, who appeared frighted at the sight of a third person. Miss Tichborne told him almost at his entrance that the lady he saw there was a perfect mistress of music, and as he passionately loved it she thought she could not oblige him more than by desiring her to play. Miss Legh very willingly sat to the harpsichord, upon which her audience decamped to the bedchamber, and left her to play over three or four lessons to herself. They returned and made what excuses they could, but said very frankly they had not heard her performance and begged her to begin again, which she complied with, and gave them the opportunity of a second retirement. Miss Legh was by this time all fire and flame to see her heavenly harmony thus slighted, and when they returned told them she did not understand playing to an empty room. Mr Edgcumbe begged 10,000 pardons, and said if she would play 'Gode'[5] it was a tune he died to hear, and it would be an obligation he should never forget. She made answer, she would do him a much greater obligation by her absence, which she supposed was all that was wanting at that time, and run downstairs in a great fury, to publish as fast as she could, and was so indefatigable in this pious design that in four and twenty hours all the people in town had heard the story, and poor Edgcumbe met with nothing wherever he went but compliments about his third tune, which is reckoned very handsome in a lover past forty.

My Lady Sunderland could not avoid hearing this gallant history, and three days after invited Miss Legh to dinner, where in the presence of her sister and all the servants in waiting, she told her she was very sorry she had been so rudely treated in her house, that it was very true Mr Edgcumbe had been a perpetual companion of her sister's this two year, and she thought it high time he should explain himself; and she expected her sister should act in this matter as discreetly as Lady K. Pelham had done in the like case, who she heard had given Mr Pelham four months to resolve in, and after that he was either to marry or lose her forever. Sir Robert Sutton interrupted her by saying that he never doubted the honour of Mr Edgcumbe and was persuaded he could have no ill design in his family.[6] The affair stands thus, and Edgcumbe has four months to provide himself elsewhere, during which time he has free egress and regress, and 'tis seriously the opinion of many that a wedding will in good earnest be brought about by this admirable conduct.[7]

I send you a novel instead of a letter, but as it is in your power to shorten it when you please by reading no farther than you like, I will make no excuses for the length of it.

[5] An aria from Handel's recently revived opera *Ottone*.

[6] Sutton, an M.P. and retired diplomatist, had married the widowed Lady Sunderland in 1724.

[7] Edgcumbe, a widower since 1721, never remarried.

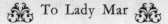

September 1727

This is a vile world, dear sister, and I can easily comprehend that whether one is at Paris or London one is stifled with a certain mixture of fool and knave that most people are composed of. I would have patience with a parcel of polite rascals or your downright honest fools. But father Adam shines through his whole progeny; he first ate the apple like a sot and then turned informer like a scoundrel. – So much for our inside. Then our outward is so liable to ugliness and distempers that we are perpetually plagued with feeling our own decays and seeing other people's – yet six pennorth of common sense divided amongst a whole nation would make our lives roll away glib enough. But then we make laws and we follow customs; by the first we cut off our own pleasures, and by the second we are answerable for the faults and extravagancies of others. All these things and five hundred more convince me (as I have the most profound adoration for the Author of nature) that we are here in an actual state of punishment. I am satisfied I have been damned ever since I was born, and in submission to divine justice don't at all doubt but I deserved it in some pre-existent state. I am very willing to soften the word damned and hope I am only in purgatory, and that after whining and grunting here a certain number of years I shall be translated to some more happy sphere where virtue will be natural and custom reasonable; that is, in short, where common sense will reign.

I grow very devout, as you see, and place all my hopes in the next life, being totally persuaded of the nothingness of this. Don't you remember how miserable we were in the little parlour at Thoresby? We thought marrying would put us at once into possession of all we wanted; then came being with child, etc., and you see what comes of being with child.[1]

Though after all I am still of opinion that 'tis extremely silly to submit to ill fortune; one should pluck up a spirit and live upon cordials when one can have no other nourishment. These are my present endeavours, and I run about though I have 5,000 pins and needles running into my heart. I try to console with a small damsel who is at present everything that I like, but alas, she is yet in a white frock. At fourteen she may run away with the butler. There's one of the blessed consequences of great disappointment; you are not only hurt by the thing present, but it cuts off all future hopes and makes your very expectations melancholy. *Quelle vie*!

[1] Edward Wortley Montagu, junior, was the cause of his mother's anguish. In the previous year the thirteen-year-old boy had run away from Westminster School to Oxford, but was soon found and put back in school. In September 1727 he ran away again: this time he successfully eluded his parents' search, including their conciliatory advertisements in newspapers. He had shipped out on a boat bound for Gibraltar, and was not returned to his parents until the following January.

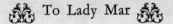

London, October 1727

I cannot deny but I was very well diverted the Coronation day.[1] I saw the procession much at my ease in a house I filled with my own company, and then got into the Hall without any trouble, where it was very entertaining to observe the variety of airs that all meant the same thing, the business of every walker there being to conceal vanity and gain admiration. For these purposes some languished and others strutted, but a visible satisfaction was diffused over every countenance as soon as the coronet was clapped on the head. But she that drew the greatest number of eyes was indisputably the Countess of Orkney.[2] She exposed behind a mixture of fat and wrinkles, and before a considerable pair of bubbies a good deal withered, a great belly that preceded her; add to this the inimitable roll of her eyes and her grey hair which by good fortune stood directly upright, and 'tis impossible to imagine a more delightful spectacle. She had embellished all this with a great deal of magnificence which made her as big again as usual, and I should have thought her one of the largest things of God's making if my Lady St John had not displayed all her charms that day. The poor Duchess of Montrose crept along with a dozen of black snakes playing round her face; and my Lady Portland (who is fallen away since her dismission from Court)[3] represented very finely an Egyptian mummy embroidered over with hieroglyphics. In general I could not perceive but the old were as well pleased as the young, and I (who dread growing wise more than anything in the world) was overjoyed to observe one can never outlive one's vanity.

I have never received the long letter you talk of, and am afraid you have only fancied that you writ it.

Adieu, my dear sister. I am affectionately yours.

[1] George II was crowned on 11 October.
[2] She had been mistress to William III, more for her intellectual than physical charms.
[3] By George II, whose children had been put in her charge when he quarrelled with his father in 1718.

❧ To Dr John Arbuthnot ❧

3 January 1735

Sir,

I have perused the last lampoon of your ingenious friend, and am not surprised you did not find me out under the name of Sappho,[1] because there is nothing I ever heard in our characters or circumstances to make a parallel, but as the town (except you who know better) generally suppose Pope means me whenever he mentions that name, I cannot help taking notice of the terrible malice he bears against the lady signified by that name, which appears to be irritated by supposing her writer of the *Verses to the Imitator of Horace*.[2] Now I can assure him they were wrote (without my knowledge) by a gentleman of great merit, whom I very much esteem, who he will never guess, and who, if he did know, he durst not attack; but I own the design was so well meant and so excellently executed that I cannot be sorry they were written.

I wish you would advise poor Pope to turn to some more honest livelihood than libelling. I know he will allege in his excuse that he must write to eat, and he is now grown sensible that nobody will buy his verses except their curiosity is piqued to it to see what is said of their acquaintance, but I think this method of gain so exceeding vile that it admits of no excuse at all. Can anything be more detestable than his abusing poor Moore scarce cold in his grave, when it is plain he kept back his poem while he lived for fear he should beat him for it.[3] This is shocking to me though of a man I never spoke to and hardly knew by sight; but I am seriously concerned at the worse scandal he has heaped on Mr Congreve,[4] who was my friend, and whom I am obliged to justify because I can do it on my own knowledge, and which is yet farther, being witness of it from those who were then often with me, that he was so far from loving Pope's rhyme, both that and his conversation were perpetual jokes to him, exceeding despicable in his opinion, and he has often made us laugh in talking of them, being particularly pleasant on that subject. As to Pope's being born of honest parents, I verily believe it, and will add one praise to his mother's character, that (though I only knew her very old) she always appeared to me to have much better sense than himself. I desire, sir, as a favour, that you would show this letter to Pope, and you will very much oblige, sir, your humble servant,

M. W. Montagu

[1] The famous lyrical poetess who lived in the seventh century B.C. In his *Epistle to Arbuthnot*, published 2 January 1735, Pope uses that pseudonym for a dangerous female wit – clearly meaning Lady Mary.

[2] This satire, published on 8 March 1733, was a bludgeoning attack on Pope written in revenge by Lady Mary assisted by Lord Hervey, who had also been ridiculed by Pope.

[3] James Moore Smythe, co-author of the satiric *One Epistle to Pope*, had died the previous October; he is mentioned several times in the *Epistle to Arbuthnot* though not with any severity.

[4] The 'worse scandal' about Congreve in the *Epistle to Arbuthnot* was merely that he had loved Pope's poetry.

To Francesco Algarotti

London, April 1736

Monday night

My Lady Stafford and myself waited for you three hours. Three hours of expectation is no small trial of patience, and I believe some of your martyrs have been canonized for suffering less. If you have repentance enough to be inclined to ask pardon you may obtain it by coming here tomorrow at seven o'clock.

Let me have a line of answer.

To Francesco Algarotti

London, August 1736

I no longer know how to write to you. My feelings are too ardent; I could not possibly explain them or hide them. One would have to be affected by an enthusiasm similar to mine to endure my letters. I see all its folly without being able to correct myself. The very idea of seeing you again gave me a shock while I read your letter, which almost made me swoon. What has become of that philosophical indifference that made the glory and the tranquillity of my former days? I have lost it never to find it again, and if that passion is healed I foresee nothing except mortal ennui. – Forgive the absurdity that you have brought into being, and come to see me.

[translation]

To Francesco Algarotti

London, September 1736

How timid one is when one loves! I am afraid of offending you by sending you this note though I mean to please you. In short I am so foolish about everything that concerns you that I am not sure of my own thoughts. My reason complains very softly of the stupidities of my heart without having the strength to destroy them. I am torn by a thousand conflicting feelings that concern you very little, and I don't know why I confide this to you. All that is certain is that I shall love you all my life in spite of your whims and my reason.

[*translation*]

To Francesco Algarotti

London, 20 September 1736

Is it possible that I have no news from you? It seems to me that you promised to write to me from Calais. I think only of that, and while I wait everything bores me, everything displeases me, and I am in a state which would draw pity even from the people who hate me most. It seems to me that it ought to have cost you less to write three or four lines to me than to spend as many hours talking to me. Philosophically, an exchange of letters with me ought to give you a kind of pleasure. You will see (what has never been seen till now) the faithful picture of a woman's heart without evasion or disguises, drawn to the life, who presents herself for what she is, and who neither hides nor glosses over anything from you. My weaknesses and my outbursts ought at least to attract your curiosity, in presenting to you the accurate dissection of a female soul. It is said that Montaigne pleases by that naturalness which reveals even his faults, and I have that merit if I have no others in your eyes. So it is not possible that my letters bore you to the extent that you renounce them so brusquely.

It would be very much worse if some accident had happened to you. – We have not heard of storms or vessels lost. – I must be enlightened at whatever cost. – I will see Lord Hervey; he should have had news of you. Ingrate though you are, I should have a moment of pleasure in knowing that you have arrived safely in Paris, where you would make fun of my letters with some beautiful Parisienne. No matter, I shall always write to you in order to please you if you love me, or to enrage you if you wish to forget me. How unhappy I am! and what a stroke of mercy a stroke of lightning would be at this moment!

This is the fourth letter I send you. You must be thoroughly bored with my complaints, but is it my duty to protect your repose when you have so little concern for mine?

[*translation*]

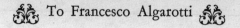

To Francesco Algarotti

London, c. 29 September 1736

Your letter came in very good time to save the small remains of
my understanding. Your silence had so far disturbed it, that
not able to bear the perplexity of my own imaginations I sent Lord
Hervey word I should be glad to speak to him. You may believe (with
his politeness) I saw him soon after, and then I was in almost as much
difficulty to draw from him what I had a mind to know; that is, whether
you were arrived safe at Paris? The question was very short, but the
way to make it very hard; and in short I said nothing of what I had a
mind to know, and all he could collect from my conversation was that I
was very near if not quite distracted. He told me very plainly that after
so much neglect as I had shown him he could not fancy I would honour
him with a message except I had something to demand of him that I
thought of importance to myself, and very generously made me all sort
of offers of services and assurances of obeying my commands, reasonable or unreasonable. This speech, which was meant to give me courage
to explain myself, made it quite impossible for me to do it. I reflected
I could not now ask him this question with an air of indifference since
he already thought nothing but the last necessity would make me ask
him any question at all, and I was reduced to confess I had something of
consequence to impart but could not prevail on myself to do it that day,
and postponed my inquiry to another.[1] I received your letter the day
following, and have now nothing farther to demand of him.

I shall go tomorrow (late as it is in the year) to my country house,
where I intend to bury myself for at least three months. People tell me
that I am going to a wilderness, because they don't know that I am
leaving one, and 'tis all one to me whether I see beasts covered with
their natural hides or embroideries; they are equally unconversable.
You have taken from me not only the taste but the sufferance of those I
see, but in recompense you have made me very entertaining to myself,
and there are some moments when I am happy enough to think over
the past till I totally forget the present.

> I have lived today; to-morrow let the Father fill the heaven with
> murky clouds, or radiant sunshine! Yet will he not render vain what-
> ever now is past, nor will he alter and undo what once the fleeting
> hour has brought.[2]

My picture is doing.

---

[1] Hervey sent Algarotti a long, caustic account of how he had at first evaded
Lady Mary's attempt to see him, and then of her painful and unsuccessful
interview.

[2] Lady Mary wrote six lines from Horace's *Odes*, here translated from the Loeb
Library.

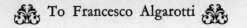

December 1736

I have sent you so many verses, this shall wait on you in the form of plain prose. My picture went last, wrapped up in poetry without fiction. I could be angry at your haste in restoring a trifle that, if you ever intend to see me again, might have been time enough delivered to my own hand. If you seriously wish to see me it will certainly happen; if your affairs do not permit your return to England mine shall be arranged in such a manner as I may come to Italy. This sounds extraordinary, and yet is not so when you consider the impression you have made on a heart that is capable of receiving no other. My thoughts of you are such as exceed the strongest panegyric that the vainest man upon earth ever wished to hear made of himself, and all conversations since I lost yours are so insipid to me that I prefer my closet meditations to all the amusements of a populous town or crowded court.

I shall endeavour to obey all your commands because they are yours, but I have so little correspondence and yet less faith in doctors of all degrees that I know not who to apply to for your old relation. I only know in general many people here have cataracts, and none are cured but by couching, which is a manual operation.[1]

You may spare the recommendation of remembering you. You are ever present to my thoughts, and half those aspirations to the B. V. [Blessed Virgin] would deserve her personal appearance to encourage so sincere a votary.

Let me know when you receive my picture. Write to me, and believe whenever you do it you are bestowing the only happiness I can be sensible of in your absence.

[1] Inserting a needle through the membrane of the eye and displacing the cataract below the axis of vision. This operation was being successfully performed by 1710.

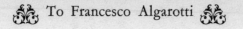

To Francesco Algarotti

London, 24 February 1738

There needs only your absence to make any place disagreeable to me, but at present we have a complication of everything in London that is contrary to my inclination: noise, crowd, division, and almost an impossibility of keeping entirely clear of the infection. Though my mind is too well filled with soft remembrances to be penetrable to the rough impressions of faction and nonsense, yet my ears are daily wounded with epidemic madness, and my person exposed to the rheums and disorders incident to this watery climate. I am forced to remember this by a cursed toothache that endeavours to torment me at this very moment, but your idea shall give me stoicism enough to resist it. This is doing a great deal, but you cannot expect me to carry it so far as to be entertaining in my present situation. 'Tis enough that you can make me insensible either to pain or politics, but I must necessarily be dull when the sun and you are both so distant from me; may the spring bring a return of both.

> You, lovely youth, shall my Apollo prove,
> Adorn my verse, and tune my soul to love.[1]

[1] Verse adapted from Elizabeth Singer, 'A Pastoral Inscribed to the Hon. Mrs. ——'.

To Lady Pomfret

26 July 1738

I hope, dear madam, you find at least some amusement in your travels, and though I cannot wish you to forget those friends in England who will never forget you, yet I should be pleased to hear you were so far entertained as to take off all anxiety from your mind. I know you are capable of many pleasures that the herd of mankind are insensible of; and wherever you go I do not doubt you will find some people that will know how to taste the happiness of your conversation. We are as much blinded in England by politics and views of interest as we are by mists and fogs, and 'tis necessary to have a very uncommon constitution not to be tainted with the distempers of our climate. I confess myself very much infected with the epidemical dullness; yet as 'tis natural to excuse one's own faults as much as possible, I am apt to flatter myself that my stupidity is rather accidental than real. At least I am sure that I want no vivacity when I think of my Lady Pomfret, and that it is with the warmest inclination as well as the highest esteem that I am ever affectionately yours,

M.W.M.

Here is no alteration since you left us except in the weather, and I would not entertain you with the journal of the thermometer. I hope to hear soon from you.

To Lady Pomfret

October 1738

Yesterday was very fortunate to me; it brought two of your ladyship's letters. I will not speak my thoughts of them, but must insist once for all that you lay aside all those phrases of *tiring me, ashamed of your dullness*, etc. etc. I can't help when I read them either doubting your sincerity or fearing you have a worse opinion of my judgment than I desire you should have. Spare me those disagreeable reflections, and be assured, if I hated you, I should read your letters with pleasure; and that I love you enough to be charmed with hearing from you though you knew not how to spell.

The delightful description of your retirement makes me wish to partake it with you, but I have been so much accustomed to wish in vain that I dare not flatter myself with so pleasing an idea. We are wrapped up in fogs, and consequential stupidity, which increases so visibly we want but little of the state of petrifaction which was said to befall an African town. However, there remains still some lively people amongst us that play the fool with great alacrity. Lady Sophia Keppel has declared her worthy choice of the amiable Captain Thomas.[1] Poor Lady Frances Montagu is on the point of renouncing the pomps and vanities of this world, and confining herself to rural shades with Sir Roger Burgoyne, whose mansion house will, I believe, perfectly resemble Mr Sullen's; but as we are in dead peace, I am afraid there is no hope of a French count to enliven her solitude.[2] It is reported a much greater, fairer lady is going to be disposed of to a much worse retreat, at least I should think so.[3] 'Tis terrible to be the fifth in rank after having been the first, but such is the hard condition of our sex: women and priests never know where they shall eat their bread.

All the polite and the gallant are either gone or preparing for the

---

[1] Captain John Thomas, later General, was an aide-de-camp to Lady Sophia's father, 1st Earl of Albemarle.

[2] A reference to George Farquhar's comedy *The Beaux' Stratagem*.

[3] Princess Mary, daughter of George II, married the Prince-Elector Frederick II of Hesse–Kassel in May 1740.

Bath. You may suppose Lady Hervey would not fail appearing there, where I am told she has made a marvellous union with the Duchess of Manchester, and writes from thence that she is charmed with her Grace's sweetness of temper.[4] The Duchess of Richmond declares a design of passing the winter at Goodwood, where she has had a succession of olios of company. It is said very gravely that this loss to the town is occasioned by the suspension of operas. We have no less than fifty-three French strollers arrived to supply their place, and Monsieur de Cambis goes about with great solemnity, negotiating to do them service.[5] These are the most important events that are come to my knowledge; perhaps I should remember some more serious if I was so happy as to be with you. I am very glad to hear of the return of Lady Sophia's health and beauty.[6] My dear Lady Pomfret has on all occasions my warmest wishes, and the truest esteem and affection of your faithful, etc. etc.

[4] Lady Mary is ironic; the Duchess had a ferocious temper.

[5] The French Ambassador needed to look after the company of French players who had arrived in London at the end of September. When they opened at the Haymarket the audience rioted, and would not let them finish.

[6] Lady Sophia Fermor was Lady Pomfret's eldest daughter, and her beauty was universally acknowledged.

❧ To Lady Pomfret ❧

November 1738

I should take your ladyship's question (whether I should always desire your friendship) very unkindly if I was in the least disposed to quarrel with you; it is very much doubting both my understanding and morals – two very tender points. But I am more concerned for your opinion of the last than the other, being persuaded 'tis easier for you to forgive an involuntary error of the head than a levity in the mind, of which (give me leave to say) I am utterly incapable; and you must give me very great proofs of my being troublesome before you will be able to get rid of me. I passed two very agreeable evenings last week with Lady Bell Finch; we had the mutual pleasure of talking of you, and joined in very sincere wishes for your company.

The reason of Lord Morpeth's leaving Caen are variously told; I believe Lady Carlisle is persuaded he was not properly used there. I hear he is with his father at Venice. The whole seems odd, but it is not possible to know the true motives of people's conduct in their families, which may be very reasonable when it does not appear so.[1]

[1] Lord Morpeth, Carlisle's son and heir, died in 1741 of consumption, though gossip attributed his death to venereal disease.

Here are some few births, but neither marriages or burials worth mentioning. Lady Townshend has entertained the Bath with a variety of lively scenes,[2] and Lady Harriet Herbert furnished the tea-tables here with fresh tattle for this last fortnight.[3] I was one of the first informed of her adventure by Lady Gage, who was told that morning by a priest that she had desired him to marry her the next day to Beard, who sings in the farces at Drury Lane.[4] He refused her that good office and immediately told Lady Gage, who (having been unfortunate in her friends) was frighted at this affair and asked my advice. I told her honestly that since the lady was capable of such *amours* I did not doubt if this was broke off she would bestow her person and fortune on some hackney-coachman or chairman, and that I really saw no method of saving *her* from ruin, and her *family* from dishonour, but by poisoning her, and offered to be at the expense of the arsenic, and even to administer it with my own hands if she would invite her to drink tea with her that evening. But on her not approving that method, she sent to Lady Montagu, Mrs Dunch, and all the relations within the reach of messengers. They carried Lady Harriet to Twickenham, though I told them it was a bad air for girls.[5] She is since returned to London, and some people believe her married; others, that he is too much intimidated by Mr Waldegrave's threats to dare to go through the ceremony. But the secret is now public, and in what manner it will conclude I know not.[6] Her relations have certainly no reason to be amazed at her constitution, but are violently surprised at the mixture of devotion that forces her to have recourse to the Church in her necessities, which has not been the road taken by the matrons of her family.[7] Such examples are very detrimental to our whole sex and are apt to influence the other into a belief that we are unfit to manage either liberty or money. These melancholy reflections make me incapable of a lively conclusion to my letter; you must accept of a very sincere one in the assurance that I am, dear madam, inviolably yours, etc.

[2] Lady Townshend was notorious for her loose morals and racy wit.

[3] Lady Henrietta, daughter of 1st Earl Waldegrave, Ambassador to France, had married Lord Edward Herbert in 1734. He died the same year.

[4] John Beard, actor and singer, then beginning his career, was approximately the same age as Lady Henrietta. His moral and social qualities were generally commended.

[5] Lady Mary is no doubt thinking of her own disobedient daughter and niece: Mary Wortley Montagu married the Earl of Bute in 1736 against her parents' wishes – though with their final, reluctant consent; and Lady Frances Pierrepont eloped with Philip Meadows in 1734.

[6] In spite of threats by Lady Henrietta's younger brother, John Waldegrave (later 3rd Earl), the marriage took place on 8 January 1739.

[7] Her grandmother, wife of 1st Lord Waldegrave, had been the illegitimate daughter of James II, and as a widow at the exiled Court of Saint-Germain had been ordered into a convent because she was pregnant and would not name her lover.

November 1738

I am too much affected by your ways of treating me. What have you seen so disobliging in my last letter? Would to God that I might receive similar marks of your attachment for me! But I am not made to inspire the tenderness that I am capable of feeling, and am wrong to be offended. You have too much wit to need any explanation. If you wish to quarrel with me, it is because you wish it. You know only too well that you are the only object in the world which pleases me. I have done everything until this moment to prove it to you, and I shall always be the same towards you; and I have so little notion of finding anything else agreeable, I would wish with all my heart, if I lose the hope of seeing you, to lose my life at the same moment.

[*translation*]

🎀 To Lady Pomfret 🎀

January 1739

Amidst the shining gallantries of the French Court I know not how you will receive a stupid letter from these regions of dull-ness, where even our ridiculous actions (which are very frequent, I confess) have a certain air of formality that hinders them from being risible, at the same time that they are absurd. I think Lady Anne Lumley's marriage may be reckoned into this number, who is going to espouse with great gravity a younger brother of Sir Thomas Frank-land's. There are great struggles and many candidates for her place.[1] Lady Anne Montagu, daughter to Lord Halifax, is one of them; and Lady Charlotte Rich, Lady Betty Herbert, and the incomparable Lady Bateman are her competitors.[2]

I saw Mrs Bridgeman the other day, who is much pleased with a letter she has had the honour to receive from your ladyship: she broke out – '*Really, Lady Pomfret writes finely!*' I very readily joined in her opinion; she continued – '*Oh, so neat, no interlineations, and such*

---

[1] Lady Anne, daughter of the 1st Earl of Scarborough, was Lady of the Bed-chamber to Princess Amelia and Princess Caroline at £300 p.a. In February she married Frederic Frankland, an M.P. and barrister. She was then between forty and fifty, ugly, and fat. In June her husband insisted on a separation because he had taken an intense aversion to her.

[2] Lady Anne Montagu succeeded her aunt as Lady of the Bedchamber.

proper distances!' This manner of praising your style made me reflect on the necessity of attention to trifles if one would please in general, a rule terribly neglected by me formerly; yet it is certain that some men are as much struck with the careless twist of a tippet as others are by a pair of fine eyes.

Lady Vane is returned hither in company with Lord Berkeley, and went with him in public to Cranford, where they remain as happy as love and youth can make them.[3] I am told that though she does not pique herself upon fidelity to any one man (which is but a narrow way of thinking), she boasts that she has always been true to her nation, and, notwithstanding foreign attacks, has always reserved her charms for the use of her own countrymen. I forget you are at Paris, and 'tis not polite to trouble you with such long scrawls as might perhaps be supportable at Monts; but you must give me leave to add that I am, with a true sense of your merit, for ever yours, in the largest extent of that expression.

[3] In 1736 Lady Vane had deserted her husband in Paris to run off with another man. As late as 1741 she was still living with Lord Berkeley at his home, Cranford Park, Middlesex. Her *Memoirs of a Lady of Quality*, published in 1751, relate some of her amatory adventures.

❧ To Lady Pomfret ❧

London, March 1739

I am so well acquainted with the lady you mention that I am not surprised at any proof of her want of judgment. She is one of those who has passed upon the world vivacity in the place of understanding; for me, who think with Boileau

Rien n'est beau que le vrai, le vrai seul est aimable,[1]

I have always thought those geniuses much inferior to the plain sense of a cook-maid, who can make a good pudding and keep the kitchen in good order.

Here is no news to be sent you from this place, which has been for this fortnight and still continues overwhelmed with politics, and which are of so mysterious a nature, one ought to have some of the gifts of Lilly or Partridge[2] to be able to write about them; and I leave all those

[1] 'Nothing is beautiful but truth; truth alone is worth loving.'
[2] William Lilly (d. 1681) was an astrologer and almanac-maker, and John Partridge (d. 1715) a cobbler turned almanac-maker. The latter was satirized by Swift.

dissertations to those distinguished mortals who are endowed with the talent of divination, though I am at present the only one of my sex who seems to be of that opinion, the ladies having shown their zeal and appetite for knowledge in a most glorious manner. At the last warm debate in the House of Lords it was unanimously resolved there should be no crowd of unnecessary auditors; consequently the fair sex were excluded, and the gallery destined to the sole use of the House of Commons. Notwithstanding which determination, a tribe of dames resolved to show on this occasion that neither men nor laws could resist them. These heroines were Lady Huntingdon, the Duchess of Queensbury, the Duchess of Ancaster, Lady Westmorland, Lady Cobham, Lady Charlotte Edwin, Lady Archibald Hamilton and her daughter, Mrs Scott, and Mrs Pendarves, and Lady Frances Saunderson. I am thus particular in their names since I look upon them to be the boldest asserters and most resigned sufferers for liberty I ever read of. They presented themselves at the door at nine o'clock in the morning, where Sir William Saunderson respectfully informed them the Lord Chancellor had made an order against their admittance. The Duchess of Queensbury, as head of the squadron, pished at the ill-breeding of a mere lawyer, and desired him to let them upstairs privately. After some modest refusals he swore by G—— he would not let them in. Her Grace, with a noble warmth, answered, by G—— they would come in, in spite of the Chancellor and the whole House. This being reported, the peers resolved to starve them out; an order was made that the doors should not be opened till they had raised their siege.

These Amazons now showed themselves qualified for the duty even of foot-soldiers; they stood there till five in the afternoon, without either sustenance or evacuation, every now and then playing volleys of thumps, kicks, and raps, against the door, with so much violence that the speakers in the House were scarce heard. When the Lords were not to be conquered by this, the two Duchesses (very well apprized of the use of stratagems in war) commanded a dead silence of half an hour; and the Chancellor, who thought this a certain proof of their absence (the Commons also being very impatient to enter) gave order for the opening of the door; upon which they all rushed in, pushed aside their competitors, and placed themselves in the front rows of the gallery. They stayed there till after eleven, when the House rose, and during the debate gave applause and showed marks of dislike not only by smiles and winks (which have always been allowed in these cases) but by noisy laughs and apparent contempts, which is supposed the true reason why poor Lord Hervey spoke miserably.[3] I beg your pardon,

[3] At this sitting of the House of Lords, on 1 March 1739, the Ministry prepared an address of thanks to the King for the Convention of El Prado with Spain, and the Opposition – supported by the ladies in the gallery – protested in vain against Spanish depredations; but the Ministry prevailed. According to another report, by Lord Orrery, Hervey 'spoke nicely and was full of peace, plenty and sugar-plumbs'.

dear madam, for this long relation, but 'tis impossible to be short on so copious a subject; and you must own this action very well worthy of record, and I think not to be paralleled in any history, ancient or modern. I look so little in my own eyes (who was at that time ingloriously sitting over a tea-table), I hardly dare subscribe myself even, yours.

❧ To Francesco Algarotti ❧

London, 16 July 1739

I am leaving to seek you. It is not necessary to accompany such a proof of an eternal attachment with an embroidery of words. I shall meet you in Venice. I had intended to meet you on the road, but I believe it is more discreet, and even more certain, to wait to see you at the end of my pilgrimage. It is for you to grant my prayers and to make me forget all my fatigues and chagrins.

Do not write to me any more in London. I shall not be there, and a letter found might have very unfortunate consequences.

I hazard this letter by another way, not being sure that you received the one which I addressed to Mr Rondeau.[1] I hope it is not necessary to beg you not to stay in London, if you arrive there.

[translation]

[1] British envoy in St Petersburg.

❧ To Francesco Algarotti ❧

London, 24 July 1739

At last I depart tomorrow with the resolution of a man well persuaded of his religion and happy in his conscience, filled with faith and hope. I leave my friends weeping for my loss and bravely take the leap for another world. If I find you such as you have sworn to me, I find the Elysian fields and happiness beyond imagining; if – but I wish to doubt no more, and at least I wish to enjoy my hopes. If you want to repay me for all that I am sacrificing, hurry to me in Venice, where I shall hasten my arrival as much as possible.

[translation]

PART V

Tourist and Expatriate
1739-1746

On her journey to Venice Lady Mary went by way of Dijon and Lyons across the Alps to Turin and Milan before reaching her destination, where she rented lodgings on the Grand Canal. By then, since Algarotti had returned to England from St Petersburg, she expected him to join her. (She was unaware that he had visited the court of the Prussian Crown Prince, and begun a friendship with a far more promising future than hers.) She found life in Venice very agreeable. She was entertained there by a few old friends and many new ones among the patricians and the diplomatic corps; and she witnessed such extravagant sights as the Carnival festivities, a great regatta in honour of the Prince of Saxony, and the gorgeous ceremony of marriage between the Republic and the Adriatic Sea.

At the end of May 1740, when Frederick succeeded his father as King of Prussia, Algarotti immediately accepted his invitation to Berlin. Once she knew this, Lady Mary decided to visit her friend Lady Pomfret in Florence. After two months there she visited Rome, moved on to Naples, back to Rome, and then to Leghorn, where she collected the immense amount of baggage (clothes, furniture, china, silver, books and manuscripts) she had prepared before leaving England. She then went to Turin, in March 1741, and for the first time in two years met Algarotti, who had been sent there on a diplomatic mission by his Royal master. Their meeting, for reasons unknown, was a disagreeable disappointment to Lady Mary, and put an end to her romantic fantasy.

Since a Spanish invasion of Italy was threatened she crossed the Alps in October and stayed in Geneva one month before going to Chambéry, where she passed a frugal and pleasant winter. Still fearful of war, she thought that the Papal State of Avignon would be safer, and so settled there in the spring of 1742, remaining for more than four years.

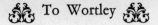

Dijon, 18 August 1739

I am at length arrived here very safe and without any bad accident, and so much mended in my health that I am surprised at it. France is so much improved it is not to be known to be the same country we passed through twenty year ago. Everything I see speaks in praise of Cardinal Fleury;[1] the roads are all mended and the greatest part of them paved as well as the streets of Paris, planted on both sides like the roads in Holland, and such good care taken against robbers that you may cross the country with your purse in your hand. But as to travelling incognito, I may as well walk incognito in the Pall Mall; there is not any town in France where there is not English, Scotch or Irish families established, and I have met with people that have seen me (though often such as I do not remember to have seen) in every town I have passed through. And I think the farther I go the more acquaintance I meet; here is in this town no less than sixteen English families of fashion. Lord Mansell lodges in the house with me, and a daughter of Lord Bathurst's (Mrs Whichcote) is in the same street. The Duke of Rutland is gone from hence some time ago, which Lady Peterborough told me at St Omers, which was one reason determined me to come here, thinking to be quiet, but I find it is impossible, and that will make me leave the place after the return of this post. The French are more changed than their roads; instead of pale yellow faces wrapped up in blankets as we saw them,[2] the villages are all filled with fresh coloured lusty peasants, in good cloth and clean linen. It is incredible, the air of plenty and content that is over the whole country.

I hope to hear as soon as possible that you are in good health.

[1] Louis XV's chief minister from 1726 to 1743.
[2] In 1718.

🎕 To Francesco Algarotti 🎕

Here I am at the feet of the Alps, and tomorrow I take the step which is to lead me into Italy. I commend myself to you in all perils like Don Quixote to his Dulcinea, and I have an imagination no less inflamed than his. Nothing frightens me, nothing diverts me a moment; absorbed in my own thoughts, neither the fatigues of the road nor the pleasures offered me in the towns have distracted me for an instant from the sweet contemplation in which I am immersed.

> Such soft ideas all my pains beguile,
> The Alps are levelled, and the deserts smile.
> These pendant rocks and ever during snow,
> These rolling torrents that eternal flow:
> Amidst this chaos that around me lies,
> I only hear your voice, and see your eyes.

[*prose translated*]

🎕 To Wortley 🎕

Venice, 25 September 1739

I am at length happily arrived here, I thank God. I wish it had been my original plan, which would have saved me some money and fatigue, though I have not much reason to regret the last, since I am convinced it has greatly contributed to the restoration of my health. I have met nothing disagreeable in my journey but too much company. I find (contrary to the rest of the world) I did not think myself so considerable as I am, for I verily believe if one of the pyramids of Egypt had travelled, it could not have been more followed, and if I had received all the visits that have been intended me I should have stopped at least a year in every town I came through.

I liked Milan so well that if I had not desired all my letters to be directed hither I think I should have been tempted to stay there. One of the pleasures I found there was the Borromean Library, where all strangers have free access, and not only so, but liberty on giving a note for it to take any printed book home with them. I saw several curious manuscripts there.[1] And as a proof of my recovery I went up to the very

---

[1] The Ambrosiana, founded by Cardinal Frederico Borromeo, was considered the best library in Italy after the Vatican.

top of the dome of the great church without any assistance. I am now in a lodging on the great canal. Lady Pomfret is not yet arrived, but I expect her very soon, and if the air does not disagree with me I intend seeing the carnival here. I hope your health continues, and that I shall hear from you very soon.

I think I have been a very good housewife to come thus far on the money I carried out with me, but you may be sure I am very near the end of it. I desire you would send me a bill of exchange enclosed in your next letter, directed to be left at the Consul Mr Browne's at Venice; he is the only person I have seen here. He tells me our old friend Grimani is Procurator of St Mark and will come to see me as soon as he hears of my arrival.[2]

[2] Pietro Grimani had been Venetian Ambassador in London 1710–13, and in Vienna 1715–20. In 1741 he was elected Doge of Venice.

To Lady Pomfret

Venice, 6 November 1739

It was with the greatest pleasure I read dear Lady Pomfret's letter half an hour ago. I cannot too soon give thanks for the delightful hopes you give me of seeing you here; and, to say truth, my gratitude is even painful to me till I try to express some part of it.

Upon my word, I have spoke my real thoughts in relation to Venice, but I will be more particular in my description, lest you should find the same reason of complaint you have hitherto experienced. It is impossible to give any rule for the agreeableness of conversation; but here is so great a variety I think 'tis impossible not to find some to suit every taste. Here are foreign ministers from all parts of the world, who, as they have no court to employ their hours, are overjoyed to enter into commerce with any stranger of distinction. As I am the only lady here at present I can assure you I am courted as if I was the only one in the world. As to all the conveniences of life, they are to be had at very easy rates; and for those that love public places, here are two playhouses and two operas constantly performed every night, at exceeding low prices. But you will have no reason to examine that article, no more than myself; all the ambassadors having boxes appointed them, and I have everyone of their keys at my service, not only for my own person, but whoever I please to carry or send. I do not make much use of this privilege, to their great astonishment.

It is the fashion for the greatest ladies to walk the streets, which are admirably paved; and a mask, price sixpence, with a little cloak and the head of a domino, the genteel dress to carry you everywhere. The greatest equipage is a gondola, that holds eight persons and is the price of an English chair. And it is so much the established fashion for everybody to live their own way that nothing is more ridiculous than censuring the actions of another. This would be terrible in London, where we have little other diversion; but for me, who never found any pleasure in malice, I bless my destiny that has conducted me to a part where people are better employed than in talking of the affairs of their acquaintance. It is at present excessive cold (which is the only thing I have to find fault with); but in recompense we have a clear bright sun, and fogs and factions things unheard of in this climate. In short, if you come, and like the way of living as well as I do, there can be nothing to be added to the happiness of, dearest madam, your faithful, etc.

To Lady Pomfret

Venice, February 1740

I must begin my letter, dear madam, with asking pardon for the peevishness of my last. I confess I was piqued at yours, and you should not wonder I am a little tender on that point. To suspect me of want of desire to see you is accusing at once both my taste and my sincerity; and you will allow that all the world are sensible upon these subjects. But you have now given me an occasion to thank you, in sending me the most agreeable young man I have seen in my travels.[1] I wish it was in my power to be of use to him; but what little services I am able to do him I shall not fail of performing with great pleasure. I have already received a very considerable one from him in a conversation where you was the subject, and I had the satisfaction of hearing him talk of you in a manner that agreed with my own way of thinking. I wish I could tell you that I set out for Florence next week; but the winter is yet so severe, and by all report, even that of your friends, the roads so bad, it is impossible to think of it.

We are now in the midst of carnival amusements, which are more than usual, for the entertainment of the Electoral Prince of Saxony,[2] and I am obliged to live in a hurry very inconsistent with philosophy,

---

[1] Charles-Juste, Prince de Beauvau; his father Prince de Craon was head of the Council of Regency that governed Tuscany.

[2] Frederick Christian, son of Augustus III, Elector of Saxony and King of Poland. He had rented a house next to Lady Mary's.

and extreme different from the life I projected to lead. But 'tis long since I have been of Prior's opinion, who, I think, somewhere compares us to cards who are but played with, do not play.[3] At least such has been my destiny from my youth upwards, and neither Dr Clarke or Lady Sundon could ever convince me that I was a free agent,[4] for I have always been disposed of more by little accidents than either my own inclinations or interest. I believe that affairs of the greatest importance are carried the same way. I seriously assure you (as I have done before), I wish nothing more than your conversation, and am downright enraged that I can appoint no time for that happiness, which however I hope will not be long delayed, and is impatiently waited for by, dear madam, your ladyship's, etc.

[3] Matthew Prior, *Alma* (1718).
[4] The churchman Samuel Clarke was considered deistical by the orthodox; Lady Sundon had been his great friend.

To Francesco Algarotti

Venice, 12 March 1740

Why so little sincerity? Is it possible that you could say you remonstrated with me against Italy? On the contrary, I still have one of your letters in which you assure me that whatever town I establish myself in you will not fail to go there yourself, and I chose Venice as that which suited you the most. You know that the least of your desires would have led me to decide even on Japan. Provence or Languedoc would have pleased me perfectly, and saved me much fatigue and expense. Recall, if you please, the conversations which we had together, and you will confess that I should naturally have believed that the journey I have made was the one to bring me closest to you. Geneva is always full of English people, consequently hardly suitable for my sojourn, Holland even less because of its proximity.

I am settled here where I have found pleasures which I had not at all expected. The Procurator Grimani (whose merit and importance you doubtless know) is so very much a friend of mine that he has made it a point of pride to render Venice agreeable to me. I am sought out by all the most considerable ladies and gentlemen here. In brief, I am miraculously much better off than in London. I should certainly leave all the conveniences of my life a second time to make the happiness of yours if I were persuaded I was necessary to it. Be honourable enough to think about this seriously. Consult your heart; if it tells you that you would be happy near me I sacrifice all for that. It is no longer a sacrifice; your friendship and your conversation will make the delights of my life. It is not possible for us to live in the same house, but you could lodge close to mine, and see me every day if you should want to. Tell me your thoughts frankly. If it is true that your inclination persuades you to choose this plan I would return to France and settle in some provincial town where we could live in tranquillity.

[*translation*]

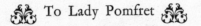

To Lady Pomfret

Venice, March 1740

I cannot deny your ladyship's letter gave me a great deal of pleasure; but you have seasoned it with a great deal of pain in the conclusion (after the many agreeable things you have said to me) that you are not entirely satisfied with me: you will not throw our separation on ill fortune, and I will not renew the conversation of the fallen angels in Milton, who in contesting on predestination and free will, we are told, 'They of the vain dispute could know no end.'[1] Yet I know that neither my pleasures, my passions, nor my interests have ever disposed of me so much as little accidents which, whether from chance or destiny, have always determined my choice. Here is weather, for example, which to the shame of all almanacs keeps on the depth of winter in the beginning of spring, and makes it as much impossible for me to pass the mountains of Bologna as it would be to wait on you in another planet if you had taken up your residence in Venus or Mercury. However, I am fully determined to give myself that happiness; but when is out of my power to decide.

You may imagine, apart from the gratitude I owe you and the inclination I feel for you, that I am impatient to hear good sense pronounced in my native tongue, having only heard my language out of the mouths of boys and governors for these five months. Here are inundations of them broke in upon us this carnival, and my apartment must be their refuge, the greater part of them having kept an inviolable fidelity to the language their nurses taught them. Their whole business abroad (as far as I can perceive) being to buy new clothes, in which they shine in some

---

[1] A paraphrase from *Paradise Lost*, ii. 558–61.

obscure coffee-house where they are sure of meeting only one another; and after the important conquest of some waiting gentlewoman of an opera queen, who perhaps they remember as long as they live, return to England excellent judges of men and manners. I find the spirit of patriotism so strong in me every time I see them that I look on them as the greatest blockheads in nature; and, to say truth, the compound of booby and *petit maître* makes up a very odd sort of animal. I hope we shall live to talk all these things over, and ten thousand more, which I reserve till the hour of meeting; which that it may soon arrive is the zealous wish of your ever faithful, etc. etc.

✂ To Lady Pomfret ✂

Venice, April 1740

Upon my word, dear madam, I seriously intend myself the happiness of being with you this summer, but it cannot be till then. While the Prince of Saxony stays here I am engaged not to move, not upon his account, as you may very well imagine, but here are many entertainments given, and to be given him by the public, which it would be disobliging to my friends here to run away from; and I have received so many civilities from the first people here I cannot refuse them the complaisance of passing the feast of the Ascension in their company, though 'tis a real violence to my inclination to be so long deprived of yours, of which I know the value, and may say that I am just to you from judgment as well as pleased with you from taste. I envy nothing more to Lady Walpole than your conversation, though I am glad you have met with hers.[1]

Have you not reasoned much on the surprising conclusion of Lord Scarborough? I confess I look upon his engagement with the duchess not as the cause, but sign, that he was mad.[2] I could wish for some authentic account of her behaviour on this occasion. I do not doubt she shines in it, as she has done in every other part of her life. I am almost

---

[1] Lady Walpole (see note on p. 144) was on unfriendly terms with her husband, and had been living on the Continent since 1734. She was now settled in Florence.

[2] He committed suicide shortly before his intended marriage to the Duchess of Manchester.

inclined to superstition on this accident, and think it a judgment for the death of a poor silly soul, that you know he caused some years ago.[3]

I had a visit yesterday from a Greek called Cantacuzena, who had the honour to see your ladyship, as he says, often at Florence, and gave me the pleasure of speaking of you in the manner I think. Prince Beauvau and Lord Shrewsbury intend to leave us in a few days for the Conclave.[4] We expect after it a fresh cargo of English but, God be praised, I hear of no ladies among them. Mrs Lethieullier was the last that gave comedies in this town, and she had made her exit before I came, which I look upon as a great blessing.

I have nothing to complain of here but too much diversion, as it is called, and which literally diverts me from amusements much more agreeable. I can hardly believe it is me dressed up at balls and stalking about at assemblies, and should not be so much surprised at suffering any of Ovid's transformations, having more disposition, as I thought, to harden into stone or timber than to be enlivened into these tumultuary entertainments, where I am amazed to find myself seated by a sovereign prince after travelling a thousand miles to establish myself in the bosom of a republic, with a design to lose all memory of kings and courts. Won't you admire the force of destiny? I remember my contracting an intimacy with a girl in a village as the most distant thing on earth from power and politics. Fortune tosses her up (in a double sense), and I am embroiled in a thousand affairs that I had resolved to avoid as long as I lived.[5] Say what you please, madam, we are pushed about by a superior hand, and there is some predestination, as well as a great deal of free will, in my being faithfully yours, etc.

[3] As a widow Lady Kingston, Lady Mary's sister-in-law, lived openly with Lord Scarborough, and had two sons by him. When she realized that he had no intention of marrying her she became speechless and died the next day.

[4] In Rome, to choose a successor to Pope Clement XII.

[5] Lady Mary refers to Maria Skerrett, who became Robert Walpole's mistress by 1724. Miss Skerrett had stayed with her at Twickenham.

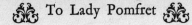

Venice, 17 May 1740

I had the happiness of a letter from your ladyship a few days since, and yesterday the pleasure of talking of you with Sir Henry Englefield. He tells me you are still in ice and snow at Florence, and we are very little better at Venice, where we remain in the state of warming beds and sitting by firesides. I begin to be of opinion that the sun is grown old; it is certain he does not ogle with so much spirit as he used to do, or our planet has made some slip unperceived by the mathematicians. For my own part, who am more passionately fond of Phoebus than ever Clymene was,[1] I have some thoughts of removing into Africa, that I may feel him once more before I die, which I shall do as surely as your olive trees if I have much longer to sigh for his absence. In the meantime I am tied here as long as the Prince of Saxony, which is an uncertain term, but I think will not be long after the Ascension, and then I intend myself the pleasure of waiting on you, where I will listen to all your reproaches, hoping you will do the same to my excuses, and that the balance will come out in my favour: though I could wish you rather here, having a strong notion Venice is more agreeable than Florence, as freedom is more eligible than slavery; and I have an insuperable aversion to courts, or the shadows of them, be they in what shapes they will.

I send you no description of the Regatta, not doubting you have been wearied with the printed one. It was really a magnificent show as ever was exhibited since the galley of Cleopatra. Instead of her Majesty we had some hundreds of Cleopatras in the windows and balconies. The operas and masks begin next Wednesday, and we persevere in gallantries and raree-shows in the midst of wars and rumours of wars that surround us. I may, however, assure you with an English plainness, these things can at most but attract my eyes, while (as the song says) you engage my heart; which I hope to convince you of when I am so happy as to tell you by word of mouth that I am sincerely and faithfully yours, etc.

[1] Beloved of Phoebus by whom she had a son, Phaethon.

❧ To Lady Pomfret ❧

Venice, June 1740

I send you this letter by so agreeable a companion that I think it a very considerable present. He will tell you that he has pressed me very much to set out for Florence immediately, and I have the greatest inclination in the world to do it; but, as I have already said, I am but too well convinced that all things are relative, and mankind was not made to follow their own inclinations. I have pushed as fair for liberty as any one; I have most philosophically thrown off all the chains of custom and subjection, and also rooted out of my heart all seeds of ambition and avarice. In such a state, if freedom could be found that lot would sure be mine, yet certain atoms of attraction and repulsion keep me still in suspense,[1] and I cannot absolutely set the day of my departure though I very sincerely wish for it and have one reason more than usual: this town being at present infested with English, who torment me as much as the frogs and lice did the palace of Pharaoh, and are surprised that I will not suffer them to skip about my house from morning till night – me, that never opened my doors to such sort of animals in England. I wish I knew a corner of the world inaccessible to *petits maîtres* and fine ladies. I verily believed when I left London I should choose my own company for the remainder of my days, which I find more difficult to do abroad than at home, and with humility I sighing own,

> Some stronger power eludes the sickly will,
> Dashes my rising hope with certain ill;
> And makes me with reflective trouble see,
> That all is destined that I fancied free.[2]

I have talked to this purpose with the bearer of this letter; you may talk with him on any subject, for though our acquaintance has been very short it has been long enough to show me that he has an understanding that will be agreeable in what light he pleases to show it.

[1] Lady Mary was undoubtedly waiting for Algarotti to answer her proposal of 12 March that he suggest a place where they could live in romantic proximity.
[2] From Matthew Prior's *Solomon* (1708).

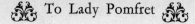

Venice, 29 June 1740

Your ladyship's letter (which I have this minute received) would have been the most agreeable thing in the world if it had been directed to another, but I can no more be charmed with it than a duellist can admire the skill by which he is mortally wounded. With all the respect I owe you, I cannot forbear saying that no woman living ever reproached another with less reason than you do me at present. You can't possibly suspect I have got my chambermaid with child myself for a pretence to stay here.[1] This is a crime of which all mankind will acquit me; and if she had any such malicious design in conceiving I can assure you she had no orders from me; but, as the song says,

> 'Tis e'en but a folly to flounce;
> 'Tis done, and it cannot be holp.

As soon as she is able to travel, I will certainly set out, notwithstanding the information of your popish priest. There's another thing; how can you pin your faith upon the sleeve of one of those gentlemen against the assurances given you by a daughter of the Church of England? After this, you are obliged to me that I do not suspect he can persuade you into a belief in all the miracles in the Legend.[2] All quarrelling apart, if neither death nor sickness intervene you will certainly see me at Florence. I talk of you every day at present with Mr Mackenzie, who is a very pretty youth,[3] much enchanted by the charms of Lady Sophia, who, I hear from all hands, so far outshines all the Florentine beauties that none of them dare appear before her. I shall take great pleasure in being spectatress of her triumphs; but yet more in your ladyship's conversation, which was never more earnestly desired by anyone than it is at this time by, dearest madam, yours, etc.

[1] Lady Mary wrote to Wortley on 17 June that she was 'a good deal vexed at a foolish accident . . . Mrs Mary [Turner] is downlying of a big belly which she has concealed till now'.
[2] The Golden Legend, a thirteenth-century collection of saints' lives.
[3] Lord Bute's only brother; he became Lady Mary's friend and correspondent.

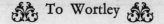

Florence, 11 September 1740

This is a very fine town, and I am much amused with visiting the Gallery, which I do not doubt you remember too well to need any description of.[1] Lord and Lady Pomfret take pains to make the place agreeable to me[2] and I have been visited by the greatest part of the people of quality. Here is an opera, which I have heard twice, but it is not so fine, neither for voices or decorations as that at Venice.

I am very willing to be at Leghorn when my things arrive, which I fear will hinder my visiting Rome this season except they come sooner than is generally expected. If I could go from thence by sea to Naples with safety I should prefer it to a land journey, which I am told is very difficult, and that it is impossible I should stay there long, the people being entirely unsociable. I do not desire much company, but would not confine myself to a place where I could get none.

I have wrote to your daughter directed to Scotland this post.[3]

[1] Lady Mary visited the Uffizi Gallery twice.

[2] Their daughter confirms this in a letter to a friend: 'we are so happy as to enjoy my Lady Mary Wortley's conversation at present. She arrived here from Venice a week past and does us the honour to accept of an apartment in our house.'

[3] Lady Bute lived with her husband at Mount Stuart, Isle of Bute.

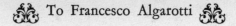

Florence, 11 October 1740

I shall write you little because I fear you will not receive my letter. I don't want to believe that you would not wish to answer it. Do me the favour of letting me know your intentions. I have left Venice and am ready to go where you wish. I await your orders to regulate my life. Remember that I have been undecided a long time, and that it is assuredly time for me to make up my mind.

Address your letter in care of the English Resident in Florence. I am leaving that city to make a small tour, while awaiting news of you.

[translation]

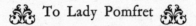 To Lady Pomfret

Rome, 22 October 1740

Dear Madam,

I flatter myself that your ladyship's goodness will give you some pleasure in hearing that I am safely arrived at Rome. It was a violent transition from your palace and company to be locked up all day with my chambermaid and sleep at night in a hovel; but my whole life has been in the Pindaric style. I am at present settled in the lodging Sir Francis Dashwood[1] recommended to me. I liked that Mr Boughton mentioned to me (which had been Sir Bourchier Wrey's)[2] much better; 'tis two sequins per month cheaper, and at least twenty more agreeable, but the landlord would not let it for a very pleasant reason. It seems your gallant knight used to lie with his wife, and as he had no hopes I would do the same he resolves to reserve his house for some young man. The only charm belonging to my present habitation is the ceiling, which is finer than that of the Gallery, being all painted by the proper hand of Zuccaro, in perfect good preservation.[3] I pay as much for this small apartment as your ladyship does for your magnificent palace; 'tis true I have a garden as large as your dressing room. I walked last night

---

[1] Later Baron Le Despencer, famous as a rake and founder of the Hell Fire Club. Lady Mary had seen him in Florence, where he visited and dined at Lady Pomfret's.

[2] Another of Lady Pomfret's visitors; described by Horace Walpole as 'a very foolish knight'.

[3] The sixteenth-century painter famous for his frescoes; his house became an inn early in the eighteenth century.

two hours in that of Borghese, which is one of the most delightful I ever saw. I have diverted myself with a plain discovery of the persons concerned in the letter that was dropped in the opera house. This is all the news I know, and I will not tire you with my thanks for the many civilities for which I am obliged to your ladyship; but I shall ever be highly sensible of them, and can never be other than, dear madam, your ladyship's most faithful humble servant.

To Lady Pomfret

Rome, 11 November 1740

I received the honour of your ladyship's letter but last night. I perceive all letters are stopped. Two that you enclosed are from dear Mr Mackenzie, pressing with the most friendly solicitude my return to Venice, and begging me to let him meet me at Bologna. I am amazed at the good nature of that youth. I could not wish a child of my own a more affectionate behaviour than he has shown to me, and that inducement is added to many others to incline me to Venice; but——. I intend for Naples next week, but as my stay there will not exceed fifteen days, I shall be again here before it is possible for you to arrive, where I wish you for your own sake.

Here are entertainments for all tastes, and whatever notions I had of the magnificence of Rome I can assure you it has surpassed all my ideas of it. I am sincerely concerned for Mr Boughton, and wish the air of Pisa may recover his health. I shall very readily tell your ladyship all I guess about the said letter. An English lady called Mrs D'Arcie (what D'Arcie I can't imagine) lodged in the house where I now am, and Sir Francis Dashwood was every day with her; she went from hence, by the way of Florence, to England. Putting this together, I supposed her the person concerned. This is all I know. You may see that I have no other advantage from this discovery but the bare satisfaction of my curiosity. The Abbé Niccolini arrived last night;[1] I believe I shall see him this evening. Here are yet no English of your acquaintance except Lord Elcho.[2] I am told Lord Lincoln[3] has taken a large house and intends to keep a table, etc.

[1] Antonio Niccolini, marchese di Ponsacco, Florentine ecclesiastic and man of letters.
[2] David Wemyss, styled Lord Elcho. Then on the Grand Tour, he stayed in Rome for six months and became an ardent Jacobite.
[3] Earl of Lincoln, later 2nd Duke of Newcastle; he was related to Lady Mary.

The life I now lead is very different from what you fancy. I go to bed every night at ten, run about all the morning among the antiquities, and walk every evening in a different beautiful villa, where if amongst the fountains I could find the waters of Lethe I should be completely happy.

> Like a deer that is wounded I bleed and run on,
> And fain I my torment would hide.
> But alas! 'tis in vain, for wherever I run
> The bloody dart sticks in my side,

and I carry the serpent that poisons the paradise I am in.[4] I beg your pardon (dear madam) for this impertinent account of myself. You ought to forgive it, since you would not be troubled with it, if I did not depend upon it that your friendship for me interests you in all my concerns, though I can no way merit it but by the sincerity with which I am, etc.

[4] The cause of Lady Mary's anguish (if any) must have been Algarotti, who was still in Berlin.

🎔 To Wortley 🎔

Naples, 12 December 1740

I have received half an hour ago two letters from you, the one dated October the sixth, the other the twenty-third. I am surprised you have received none from me during the whole month of August, having wrote several, but I perceive all letters are stopped and many lost. I gave my daughter a direction to me long since, but as far as I can find she has never received neither that nor another which I directed to her in Scotland.

The town lately discovered[1] is at Portici, about three mile from this place. Since the first discovery no care has been taken, and the ground fallen in that the present passage to it is, as I am told by everybody, extreme dangerous, and of some time nobody ventures into it. I have been assured by some English gentlemen that were let down into it the

[1] Herculaneum, destroyed by the same eruption of Vesuvius that engulfed Pompeii. Its official excavation had been under way since the autumn of 1738.

last year that the whole account given in the newspapers is literally true. Probably great curiosities might be found there, but there has been no expense made either by propping the ground or clearing a way into it, and as the earth falls in daily it will possibly be soon stopped up as it was before.

I wrote to you last post a particular account of my reasons for not choosing my residence here, though the air is very agreeable to me and I see I could have as much company as I desire. But I am persuaded the climate is much changed since you knew it; the weather is now very moist and misty, and has been so for a long time. However, it is much softer than in any other place I know.

I desire you would direct to Mons. Belloni, banker at Rome; he will forward your letters wherever I am. The present uncertain situation of affairs all over Europe makes every correspondence precarious.

I am sorry to trouble you with the enclosed to my daughter, but as she seems concerned for not hearing from me, and I have reason to fear that no letter directed to her in Scotland will arrive safe, I send her these few lines.

To Mme Chiara Michiel

Leghorn, 25 February 1741

I arrived here yesterday evening, where I had the honour of finding your kind letter. I do not want to delay a moment in showing my gratitude, although I am quite surrounded with packages, and confounded by merchants' bills, etc. Despite all the obliging things that you tell me I must reproach you for your forbidding me to dwell upon your praises. You want then, madam, to deprive me of my most acute pleasure, but it is no use, and I will speak well of you everywhere, even if you should be angry.

I am delighted that Mr Mackenzie is making himself worthy of your kindness; and frankly I think I have spent my life with vulgar prejudices about people of his age. I had preconceptions that they were all thoughtless and should well be avoided, which I have always done, until my travels forced me to keep company with them; and I assure you that I have found among them good faith and honour, which is rare enough elsewhere, and naturally it must be thus. There are few people endowed with a strong enough virtue to preserve themselves in the dealings of the world; young people still have a remnant of sincerity, which, joined to the maxims of a noble education, renders them more estimable than people of an advanced age, who are ordinarily corrupted by bad examples. You see that it is not my own praise that I sing; as for you, madam, you enjoy that brilliant season at which the mind has matured without the face's suffering from it. I would that Heaven might perform a miracle in your favour, and that you could be such as you are for two or three hundred years to come.

I do not know what my wandering destiny will require of me; one way or another my heart tells me that we shall see each other again. I come from Rome, which I have seen in all its charms during the last days of the carnival, but the embroiderers and bath-keepers are wasted on those people. Perhaps it is a grace that St Peter accords to the state of the Church, but I have never seen faces so formed to inspire chastity. Indeed the city is so sparsely peopled that one understands it endures only through pure conjugal duty.

Allow me, madam, to beg you to pay very cordial and very sincere compliments to the Procurator Grimani on my behalf; and be convinced that in all countries where I shall be, I am inviolably, my very dear madam, your excellency's very humble and very obedient servant,

M. W. Montagu

[*translation*]

To Francesco Algarotti

Turin, May 1741

Yes, I would spend the morning writing to you even if you should be furious. I have begun to scorn your scorn, and in that vein I no longer wish to restrain myself. In the time (of foolish memory) when I had a frantic passion for you the desire to please you (although I understood its entire impossibility) and the fear of boring you almost stifled my voice when I spoke to you, and all the more stopped my hand five hundred times a day when I took up my pen to write to you. At present it is no longer that. I have studied you, and studied so well, that Sir Isaac Newton did not dissect the rays of the sun with more exactness than I have deciphered the sentiments of your soul. Your eyes served me as a prism to discern the ideas of your mind. I watched it with such great intensity that I almost went blind (for these prisms are very dazzling). I saw that your soul is filled with a thousand beautiful fancies but all together makes up only indifference. It is true that separately – divide that indifference (for example) into seven parts, on some objects at certain distances – one would see the most lively taste, the most refined sentiments, the most delicate imagination etc. Each one of these qualities is really yours. About manuscripts, statues, pictures, poetry, wine, conversation, you always show taste, delicacy, and vivacity. Why then do I find only churlishness and indifference? Because I am dull enough to arouse nothing better, and I see so clearly the nature of your soul that I am as much in despair of touching it as Mr Newton was of enlarging his discoveries by means of telescopes, which by their own powers dissipate and change the light rays.[1]

[*translation*]

[1] In general Lady Mary alludes to Algarotti's graceful Italian dialogues explaining Newton's *Optics*, translated into English as *Sir Isaac Newton's Philosophy Explain'd for the Use of the Ladies* (1739).

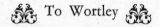

To Wortley

Genoa, 25 August 1741

I received yours of the 27th July this morning. I had that of March 19, which I answered very particularly the following post, with many thanks for the increase of my allowance.[1] It appears to me that the letters I wrote between the 11th of April and 31st of May were lost, which I am not surprised at. I was then at Turin, and that Court in a very great confusion and extreme jealous of me, thinking I came to examine their conduct. I have some proof of this, which I do not repeat lest this should be stopped also.

The manners of Italy are so much altered since we were here last, the alteration is scarce credible. They say it has been by the last war; the French being masters introduced all their customs, which were eagerly embraced by the ladies and I believe will never be laid aside, yet the different governments make different manners in every state. You know, though the Republic is not rich, here are many private families vastly so, and live at a great superfluous expense. All the people of the first quality keep coaches as fine as the Speaker's,[2] and some of them two or three, though the streets are too narrow to use them in the town; but they take the air in them, and their chairs carry them to the gates. The liveries are all plain, gold or silver being forbidden to be worn within the walls. The habits are all obliged to be black, but they wear

[1] To £1,100 a year, a generous amount.
[2] Of the House of Commons.

exceeding fine lace and linen, and in their country houses, which are generally in the *faubourg*, they dress very rich and have extreme fine jewels.

Here is nothing cheap but houses; a palace fit for a prince may be hired for £50 per annum – I mean unfurnished. All games of chance are strictly prohibited, and it seems to me the only law they do not try to evade. They play at quadrille, piquet, etc., but not high. Here are no regular public assemblies. I have been visited by all of the first rank, and invited to several fine dinners, particularly to the wedding of one of the House of Spinola, where there was ninety-six sat down to table, and I think the entertainment one of the finest I ever saw. There was the night following, a ball and supper for the same company with the same profusion. They tell me all their great marriages are kept in the same public manner. Nobody keeps more than two horses, all their journeys being post. The expense of them including the coachman is (I am told) £50 per annum. A chair is very near as much; I give eighteen francs a week for mine. The Senators can converse with no strangers during the time of their magistracy, which lasts two years. The number of servants are regulated and almost every lady has the same, which is two footmen, a gentleman usher, and a page, which follow her chair.

To Wortley

Geneva, 12 October 1741

I arrived here last night, where I find everything quite different from what it was represented to me. It is not the first time it has happened to me in my travels. Everything is as dear as it is at London; 'tis true as all equipages are forbidden that expense is entirely retrenched. I have been visited this morning by some of the chief people in the town, who seem extreme good sort of people, which is their general character, very desirous of attracting strangers to inhabit with them, and consequently very officious in all they imagine can please them. The way of living is absolutely the reverse of that in Italy. Here is no show and a great deal of eating; there is all the magnificence imaginable, and no dinners but on particular occasions, yet the difference of the prices renders the total expense very near equal. As I am not yet determined whether I shall make any considerable stay I desire not to have the money you intend me till I ask for it.

If you have any curiosity for the present state of any of the States of Italy, I believe I can give you a truer account than perhaps any other traveller can do, having always had the good fortune of a sort of intimacy with the first persons in the governments where I resided, and they not guarding themselves against the observations of a woman as they would have done from those of a man.

To Wortley

Geneva, 5 November 1741

I have now been here a month. I have wrote to you three times without hearing from you, and cannot help being uneasy at your silence. I think this air does not agree with my health. I have had a return of many complaints from which I had an entire cessation during my stay in Italy, which makes me incline to return thither, though a winter journey over the Alps is very disagreeable. The people here are very well to be liked, and this little republic has an air of the simplicity of old Rome in its earliest age. The magistrates toil with their own hands, and their wives literally dress their dinners against their return from their little Senate. Yet without dress or equipage 'tis as dear living here for a stranger as in places where one is obliged to both, from the price of all sort of provision, which they are forced to buy from their neighbours, having almost no land of their own.

I am very impatient to hear from you. Here are many reports concerning the English affairs, which I am sometimes splenetic enough to give credit to.

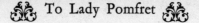

To Lady Pomfret

At length, dear madam, I have the pleasure of hearing from you; I hope you have found everything in London to your satisfaction. I believe it will be a little surprise to you to hear that I am fixed for this winter in this little obscure town, which is generally so much unknown that a description of it will at least have novelty to recommend it. Here is the most profound peace and unbounded plenty that is to be found in any corner of the universe; but not one rag of money. For my part, I think it amounts to the same thing, whether one is obliged to give several pence for bread, or can have a great deal of bread for a penny, since the Savoyard nobility here keep as good tables, without money, as those in London who spend in a week what would be here a considerable yearly revenue. Wine, which is equal to the best burgundy, is sold for a penny a quart, and I have a cook for very small wages that is capable of rivalling Chloé.[1] Here are no equipages, but chairs, the hire of which is about a crown a week, and all other matters proportionable. I can assure you I make the figure of the Duchess of Marlborough by carrying gold in my purse, there being no visible coin but copper. Yet we are all people that can produce pedigrees to serve for the Order of Malta. Many of us have travelled, and 'tis the fashion to love reading. We eat together perpetually, and have assemblies every night for conversation. To say truth, the houses are all built after the manner of the old English towns, nobody having had money to build for two hundred years past. Consequently the walls are thick, the roofs low, etc., the streets narrow and miserably paved. However, a concurrence of circumstances obliges me to this residence for some time.

You have not told me your thoughts of Venice. I heartily regret the loss of those letters you mention, and have no comfort but in the hopes of a more regular correspondence for the future. I cannot compassionate the countess, since I think her insolent character deserves all the mortifications Heaven can send her. It will be charity to send me what news you pick up, which will be always shown advantageously by your relation. I must depend upon your goodness for this, since I can promise you no return from hence but the assurances that I am ever faithfully yours.

Be pleased to direct as before to Mons. Villette, as the super-direction. Here are no such vanities as gilt paper, therefore you must excuse the want of it.

[1] The famous French cook employed by the Duke of Newcastle.

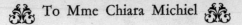

To Mme Chiara Michiel

Avignon, 20 May 1742

Excellency,

It seems to me a hundred years since I had news of you, my beautiful ambassadress, but I could never forget the charms of your conversation, and all the graces that I have admired in your person.

Here I am settled for some time at Avignon. It was with great regret that I left delightful Italy, but it is going (they say) to become the theatre of war, and I did not dare remain there. I have at least the consolation of being under the dominion of an Italian prince,[1] and (between us, let it be said) of the only prince whom I esteem because he is the only one who appears to me to consider his subjects as being under his protection, and he makes an effort to relieve them, whilst the other sovereigns consider them solely as beings created to serve their passions.

I sometimes have letters from poor Mr Mackenzie, who is very bored in his dreary country and who speaks to me eternally of Venice. We are here entirely surrounded by Spaniards; God knows what will happen. I confess that except for my friends (in whom I have a lively interest) the fate of mankind is as indifferent to me as that of butterflies, whether the blue beat the green, or the red the yellow. All these events seem to me unworthy of consideration, and I wrap myself up in a philosophy that gives me great tranquillity despite the tumults of Europe. But this quietude does not go so far as to make me indifferent to your memory, and I should be in despair if I did not flatter myself that you honour me sometimes with your thoughts, as being as much as it is possible to be (my dear madam) your excellency's very humble and very obedient servant,

M. W. Montagu

[*translation*]

[1] Pope Benedict XIV.

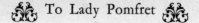

Avignon, 4 November 1742

I am very much obliged to your ladyship for judging so rightly both of my taste and inclinations as to think it impossible I should leave a letter of yours unanswered. I never received that which you mention, and am not surprised at it since I have lost several others, and all for the same reason – I mean mentioning political transactions; and 'tis the best proof of wisdom that I know of our reigning ministers, that they will not suffer their fame to travel into foreign lands. Neither have I any curiosity for their proceedings, being long ago persuaded of the truth of that histori-prophetical verse which says,

> The world will still be ruled by knaves
> And fools contending to be slaves.[1]

I desire no other intelligence from my friends but tea-table chat, which has been allowed to our sex by so long a prescription, I believe no lady will dispute it at present. I am very much diverted with her grace's passion, which is perhaps excited by her devotion, being piously designed to take a strayed young man out of the hands of a wicked woman. I wish it may end as those projects often do, in making him equally despise both, and take a bride as charming as Lady Sophia, who, I am glad, has had a legacy from Mrs Bridgman, though I could have wished it had been more important. I hear the Duke of Cleveland will be happily disposed of to Miss Gage, who, I do not doubt, will furnish his family with a long posterity, or I have no skill in airs and graces.[2]

This place affords us no news worth telling. I suppose you know Lady Walpole has been near dying;[3] and that Mrs Goldsworthy being detected *flagrante délit* is sent back to England with her children, some of which I hear he disowns.[4] I think her case not unlike Lady Abergavenny's, her loving spouse being very well content with her gallantries while he found his account in them, but raging against those that brought him no profit.[5] Be pleased to direct your next to Avignon, and I believe it will come safe to your ladyship's faithful humble servant,

M.W.M.

[1] By John How.

[2] The young Duchess of Cleveland had died in April, but the Duke did not marry Miss Gage (or anyone else), and thus remained without heirs.

[3] Margaret, Horace's sister-in-law, lived until 1781.

[4] Philippia Goldsworthy, wife of the British consul at Leghorn, had been the mistress of General von Wachtendonck, commander of the Emperor's Tuscan forces. Their liaison lasted from about 1737 until his death in August 1741, when it was discovered that he had been paying her for her services. Lady Mary's gossip is only partially true; Mrs Goldsworthy had returned to England with her children in August.

[5] In 1729 Lady Abergavenny was detected *in flagrante* with a friend of her husband's. She was driven from her house, and died soon after. The following year her husband was awarded damages of £10,000 from his adulterous friend.

❧ To James Stuart Mackenzie ❧

Avignon, 27 March 1743

You have certainly forgot that I wrote you word long since that I had desired from Lady Oxford preferment for your friend in the strongest manner, and she answered me that she had put his name in her table-book, and would certainly remember him the first occasion that offered, but knew of none likely to fall at present.[1] You may be assured of all my possible services as long as I live, and 'tis no compliment to tell you I have the most sincere esteem for you, and know in the whole world so few people that I can esteem that I verily believe I have more value for you than you have for yourself, from the comparisons I often make between your character and those I daily see and hear of.

Your citation is so just and well applied, there is nothing to be added to it. It is not surprising that at my age I make those reflections, but 'tis a very uncommon merit, in all the bloom of youth and affluence of fortune, that you should see through the tinsel glitter of the world, and despise the rotten hearts under the gaudy appearances. I am afraid every year will confirm you in these melancholy notions, for which I know no remedy but the advice of Solomon and Epicurus. Let us eat and drink, for tomorrow we die, which last reflection I think far from melancholy to any honest mind, being fully persuaded whatever future state is allotted for us it cannot be worse than this. Perhaps we are to go the round of the planets, and then, do but imagine what lively creatures we shall be in Mercury or Venus; I dare swear the inhabitants are entirely unacquainted with spleen and vapours. A Frenchman drunk with champagne is a dull animal to them. They have undoubtedly many sensations that raise them more above us than we are above trouts. For my part, I am determined for my present satisfaction to hope to meet you there if we are destined never to meet again here; and I expect to see you with some distinguished rays of light as the due reward of your virtue.

---

[1] Lady Oxford, recently widowed, had been a girlhood friend. During Lady Mary's residence abroad she and Lady Oxford carried on a decorous correspondence for about ten years.

Avignon, 20 December 1743

I received yours of the twenty-fourth of Nov. O.S. yesterday. I send you the enclosed for my son, not knowing where to direct to him. I have endeavoured to write it according to your minutes, which are entirely just and reasonable.

You may perhaps hear of a trifle which makes a great noise in this part of the world, which is that I am building, but the whole expense which I have contracted for is but £26 sterling.

You know the situation of this town is on the meeting of the Rhône and Durance. On one side of it within the walls was formerly a fortress built on a very high rock.[1] They say it was destroyed by lightning. One of the towers was left part standing, the walls being a yard in thickness. This was made use of sometime for a public mill, but the height making it inconvenient for the carriage of meal it has stood useless many years. Last summer in the hot evenings I walked often thither, where I always found a fresh breeze and the most beautiful land prospect I ever saw (except Wharncliffe),[2] being a view of the windings of two great rivers, and overlooking the whole county, with part of Languedoc and Provence. I was so much charmed with it that I said in company that if that old mill was mine I would turn it into a belvedere. My words were repeated, and the two consuls waited on me soon after with a donation from the town of the mill and the land about it. I have added a dome to it and made it a little rotunda, for the foresaid sum. I have also amused myself with patching up an inscription, which I have communicated to the Archbishop, who is much delighted with it; but it is not placed and perhaps never shall be.

[Inscription in Latin verse omitted]

You will know how I picked up these verses,[3] though the Archbishop did not.

---

[1] The Rocher-des-Doms, the windswept acropolis of Avignon.

[2] Wortley's father had lived at Wharncliffe Lodge (at Wortley). The house, as described by Lady Mary's granddaughter, was placed 'like an eagle's nest, upon the very summit of a steep rock'.

[3] The Latin inscription was adapted by Lady Mary from Abraham Cowley. In their early courtship letters Wortley had mentioned Cowley to Lady Mary, and her library sent abroad in 1739 included a two-volume edition of his works.

Avignon, 17 February 1744

I am very sorry you have given yourself so much trouble about the inscription. I find I expressed myself ill if you understood by my letter that it was placed. I never intended it without your approbation, and then would have put it in the inside of the dome. The word *pauperie* is meant as is shown by the whole line

Non indecora pauperie nitens[1]

to be a life rather distant from ostentation than in poverty, and which answers very well to my way of living, which though decent is far from the show which many families make here.

The nobility consists of about two hundred houses; amongst them are two dukes, that of Crillon and of Guadagna, the last an Italian family, the other French. The Count of Suze (who also values himself very much on his pedigree) keeps a constant open table, as do several others. You will judge by that, the provisions are exceeding cheap, but it is otherwise, the price of everything being high for strangers; but as all the gentlemen keep their land in their own hands and sell their wine, oil, and corn, their housekeeping looks very great at a small expense. They have also all sort of *gibier* from their own lands, which enables them to keep a splendid table. Their estates have never been taxed, the Pope drawing (as I am assured) no revenue from hence. The Vice-Legate has a court of priests, and sees little other company, which I believe is partly owing to the little respect the nobility show him, who despise his want of birth. There is a new one expected this spring, nephew to the Cardinal Acquaviva. He is young, and they say intends to live with great magnificence.

Avignon was certainly no town in the time of the Romans, nor is there the smallest remains of any antiquity but what is entirely Gothic.[2] The town is large, but thinly peopled. Here are fourteen large convents, beside others. It is so well situated for trade and the silk so fine and plentiful that if they were not curbed by the French not permitting them to trade, they would certainly ruin Lyons; but as they can sell none of their manufactures out of the walls of the town, and the ladies here (as everywhere else) preferring foreign stuffs to their own, the tradespeople are poor and the shops ill furnished. The people of quality all affect the French manner of living, and here are many good houses. The climate would be as fine as that of Naples if we were not persecuted by the north wind, which is almost a constant plague. Yet by the great age and surprising health I see many of them enjoy I am persuaded the air is

---

[1] 'With decent poverty content.'

[2] It had been a Roman city; and Lady Mary mentions its ruins in her letter of 12 July 1744.

very wholesome. I see of both sexes past eighty who appear in all the assemblies, eat great suppers and keep late hours, without any visible infirmity.

It is today Shrove Tuesday. I am invited to sup at the Duchess of Crillon's, where I do not doubt I shall see near fifty guests who will all of them, young and old (except myself), go masked to the ball that is given in the town house. It is the sixth given this carnival by the gentlemen gratis. At the first there was 1,200 tickets given out, many coming from the neighbouring towns of Carpentras, Lisle, Orange, and even Aix and Arles, on purpose to appear there.

Don Philip is expected here the 22nd. I believe he will not stay any time, and if he should, I think (in the present situation) it would be improper for me to wait on him.[3] If he goes into company, I suppose I may indifferently see him at an assembly.

[3] He was the son of Philip V of Spain, with whom England was at war.

🎕 To Wortley 🎕

Avignon, 25 March 1744

I take this opportunity of informing you in what manner I came acquainted with the secret I hinted at in my letter of the 5th of Feb. The Society of Freemasons at Nîmes presented the Duke of Richelieu, governor of Languedoc, with a magnificent entertainment. It is but one day's post from hence, and the Duchess of Crillon with some other ladies of this town resolved to be at it, and almost by force carried me with them, which I am tempted to believe an act of Providence, considering my great reluctance and the service it proved to be to unhappy, innocent people.

The greatest part of the town of Nîmes are secret Protestants, which are still severely punished according to the edicts of Louis XIV whenever they are detected in any public worship. A few days before we came they had assembled; their minister and about a dozen of his congregation were seized and imprisoned. I knew nothing of this, but I had not been in the town two hours when I was visited by two of the most considerable of the Huguenots, who came to beg of me with tears to speak in their favour to the Duke of Richelieu, saying none of the Catholics would do it and the Protestants durst not, and that God had sent me for their protection, [that] the Duke of Richelieu was too well bred to refuse to listen to a lady, and I was of a rank and nation to have liberty to say what I pleased. They moved my compassion so much I resolved to use my endeavours to serve them, though I had little hope of succeeding.

I would not therefore dress myself for the supper, but went in a domino to the ball, a mask giving opportunity of talking in a freer manner than I could have done without it. I was at no trouble in engaging his conversation. The ladies having told him I was there, he immediately advanced towards me, and I found from a different motive he had a great desire to be acquainted with me, having heard a great deal of me. After abundance of compliments of that sort, I made my request for the liberty of the poor Protestants. He with great freedom told me that he was so little a bigot, he pitied them as much as I did, but his orders from Court were to send them to the galleys. However, to show how much he desired my good opinion he was returning and would solicit their freedom (which he has since obtained). This obligation occasioned me to continue the conversation, and he asked me what party the Pretender had in England. I answered, as I thought, a very small one. 'We are told otherwise at Paris,' said he; 'however, a bustle at this time may serve to facilitate our other projects, and we intend to attempt a descent. At least it will cause the troops to be recalled, and perhaps Admiral Mathews will be obliged to leave the passage open for Don Philip.'[1]

You may imagine how much I wished to give you immediate notice of this, but as all letters are opened at Paris it would have been to no purpose to write it by the post and have only gained me a powerful enemy in the Court of France, he being so much a favourite of the King's, he is supposed to stand candidate for the ministry. In my letter to Sir Robert Walpole from Venice I offered my service, and desired to know in what manner I could send intelligence if anything happened to my knowledge that could be of use to England. I believe he imagined that I wanted some gratification, and only sent me cold thanks.[2]

I have wrote to you by the post an account of my servants' leaving me; as that is only a domestic affair I suppose the letter may be suffered to pass.

I have had no letter from my son, and am very sure he is in the wrong whenever he does not follow your direction, who (apart from other considerations) have a stronger judgment than any of his advisers.

[1] That is, while the British fleet blockading Italy would be diverted to prevent an invasion of England, Don Philip would invade Italy.
[2] In 1740, Hervey had answered for Walpole, with an elaborately polite refusal.

❧ To Mme Chiara Michiel ❧

Avignon, 12 July 1744

I have not congratulated you (my dear and charming friend) on the renewal of our alliance.[1] Since I believe all the advantage ours, it is for me to receive the felicitations. I was always ashamed of our silly disagreement; (between us be it said) I regard almost all quarrels of princes on the same footing, and I see nothing that marks man's unreason so positively as war. Indeed, what folly to kill one another for interests often imaginary, and always for the pleasure of persons who do not think themselves even obliged to those who sacrifice themselves for them! If kings wanted to play at basset for towns and provinces, patience! As between master and master there is only the hand of cards, I should not be too angry to see the Queen of Hungary and her allies hold the bank, and the Emperor punt with his.[2] One would perhaps see Munich on one card; a double-stake would bring Prague, Linz, and Passau, without these terrible massacres and fires which horrify all those who wish well to mankind in general. If I were a plenipotentiary I would make this proposition to the first congress that was held; but alas, I fear that I should find few people as peace-loving as I.

How pleased I should be (my beautiful ambassadress) to see you in London! You will succeed everywhere, but I dare flatter myself that you will find people among us who will know your value, and consequently will be more assiduous to pay you court than anywhere else. But never will anyone take more pleasure in doing justice to you than (my very dear lady) your very humble, etc.

[translation]

[1] England had broken diplomatic relations with the Venetian Republic in 1737 because of honours paid to the Pretender's son.
[2] Maria Theresa and the newly elected Emperor Charles VII (Elector of Bavaria) were two principal antagonists in the War of the Austrian Succession, to which Lady Mary refers.

❧ To Lady Promfret ❧

Avignon, 12 July 1744

It is but this morning that I have received the honour of your ladyship's obliging letter of the 31st of May; the other you mention never reached me, and this has been considerably retarded in its passage. It is one of the sad effects of war, for us miserable exiles, the difficulty of corresponding with the few friends who are generous enough to remember the absent. I am very sorry and surprised to hear your good constitution has had such an attack. In lieu of many other comforts I have that of a very uncommon share of health, in all my wanderings having never had one day's sickness, though nobody ever took less care to prevent it.

If any marriage can have a prospect of continued happiness it is that of Lord and Lady Carteret.[1] She has fortunately met with one that will know how to value her, and I know no other place where he could have found a lady of her education, which in her early youth has given her all the advantages of experience, and her beauty is her least merit. I do not doubt that of Lady Charlotte will soon procure her a happy settlement.[2] I am much pleased with my niece's meeting with Lord Gowran; he visited me at Venice, and seemed one of the most reasonable young men I have seen.[3]

I endeavour to amuse myself here with all sorts of monastic employments, the conversation not being at all agreeable to me, and friendship in France as impossible to be attained as orange trees on the mountains of Scotland – it is not the product of the climate – and I try to content myself with reading, working, walking, and what you'll wonder to hear me mention, building. I know not whether you saw when you were at Avignon the Rock of Doms, at the foot of which is the Vice-Legate's palace; from the top of it you may see the four provinces of Venaissin, Provence, Languedoc and Dauphiné, with the distant mountains of Auvergne, and the near meeting of the Durance and Rhône which flow under it. In short, it is the most beautiful land prospect I ever saw. There was anciently a temple of Diana, and another of Hercules of Gaul, whose ruins were turned into a fort, where the powder and ammunition of the town were kept, which was destroyed by lightning about eighty years since. There remained an ancient round tower, which I said in presence of the Consul I would make a very agreeable belvedere if it was mine. I expected no consequence from this accidental speech of mine, but he proposed to the Hôtel de Ville the next day, making me a present of it, which was done *nemine contradicente*. Partly to show myself sensible of that civility and partly for my own amusement I have fitted up a little

---

[1] In April 1744 Lady Sophia Fermor, Lady Pomfret's eldest daughter, had married Carteret, a widower thirty years her senior.
[2] In 1746 she married William Finch, brother of the Earl of Winchilsea.
[3] Evelyn Leveson-Gower had married Lord Gowran in June 1744.

pavilion, which Lord Burlington would call a temple, being in the figure of the Rotunda, where I keep my books and generally pass all my evenings.[4]

If the winds were faithful messengers they would bring you from thence many sighs and good wishes. I have few correspondents in England, and you that have lived abroad know the common phrases that are made use of: 'As I suppose you know everything that passes here'; or, 'Here is nothing worth troubling you with'; this is all the intelligence I receive. You may judge then how much I think myself obliged to you, dear madam, when you tell me what passes amongst you. I am so ignorant, I cannot even guess at the improper marriages you mention. If it is Lady Mary Grey that has disposed of herself in so dirty a manner I think her a more proper piece of furniture for a parsonage-house than a palace;[5] and 'tis possible she may have been the original product of a chaplain.

I believe your ladyship's good nature will lament the sudden death of the poor Marquis of Beaufort, who died of an apoplectic fit. He is a national loss to the English, being always ready to serve. . . . [*sic*]

---

[4] Burlington was a noted enthusiast for Palladian architecture. Lady Mary probably had in mind Chiswick House, his villa described by Hervey as 'too little to live in, and too large to hang to one's watch'.

[5] A daughter of the Duke of Kent, she married (in March 1744) the Rev. Dr David Gregory, a canon of Christ Church, Oxford. She was something of a bluestocking.

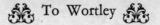

Avignon, 20 March 1746

I have not heard from you so long that I should be in great pain for your health if I had not had this post a letter from my daughter, who informs me that you are well. I am afraid my letters have all miscarried for some months past, though I have sent them by various ways, and I am sure there is never anything in them that should give occasion for their being stopped. I had a letter from my son the last post, very much to his own advantage (if he tells truth). He says that the governor (to whom he was aide-de-camp) has wrote to Prince Charles in his favour.[1] I have sent him a very kind letter, believing it proper to give him some encouragement if his behaviour deserves it.

The King of France has employed a great number of workmen to remove the earth round the ancient temple of Diana that is near Nîmes. They have made great discoveries, particularly the foundation of a very large palace which is supposed that of Agrippa when he was Governor of Gallia Narbonensis. They have found many medals and other pieces of antiquity. The greatest part are carried to the King, and some privately sold in this country. A peasant brought me a very curious piece of a mixed metal on which are the figures of justice, a Roman officer, and several other groups. I have shown it several persons who cannot guess for what use it was designed. I will send it to you by the first opportunity. I will not pretend to decide the value, but I think I can be sure it was really found very deep amongst the ruins of the palace I have mentioned.

I am fallen into the same distress that gave me so much trouble in Italy. The man and maid servant who I had taken in place of William and Mary have followed their example. They are married and she big with child. I find it impossible to have a family small enough to consist of reasonable creatures.

[1] In the autumn of 1745 Montagu had been appointed aide-de-camp to Ligonier, Commander of the British army in the Netherlands. Neither Wortley nor Lady Mary yet knew that on 4 March he had been captured by the French. Prince Charles of Lorraine was Governor-General of the Low Countries.

PART VI

Italian Retirement
1746–1756

By the summer of 1746 Avignon was no longer a peaceful haven, for Jacobites had flocked there after their abortive rising in Scotland the previous year; and so under the protection of Count Palazzi, an Italian she had met there, Lady Mary travelled across Italy to Brescia, where his family lived. During the next ten years she stayed in the peaceful Venetian province, enjoying – except for several bouts of serious illness – her rural retirement and pastimes. She had never since girlhood ceased scribbling, and here she continued to write for her private amusement. In England her reputation as a poet was spread in 1747 with the publication of her poems through Horace Walpole, who had transcribed them in Florence.

Although Wortley made several trips abroad during this decade, one as far as Vienna and Hungary, he made no attempt to see her, nor did she expect him to. She dutifully communicated with him by letter, mainly to discuss their son. Young Wortley's career had taken a new, favourable turn when he entered the army, and after his release he served as a secretary in the preliminaries to the treaty of Aix-la-Chapelle in 1748. But his reformation was shortlived, and before long he resumed the career that has put his modern biography into a series called *The Rogues' Gallery*.

Lady Mary's relations with her daughter, Lady Bute, had by now become warmly maternal, and she lavished long, affectionate letters on her. By the summer of 1756 when she became aware of the full extent of Palazzi's lies and swindles she decided to remove herself from his reach.

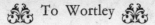

Brescia, 23 August 1746

You will be surprised at the date of this letter, but Avignon has been long disagreeable to me on many accounts, and now more than ever from the concourse of Scotch and Irish rebels that choose it for their refuge, and are so highly protected by the Vice-Legate that it is impossible to go into any company without hearing a conversation that is improper to be listened to and dangerous to contradict. The war with France hindered my settling there for reasons I have already told you, and the difficulty of passing into Italy confined me, though I was always watching an opportunity of returning thither. Fortune at length presented me one.

I believe I wrote you word when I was at Venice that I saw there the Count of Wackerbarth (who was governor to the Prince of Saxony and is favourite of the King of Poland) and of the many civilities I received from him as an old friend of his mother's.[1] About a month since came to Avignon a Gentleman of the Bedchamber of the Prince, who is a man of the first quality in this province, I believe charged with some private commission from the Polish Court.[2] He brought me a letter of recommendation from Count Wackerbarth which engaged me to show him what civilities lay in my power. In conversation I lamented to him the impossibility of my attempting a journey to Italy, where he was going. He offered me his protection, and represented to me that if I would permit him to wait on me I might pass under the notion of a Venetian lady. In short, I ventured upon it, which has succeeded very well, though I met with more impediments in my journey than I expected.

We went by sea to Genoa, where I made a very short stay and saw nobody, having no passport from that state and fearing to be stopped if I was known. We took post-chaises from thence the 16th of this month, and was very much surprised to meet on the *bochetta*[3] the baggage of the Spanish army with a prodigious number of sick and wounded soldiers and officers, who marched in a very great hurry.[4] The Count of Palazzi ordered his servants to say we were in haste for the service of Don Philip, and without further examination they gave us place everywhere, notwithstanding which the multitude of carriages and loaded mules which we met in those narrow roads made it impossible for us to reach Seravalle till it was near night. Our surprise was great to find coming out of that town a large body of troops surrounding a body of guards in the midst of which was Don Philip in person,

---

[1] Lady Mary had met the countess in Vienna in 1716, and corresponded with her.

[2] Count Ugolino Palazzi, the thirty-year-old heir of an impoverished Brescian family.

[3] A term for a mountain pass.

[4] The Spanish army was in retreat before the Austrians and Sardinians, who were England's allies.

going a very round trot, looking down, and pale as ashes. The army was in too much confusion to take notice of us, and the night favouring us we got into the town, but when we came there it was impossible to find any lodging, all the inns being filled with wounded Spaniards. The count went to the governor and asked a chamber for a Venetian lady, which he granted very readily, but there was nothing in it but the bare walls, and in less than a quarter of an hour after, the whole house was empty both of furniture and people, the governor flying into the citadel and carrying with him all his goods and family. We were forced to pass the night without beds or supper.

About daybreak the victorious Germans entered the town. The count went to wait on the generals (to whom I believe he had a commission). He told them my name, and there was no sort of honour or civility they did not pay me. They immediately ordered me a guard of hussars (which was very necessary in the present disorder) and sent me refreshments of all kinds. Next day I was visited by the Prince of Baden–Durlach, the Prince of Löwenstein, and all the principal officers, with whom I passed for a heroine, showing no uneasiness though the cannon of the citadel (where was a Spanish garrison) played very briskly. I was forced to stay there two days for want of post-horses, the postmaster being fled with all his servants, and the Spaniards having seized all the horses they could find. At length I set out from thence the 19th instant with a strong escort of hussars, meeting with no further accident on the road except at the little town of Voghera, where they refused post-horses till the hussars drew their sabres.

The 20th I arrived safe here. It is a very pretty place, where I intend to repose myself (at least) during the remainder of the summer. This journey has been very expensive, but I am very glad I have made it. I am now in a neutral country under the protection of Venice. The Doge is our old friend Grimani,[5] and I do not doubt meeting with all sort of civility. When I set out I had so bad a fluxion on my eyes I was really afraid of losing them. They are now quite recovered and my health better than it has been for some time. I hope yours continues good and that you will always take care of it.

Direct for me at Brescia by way of Venice.

[5] See above, p. 171, n. 2.

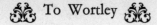

Brescia, 24 November 1746

I bragged too soon of my good health, which lasted but two days after my last letter. I was then seized with so violent a fever that I am surprised a woman of my age could be capable of it. I have kept my bed two months, and am now out of it but a few hours in the day. I did not mention in my last (thinking it an insignificant circumstance) that Count Palazzi had wrote to his mother (without my knowledge) to advertise her of my arrival.[1] She came to meet me in her coach and six, and it was impossible to resist her importunity of going to her house, where she would keep me till I had found a lodging to my liking. I had chose one when I wrote to you and counted upon going there the beginning of the week following, but my violent illness (being as all the physicians thought in the utmost danger) made it utterly impossible. The Countess Palazzi has taken as much care of me as if I had been her sister, and omitted no expense or trouble to serve me. I am still with her, and indeed in no condition of moving at present. I am now in a sort of milk diet which is prescribed me to restore my strength. From being as fat as Lady Bristol I am grown leaner than anybody I can name. For my own part, I think myself in a natural decay. However, I do what I am ordered. I know not how to acknowledge enough my obligations to the countess, and I reckon it a great one from her, who is a devotee, that she never brought any priest to me. My woman, who is a zealous French Huguenot, I believe would have tore his eyes out; during my whole illness it seemed her chief concern. I hope your health continues good.

[1] About ten years later Lady Mary dictated the 'Italian Memoir', a document explaining her financial involvement with Palazzi, emphasizing that his generosity at this time, and subsequently, was distinctly mercenary.

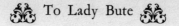 To Lady Bute

Gottolengo, Brescia, 5 January 1748

Dear Child,

I am glad to hear that yourself and family are in good health. As to the alteration you say you find in the world, it is only owing to your being better acquainted with it. I have never, in all my various travels, seen but two sorts of people (and those very like one another); I mean men and women, who always have been, and ever will be, the same. The same vices and the same follies have been the fruit of all ages, though sometimes under different names. I remember (when I returned from Turkey) meeting with the same affectation of youth amongst my acquaintance that you now mention amongst yours, and I do not doubt but your daughter will find the same twenty years hence amongst hers. One of the greatest happinesses of youth is the ignorance of evil, though it is often the ground of great indiscretions, and sometimes the active part of life is over before an honest mind finds out how one ought to act in such a world as this. I am as much removed from it as it is possible to be on this side the grave, which is from my own inclination, for I might have even here a great deal of company, the way of living in this province being what I believe it is now in the sociable part of Scotland and was in England a hundred years ago.

I had a visit in the beginning of these holidays of thirty horse of ladies and gentlemen with their servants (by the way, the ladies all ride like the late Duchess of Cleveland).[1] They came with the kind intent of staying with me at least a fortnight, though I had never seen any of them before; but they were all neighbours within ten mile round. I could not avoid entertaining them at supper, and by good luck had a large quantity of game in the house, which with the help of my poultry furnished out a plentiful table. I sent for the fiddles; and they were so obliging to dance all night, and even dine with me next day, though none of them had been in bed, and were much disappointed I did not press them to stay, it being the fashion to go in troops to one another's houses, hunting and dancing together, a month in each castle. I have not yet returned any of their visits, nor do not intend it of some time, to avoid this expensive hospitality. The trouble of it is not very great, they not expecting any ceremony. I left the room about one o'clock, and they continued their ball in the salon above stairs without being at all offended at my departure. The greatest diversion I had was to see a lady of my own age comfortably dancing with her own husband some years older, and I can assure you she jumps and gallops with the best of them.

May you always be as well satisfied with your family as you are at present, and your children return in your age the tender care you have of their infancy. I know no greater happiness that can be wished for you by your most affectionate mother,   M. Wortley

My compliments to Lord Bute and blessing to my grandchildren.

[1] Italian ladies rode astride.

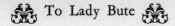

Gottolengo, 3 February 1748

My dear Child,

I return you thanks for the news you send me. I am always amused with the changes and chances that happen amongst my acquaintance. I pity the Duchess of Devonshire and admire the greatness of mind that makes her refuse an addition to her own estate, but am surprised she can relinquish the care of her children who are yet unsettled.[1] Lady Thanet's behaviour has always been without any regard to public censure, but I am ever astonished (though I have frequently seen it) that women can so far renounce all decency as to endeavour to expose a man whose name they bear.[2] Lady Burlington has made a lucky choice for her daughter. I am well acquainted with Lord Hartington and do not know any man so fitted to make a wife happy, with so great a vocation for matrimony that I verily believe if it had not been established before his time he would have had the glory of the invention.[3]

I hear the carnival is very bright at Brescia. I have not yet been to partake of it, but intend to go see the opera, which I hear much commended. Some ladies in the neighbourhood favoured me last week with a visit in masquerade. They were all dressed in white like vestal virgins, with garlands on their heads. They came at night with violins and flambeaux, but did not stay more than one dance, pursuing their way to another castle some miles from hence.

I suppose you are now in London. Wherever you are, you have the good wishes of your most affectionate mother,

M. Wortley M.

My compliments to Lord Bute and blessing to my grandchildren.

[1] According to Horace Walpole, the Duke of Devonshire parted from his wife for breaking a promise he had given her of not marrying their eldest son, Lord Hartington, to Burlington's daughter, but they were reconciled the next year. Of their seven children, three sons and one daughter were still under age.

[2] A separation between Lord and Lady Thanet had been rumoured in 1745.

[3] The only surviving daughter of Lady Burlington married Hartington in March 1748. Lady Mary had known him in Venice.

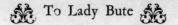

Gottolengo, 10 May 1748

I give you thanks (dear child) for your entertaining account of your present diversions. I find the public calamities have no influence on the pleasures of the town. I remember very well the play of *The Revenge*, having been once acquainted with a party that intended to represent it (not one of which is now alive). I wish you had told me who acted the principal parts. I suppose Lord Bute was Alonzo by the magnificence of his dress.[1] I think they have mended their choice in *The Orphan*. I saw it played at Westminster School, where Lord Erskine was Monimia, and then one of the most beautiful figures that could be seen.[2]

I have had here (in low life) some amusements of the same sort. I believe I wrote you word I intended to go to the opera at Brescia, but the weather being cold and the roads bad prevented my journey, and the people of this village (which is the largest I know – the curate tells me he has two thousand communicants) presented me a petition for leave to erect a theatre in my salon. This house had stood empty many years before I took it, and they were accustomed to turn the stables into a playhouse every carnival. It is now occupied by my horses, and they had no other place proper for a stage. I easily complied with their request, and was surprised at the beauty of their scenes, which though painted by a country painter are better coloured and the perspective better managed than in any of the second-rate theatres in London. I liked it so well, it is not yet pulled down. The performance was yet more surprising, the actors being all peasants, but the Italians have so natural a genius for comedy, they acted as well as if they had been brought up to nothing else, particularly the Harlequin, who far surpassed any of our English, though only the tailor of the village, and I am assured never saw a play in any other place. It is pity they have not better poets, the pieces being not at all superior to our drolls. The music, habits and illumination were at the expense of the parish, and the whole entertainment (which lasted the three last days of the carnival) cost me only a barrel of wine, which I gave the actors, and is not so dear as small beer in London. At present, as the old song says,

> ——— all my whole care
> Is my farming affair,
> To make my corn grow, and my apple trees bear.[3]

My improvements give me great pleasure, and so much profit that if I could live a hundred years longer I should certainly provide for all my

---

[1] In the 1720s Lady Mary had known and patronized Edward Young, author of *The Revenge*. Lord Bute was fond of amateur dramatics.

[2] In 1720 Erskine, Lady Mar's stepson, had acted in Thomas Otway's *The Orphan*.

[3] From Thomas D'Urfey's *Don Quixote* (1729).

grandchildren; but alas, as the Italians say, h'o sonato venti e quatro 'ora;[4] and it is not long I must expect to write myself your most affectionate mother,

M. Wortley

My compliments to Lord Bute and blessing to your little ones.

[4] 'I have dreamed for four and twenty hours.'

To Lady Bute

Gottolengo, 10 July 1748

Dear Child,

I received yours of May the 12th but yesterday, July the 9th. I am surprised you complain of my silence. I have never failed answering yours the post after I received them, but I fear, being directed to Twickenham (having no other direction from you), your servants there may have neglected them.

I have been this six weeks, and still am, at my dairy house, which joins to my garden. I believe I have already told you it is a long mile from the castle, which is situate in the midst of a very large village (once a considerable town, part of the walls still remaining) and has not vacant ground enough about it to make a garden, which is my greatest amusement;[1] and it being now troublesome to walk or even go in the chaise till the evening, I have fitted up in this farm-house a room for myself, that is to say, strewed the floor with rushes, covered the chimney with moss and branches, and adorned the room with basins of earthenware (which is made here to great perfection) filled with flowers, and put in some straw chairs and a couch-bed, which is my whole furniture.

This spot of ground is so beautiful I am afraid you will scarce credit the description, which, however, I can assure you shall be very literal, without any embellishment from imagination. It is on a bank forming a kind of peninsula raised from the River Oglio fifty foot, to which you may descend by easy stairs cut in the turf, and either take the air on the river, which is as large as the Thames at Richmond, or by walking an avenue two hundred yards on the side of it you find a wood of a hundred acres, which was already cut into walks and ridings when I took it. I have only added fifteen bowers in different views, with seats of turf. They were easily made, here being a large quantity of underwood and a

[1] After moving to Brescia, Lady Mary had rented and then bought Palazzi's house – which she calls the 'shell of a palace' – in Gottolengo; and later at his insistence she bought from an old priest the farm here described.

great number of wild vines which twist to the top of the highest trees, and from which they make a very good sort of wine they call *brusco*. I am now writing to you in one of these arbours, which is so thick shaded the sun is not troublesome even at noon. Another is on the side of the river, where I have made a camp kitchen, that I may take the fish, dress and eat it immediately, and at the same time see the barks which ascend or descend everyday, to or from Mantua, Guastalla or Pontevico, all considerable towns. This little wood is carpeted (in their succeeding seasons) with violets and strawberries, inhabited by a nation of nightingales, and filled with game of all kinds excepting deer and wild boar, the first being unknown here, and not being large enough for the other.

My garden was a plain vineyard when it came into my hands not two year ago, and it is with a small expense turned into a garden that (apart from the advantage of the climate) I like better than that of Kensington. The Italian vineyards are not planted like those in France, but in clumps fastened to trees planted in equal ranks (commonly fruit trees) and continued in festoons from one to another, which I have turned into covered galleries of shade, that I can walk in the heat without being incommoded by it. I have made a dining-room of verdure, capable of holding a table of twenty covers. The whole ground is three hundred and seventeen feet in length and two hundred in breadth. You see it is far from large, but so prettily disposed (though I say it) that I never saw a more agreeable rustic garden, abounding with all sort of fruit, and produces a variety of wines. I would send you a piece if I did not fear the custom would make you pay too dear for it. I believe my description gives you but an imperfect idea of my garden.

Perhaps I shall succeed better in describing my manner of life, which is as regular as that of any monastery. I generally rise at six, and as soon as I have breakfasted, put myself at the head of my weeder women, and work with them till nine. I then inspect my dairy and take a turn amongst my poultry, which is a very large inquiry. I have at present two hundred chicken, besides turkeys, geese, ducks, and peacocks. All things have hitherto prospered under my care. My bees and silk worms are doubled, and I am told that without accidents my capital will be so in two years' time. At eleven o'clock I retire to my books. I dare not indulge myself in that pleasure above an hour. At twelve I constantly dine, and sleep after dinner till about three. I then send for some of my old priests and either play at picquet or whist till 'tis cool enough to go out. One evening I walk in my wood, where I often sup, take the air on horseback the next, and go on the water the third. The fishery of this part of the river belongs to me, and my fisherman's little boat (where I have a green lutestring awning) serves me for a barge. He and his son are my rowers, without any expense, he being very well paid by the profit of the fish, which I give him on condition of having everyday one dish for my table. Here is plenty of every sort of freshwater fish excepting salmon, but we have a large trout so like it that I, that have almost forgot the taste, do not distinguish it.

We are both placed properly in regard to our different times of life: you amidst the fair, the gallant and the gay, I in a retreat where I enjoy every amusement that solitude can afford. I confess I sometimes wish for a little conversation, but I reflect that the commerce of the world gives more uneasiness than pleasure, and quiet is all the hope that can reasonably be indulged at my age.

My letter is of an unconscionable length. I should ask your pardon for it, but I had a mind to give you an idea of my passing my time. Take it as an instance of the affection of, dear child, your most affectionate mother,

M. Wortley

My compliments to Lord Bute and blessing to my grandchildren.

To Lady Bute

Dairy House, Gottolengo, 26 July 1748

I am really as fond of my garden as a young author of his first play when it has been well received by the town, and can no more forbear teasing my acquaintance for their approbation. Though I gave you a long account of it in my last, I must tell you I have made two little terraces, raised twelve steps each, at the end of my great walk. They are just finished and a great addition to the beauty of my garden. I enclose to you a rough draught of it, drawn (or more properly scrawled) by my own hand, without the assistance of rule or compasses, as you will easily perceive. I have mixed in my espaliers as many rose and jasmine trees as I can cram in, and in the squares designed for the use of the kitchen have avoided putting anything disagreeable either to sight or smell (having another garden below for cabbage, onions, garlic etc.). All the walks are garnished with beds of flowers, beside the parterres which are for a more distinguished sort. I have neither brick nor stone walls; all my fence is a high hedge mingled with trees, but fruit so plentiful in this country nobody thinks it worth stealing. Gardening is certainly the next amusement to reading; and as my sight will now permit me little of that I am glad to form a taste that can give me so much employment, and be the plaything of my age, now my pen and needle are almost useless to me.

I am very glad you are admitted into the conversation of the Prince and Princess.[1] It is a favour that you ought to cultivate for the good of your family, which is now numerous, and it may one day be of great advantage. I think Lord Bute much in the right to endeavour the continuance of it, and it would be imprudent in you to neglect what may be of great use to your children. I pray God bless both you and them; it is the daily prayer of your most affectionate mother,

M. Wortley M.

Now the sea is open we may send packets to one another.[2] I wish you would send me Campbell's book of prints of the English houses, and that Lord Bute would be so good to choose me the best book of practical gardening extant. I shall trouble you with some more commissions but insist on it that you would take from Child whatever money they may come to.[3] If you consign them to the English consul at Venice directed to me, they will come very safe.

[1] Only the year before, Bute had begun a close friendship with Frederick, Prince of Wales, and his wife.
[2] Preliminaries for a peace treaty between England and France had been signed at Aix-la-Chapelle that spring.
[3] Child & Co. were Lady Mary's bankers in London.

🎄 To Lady Bute 🎄

Gottolengo, February 1749

Dear Child,

I have wrote you so many letters without any return that if I loved you at all less than I do I should certainly give over writing. I received a kind letter last post from Lady Oxford, which gives me hopes I shall at length receive yours, being persuaded you have not neglected our correspondence, though I am not so happy to have the pleasure of it.

I have little to say from this solitude, having already sent you a description of my garden, which, with my books, takes up all my time. I made a small excursion last week to visit a nunnery twelve mile from hence, which is the only institution of the kind in all Italy. It is in a town in the state of Mantua, founded by a Princess of the House of Gonzaga, one of which (now very old) is the present abbess.[1] They are

[1] The Convent of Saint Ursula was founded in 1599 by Margarita Gonzaga, daughter of the Duke of Mantua. Its abbess in 1749 was probably Clara Clarina, illegitimate daughter of the last Duke.

dressed in black, and wear a thin cypress veil at the back of their heads, excepting which they have no mark of a religious habit, being set out in their hair and having no gimp, but wearing *des collets montés*, for which I have no name in English, but you may have seen them in very old pictures, being in fashion both before and after ruffs. Their house is a very large handsome building, though not regular, every sister having liberty to build her own apartment to her taste, which consists of as many rooms as she pleases. They have each a separate kitchen and keep cooks and what other servants they think proper. Though there is a very fine public refectory they are permitted to dine in private whenever they please. Their garden is very large, and the most adorned of any in these parts. They have no grates, and make what visits they will, always two together, and receive those of the men as well as ladies. I was accompanied when I went with all the nobility of the town, and they showed me all the house without excluding the gentlemen. But what I think the most remarkable privilege is a country house which belongs to them, three mile from the town, where they pass every vintage, and at any time any four of them may take their pleasure there for as many days as they choose. They seem to differ from the *chanoinesses* of Flanders only in their vow of celibacy. They take pensioners, but only those of quality. I saw here a niece of General Browne.[2] Those that profess are obliged to prove a descent as noble as the Knights of Malta.

Upon the whole I think it the most agreeable community I have seen, and their behaviour more decent than that of the cloistered nuns, who I have heard say themselves that the grate permits all liberty of speech since it leaves them no other, and indeed they generally talk according to that maxim. My house at Avignon joined to a monastery, which gave me occasion to know a great deal of their conduct, which (though the convent of the best reputation in that town, where there is fourteen) was such as I would as soon put a girl into the playhouse for education as send her amongst them.

My paper is at an end, and hardly leaves room for my compliments to Lord Bute, blessing to my grandchildren, and assurance to yourself of being your most affectionate mother,

M. Wortley

[2] Maximilian Ulysses von Browne, of Irish descent and in the Austrian service.

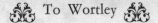

Gottolengo, 1 May 1749

I wish you joy of your new seat. I have been told that the gardens and plantations are in the best taste of any in that country.[1] Long may you enjoy it in health and happiness!

I give you many thanks for the ale, which is in great esteem here by reputation, for it is otherwise quite unknown. I would send you some wine of my own making in return if I thought it would arrive good and be worth paying the custom.

I cannot readily answer your question concerning the passage of letters, being eighteen mile from Brescia, and there is nobody in this neighbourhood that has any foreign correspondence. I will not fail to inquire the first opportunity, and let you know it. I have always dated my letters from Brescia, being the nearest post town, but have been there but twice, and that only for a few days, since my recovery from that terrible fit of sickness at my arrival. I find this air agree very well with me, and amuse myself with my little country business.

I am very glad my daughter's conduct answers the opinion I ever had of her understanding. I do not say it to lessen the praise she deserves, but I really think there is some due to Lord Bute. It is seldom that the affections of a man of his age continue so many years. May she always possess them and every other blessing! I think her much in the right to cultivate the Princess's favour, but in general have no great faith in court friendships, and remember Lord Bathurst's epigram, that princes are the sons of kings.

[1] Wortley had inherited from a cousin the estate of Newbold Verdon, Leics.

To Lady Bute

Lovere, 24 July [?1749]

Dear Child,

I am now in a place the most beautifully romantic I ever saw in my life.[1] It is the Tunbridge of this part of the world, to which I was sent by the doctor's order, my ague often returning notwithstanding the loads of bark I have taken. To say truth I have no reason to repent my journey, though I was very unwilling to undertake it, it being forty mile, half by land and half by water, the land so stony I was almost shook to pieces; and I had the ill luck to be surprised with a storm on the lake that if I had not been near a little port (where I passed a night in a very poor inn) the vessel must have been lost. A fair wind brought me hither next morning early.

I found a very good lodging, a great deal of good company, and a village in many respects resembling Tunbridge Wells, not only in the quality of the waters (which is the same) but in the manner of the buildings, most of the houses being separate at little distances, and all built on the sides of hills, which indeed are far different from those of Tunbridge, being six times as high. They are really vast rocks of different figures covered with green moss or short grass, diversified by tufts of trees, little woods, and here and there vineyards, but no other cultivation except gardens like those on Richmond Hill. The whole lake, which is twenty-five mile long and three broad, is all surrounded with these impassable mountains, the sides of which, towards the bottom, are so thick set with villages (and in most of them gentlemen's seats) that I do not believe there is anywhere above a mile distance one from another, which adds very much to the beauty of the prospect.

We have an opera here which is performed three times in the week. I was at it last night, and should have been surprised at the neatness of the scenes, goodness of the voices, and justness of the actors if I had not remembered I was in Italy. Several gentlemen jumped into the orchestra and joined in the consort, which I suppose is one of the freedoms of the place, for I never saw it in any great town. I was yet more amazed (while the actors were dressing for the farce that concluded the entertainment) to see one of the principal amongst them (and as arrant a *petit maître* as if he had passed all his life at Paris) mount the stage and present us with a cantata of his own performing. He had the pleasure of being almost deafened with applause. The ball begun afterwards, but I was not witness of it, having accustomed myself to such early hours that I was half asleep before the opera finished. It begins at ten o'clock, so that it was one before I could get to bed, though I had supped before I went, which is the custom.

I am much better pleased with the diversions on the water, where all

---

[1] Lovere, at the northern end of Lago d'Iseo, was recommended by Brescian doctors for its salubrious air and mineral waters.

the town assembles every night, and never without music; but we have none so rough as trumpets, kettledrums, and French horns – they are all violins, lutes, mandolins and *flûtes douces*. Here is hardly a man that does not excel in some of these instruments, which he privately addresses to the lady of his affections, and the public has the advantage of it by his adding to the number of the musicians. The fountain where we drink the waters rises between two hanging hills, and is overshadowed with large trees that give a freshness in the hottest time of the day. The provisions are all excellent, the fish of the lake being as large and well tasted as that of Geneva, and the mountains abounding in game, particularly black cocks, which I never saw in any other part of Italy.

But none of the amusements here would be so effectual to raising my spirits as a letter from you. I have received none since that of Feb. 27. I do not blame you for it but my ill fortune that will not let me have that consolation. The newspaper informs me that the Chevalier Gray (so he is styled) is appointed minister at Venice. I wish you would let me know who he is, intending to settle our correspondence through his hands. I did not care to ask that favour of Lord Holdernesse.[2]

Dear child, I am ever your most affectionate mother,

M. Wortley M.

My compliments to Lord Bute and blessing to all your little ones. Direct as usual.

[2] Sir James Gray had previously been Secretary of the Embassy. Holdernesse had been Ambassador since 1744.

🪷 To Lady Bute 🪷

Lovere, 5 September 1749

Dear Child,

I have once more recovered my health by the use of these waters, and can say I am at this present writing in a better state of health than I have been for some years. I rise early, take the air on the water every evening, and generally land at some part of its banks and always find some new walk amongst the mountains, which are covered with vines and fruit trees, mixed with several natural cascades and embellished with variety of beautiful prospects. I think I have already described this place to you. It really answers all the delightful ideas of romance. I could not be persuaded to leave it for the fair of Bergamo, though half engaged to do so. I play at whist an hour or two every afternoon. The fashion here is to play for the collation; the losers have at least the consolation of eating part of their money.

I am extremely pleased with your father's kindness to you. I do not doubt of your gratitude and affection. He speaks to me much of the beauty of your sons.[1] I cannot help wishing it had fallen to the share of your daughters, but I believe it is the destiny of Lord Bute's family. I never heard his mother's much celebrated, though both her brothers have been remarkable for their figure.[2]

My dear child, God bless you and yours. I am ever your most affectionate mother,

M. Wortley

My compliments to Lord Bute. I hope you will remember to send me the third volume of architecture with any other amusing books. Direct them to the English Minister at Venice, Sir James Gray.

[1] John was five, and James Archibald nearly two years old.
[2] Lord Bute's mother was the daughter of the 1st Duke of Argyll. Her two brothers were successively 2nd and 3rd Dukes; the former was thought to be very handsome and graceful, but the latter 'slovenly in his person' (according to Horace Walpole).

Gottolengo, 1 October 1749

My dear Child,

I have at length received the box with the books enclosed, for which I give you many thanks, as they amused me very much. I gave a very ridiculous proof of it, fitter indeed for my granddaughter than myself. I returned from a party on horseback, and after having rode twenty mile, part of it by moonshine, it was ten at night, when I found the box arrived. I could not deny myself the pleasure of opening it, and falling upon Fielding's works was fool enough to sit up all night reading. I think *Joseph Andrews* better than his *Foundling*.[1] I believe I was the more struck with it, having at present a Fanny in my own house, not only by the name, which happens to be the same,[2] but the extraordinary beauty, joined with an understanding yet more extraordinary at her age, which is but few months past sixteen. She is in the post of my chambermaid. I fancy you will tax my discretion for taking a servant thus qualified, but my woman, who is also my housekeeper, was always teasing me with her having too much work and complaining of ill health, which determined me to take her a deputy; and when I was at Lovere (where I drank the waters) one of the most considerable merchants there pressed me to take this daughter of his. Her mother has an uncommon good character, and the girl has had a better education than is usual for those of her rank. She writes a good hand and has been brought up to keep accounts, which she does to great perfection, and had herself such a violent desire to serve me that I was persuaded to take her. I do not yet repent it from any part of her behaviour; but there has been no peace in the family ever since she came into it – I might say the parish, all the women in it having declared open war with her and the men endeavouring at treaties of a different sort. My own woman puts herself at the head of the first party, and her spleen is increased by having no reason for it, the young creature never stirring from my apartment, always at her needle, and never complaining of anything. You will laugh at this tedious account of my domestics (if you have patience to read it over), but I have few other subjects to talk of.

I am sorry you did not take the money for the books from Child. I write him this post to pay it to you, but you will wait longer for it than I could wish.

I am much pleased at your account of your children. May they ever be as agreeable to you as they are at present!

The waters have very much mended my health. I endeavour to preserve it by constant riding, and am a better horsewoman than ever

---

[1] *Joseph Andrews* had been published in February 1742, and *Tom Jones, A Foundling* in February 1749.

[2] Chechina, a diminutive of Francesca; she stayed with Lady Mary for less than a year.

I was in my life, having complied with the fashion of this country, which is everyway so much better than ours I cannot help being amazed at the obstinate folly by which the English ladies venture everyday their lives and limbs.

My paper only allows me to add I am your most affectionate mother,

M.W.

My compliments to Lord Bute and blessing to your little ones.

❧ To Lady Bute ❧

Gottolengo, 27 November 1749

Dear Child,

By the account you give me of London I think it very much reformed. At least you have one sin the less (and it was a very reigning one in my time): I mean scandal. It must be literally reduced to a whisper since the custom of living altogether. I hope it has also banished the fashion of talking all at once (which was very prevailing when I was in town) and may perhaps contribute to brotherly love and unity, which was so much declined in my memory that it was hard to invite six people that would not, by cold looks or piqueing reflections, affront one another. I suppose parties are at an end, though I fear it is the consequence of the old almanac prophecy – poverty brings peace – and I fancy you really follow the French mode, and the lady keeps an assembly, that the assembly may keep the lady, and card money pay for clothes and equipage as well as cards and candles. I find I should be as solitary in London as I am here in the country, it being impossible for me to submit to live in a drum, which I think so far from a cure of uneasiness that it is, in my opinion, adding one more to the heap. There are so many attached to humanity, 'tis impossible to fly from them all, but experience has confirmed to me (what I always thought), that the pursuit of pleasure will be ever attended with pain, and the study of ease be most certainly accompanied with pleasures.

I have had this morning as much delight in a walk in the sun as ever I felt formerly in the crowded Mall even when I imagined I had my share of the admiration of the place, which was generally soured before I slept by the informations of my female friends, who seldom failed to tell me it was observed I had showed an inch above my shoe heels, or some other criticism of equal weight, which was construed affectation, and utterly destroyed all the satisfaction my vanity had given me. I have now no other but in my little housewifery, which is easily gratified in this country, where (by the help of my receipt book) I make a very shining figure amongst my neighbours by the introduction of custards, cheese-cakes and minced pies, which were entirely unknown in these parts and are received with universal applause, and I have reason to believe will preserve my memory even to future ages, particularly by the art of butter-making, in which I have so improved them that they now make as good as in any part of England.

My paper is at an end, which I do not doubt you are glad of. I have hardly room for my compliments to Lord Bute, blessing to my grand-children, and to assure you that I am ever your most affectionate mother,

M.W.

To Lady Bute

Gottolengo, January 1750

My dear Child,

I am extremely concerned to hear you complain of ill health at a time of life when you ought to be in the flower of your strength. I hope I need not recommend to you the care of it. The tenderness you have for your children is sufficient to enforce you to the utmost regard for the preservation of a life so necessary to their well-being. I do not doubt your prudence in their education; neither can I say anything particular relating to it at this distance, different tempers requiring different management. In general, never attempt to govern them (as most people do) by deceit. If they find themselves cheated (even in trifles) it will so far lessen the authority of their instructor as to make them neglect all their future admonitions. And (if possible) breed them free from prejudices; those contracted in the nursery often influence the whole life after, of which I have seen many melancholy examples.

I shall say no more of this subject, nor would have said this little if you had not asked my advice. 'Tis much easier to give rules than to practise them. I am sensible my own natural temper is too indulgent. I think it the least dangerous error, yet still it is an error. I can only say with truth that I do not know in my whole life having ever endeavoured to impose on you or give a false colour to anything that I represented to you. If your daughters are inclined to love reading, do not check their inclination by hindering them of the diverting part of it. It is as necessary for the amusement of women as the reputation of men; but teach them not to expect or desire any applause from it. Let their brothers shine, and let them content themselves with making their lives easier by it, which I experimentally know is more effectually done by study than any other way. Ignorance is as much the fountain of vice as idleness, and indeed generally produces it. People that do not read or work for a livelihood have many hours they know not how to employ, especially women, who commonly fall into vapours or something worse. I am afraid you'll think this letter very tedious. Forgive it as coming from your most affectionate mother,

M.W.

My compliments to Lord Bute and blessing to my grandchildren.

To Lady Bute

Gottolengo, 19 February 1750

My dear Child,

I gave you some general thoughts on the education of your children in my last letter, but fearing you should think I neglected your request by answering it with too much conciseness, I am resolved to add to it what little I know on that subject, and which may perhaps be useful to you in a concern with which you seem so nearly affected.

People commonly educate their children as they build their houses, according to some plan they think beautiful, without considering whether it is suited to the purposes for which they are designed. Almost all girls of quality are educated as if they were to be great ladies, which is often as little to be expected as an immoderate heat of the sun in the north of Scotland. You should teach yours to confine their desires to probabilities, to be as useful as is possible to themselves, and to think privacy (as it *is*) the happiest state of life.

I do not doubt your giving them all the instructions necessary to form them to a virtuous life, but 'tis a fatal mistake to do this without proper restrictions. Vices are often hid under the name of virtues, and the practice of them followed by the worst of consequences. Sincerity, friendship, piety, disinterestedness, and generosity are all great virtues, but pursued without discretion become criminal. I have seen ladies indulge their own ill humour by being very rude and impertinent, and think they deserved approbation by saying, 'I love to speak truth'. One of your acquaintance made a ball the next day after her mother died, to show she was sincere. I believe your own reflection will furnish you with but too many examples of the ill effects of the rest of the sentiments I have mentioned, when too warmly embraced. They are generally recommended to young people without limits or distinction, and this prejudice hurries them into great misfortunes while they are applauding themselves in the noble practice (as they fancy) of very eminent virtues.

I cannot help adding (out of my real affection to you) I wish you would moderate that fondness you have for your children. I do not mean you should abate any part of your care, or not do your duty to them in its utmost extent, but I would have you early prepare yourself for disappointments, which are heavy in proportion to their being surprising. It is hardly possible in such a number that none should be unhappy. Prepare yourself against a misfortune of that kind. I confess there is hardly any more difficult to support, yet it is certain imagination has a great share in the pain of it, and it is more in our power (than it is commonly believed) to soften whatever ills are founded or augmented by fancy. Strictly speaking, there is but one real evil: I mean acute pain . All other complaints are so considerably diminished by time that it is plain the grief is owing to our passion, since the sensation of it vanishes when that is over.

There is another mistake I forgot to mention usual in mothers. If any of their daughters are beauties they take great pains to persuade them that they are ugly, or at least that they think so, which the young woman never fails to believe springs from envy, and is (perhaps) not much in the wrong. I would, if possible, give them a just notion of their figure, and show them how far it is valuable. Every advantage has its price, and may be either over or undervalued. It is the common doctrine of (what are called) good books to inspire a contempt of beauty, riches, greatness etc., which has done as much mischief amongst the young of our sex as an over-eager desire of them. They should look on these things as blessings where they are bestowed, though not necessaries that it is impossible to be happy without. I am persuaded the ruin of Lady Frances Meadows was in great measure owing to the notions given her by the sillily good people that had the care of her.[1] 'Tis true her circumstances and your daughters' are very different. They should be taught to be content with privacy, and yet not neglect good fortune if it should be offered them.

I am afraid I have tired you with my instructions. I do not give them as believing my age has furnished me with superior wisdom, but in compliance with your desire, and being fond of every opportunity that

---

[1] Lady Frances Pierrepont, Lady Mary's niece and a great heiress, had lived with Lady Cheyne until 1732 and thereafter with Lady Mary until she eloped with the impecunious Philip Meadows in 1734.

gives a proof of the tenderness with which I am ever your affectionate mother,

M. Wortley

I should be glad you sent me the third volume of architecture, and with it any other entertaining books. I have seen the Duchess of Marlborough's,[2] but should be glad of the *Apology for a Late Resignation*.[3] As to the ale, 'tis now so late in the year it is impossible it should come good.

You do not mention your father. My last letter from him told me he intended soon for England.[4] I am afraid several of mine to him have miscarried, though directed as he ordered.

I have asked you so often the price of raw silk that I am weary of repeating it.[5] However, I once more beg you would send me that information.

[2] *Account of the Conduct of the Dowager Duchess of Marlborough, from her first coming to Court, to the year 1710* (1742).

[3] Published anonymously (1748), it defended Chesterfield's resignation as Secretary of State.

[4] Wortley had been in France since the summer of 1749.

[5] Lady Mary was raising silk worms on her farm, and planned to send the silk to be sold in England.

To Lady Bute

Gottolengo, 19 June 1751

My dear Child,

I received yesterday yours of May 16th, in which was enclosed the captain's bill for the box. I am much obliged to Lord Bute for thinking of me so kindly. To say truth, I am as fond of baubles as ever and am so far from being ashamed of it, it is a taste I endeavour to keep up with all the art I am mistress of. I should have despised them at twenty for the same reason that I would not eat tarts or cheese-cakes at twelve year old, as being too childish for one capable of more solid pleasures. I now know (and alas, have long known) all things in this world are almost equally trifling, and our most serious projects have scarce more foundation than those edifices that your little ones raise in cards. You see to what period the vast fortunes of the Duke and Duchess of Marlborough and Sir Robert Walpole are soon arrived. I believe, as you do, that Lady Orford is a joyful widow, but am persuaded she has as much reason to weep for her husband as ever any woman has had, from

Andromache[1] to this day. I never saw any second marriage that did not appear to me very ridiculous; hers is accompanied with circumstances that render the folly complete.[2]

Sicknesses have been very fatal in this country as well as England. I should be glad to know the names of those you say are deceased. I believe I am ignorant of half of them, the Dutch news [papers] being forbid here. I would not have you give yourself the trouble, but order one of your servants to transcribe the catalogue. You will perhaps laugh at this curiosity. If you ever return to Bute, you will find that what happens in the world is a considerable amusement in solitude. The people I see here make no more impression on my mind than the figures in the tapestry. While they are directly before my eyes, I know one is clothed in blue and another in red, but out of sight they are so entirely out of memory I hardly remember whether they are tall or short. I sometimes call myself to account for this insensibility, which has something of ingratitude in it, this little town thinking themselves highly honoured and obliged by my residence. They intended me an extraordinary mark of it, having determined to set up my statue in the most conspicuous place. The marble was bespoke and the sculptor bargained with before I knew anything of the matter, and it would have been erected without my knowledge if it had not been necessary for him to see me to take the resemblance. I thanked them very much for the intention, but utterly refused complying with it, fearing it would be reported (at least in England) that I had set up my own statue. They were so obstinate in the design, I was forced to tell them my religion would not permit it. I seriously believe it would have been worshipped (when I was forgotten) under the name of some saint or other, since I was to have been represented with a book in my hand, which would have passed for a proof of canonization.

This compliment was certainly founded on reasons not unlike those that first framed goddesses: I mean being useful to them, in which I am second to Ceres. If it be true she taught the art of sowing wheat it is sure I have learned them to make bread, in which they continued in the same ignorance Misson complains of (as you may see in his letter from Padua).[3] I have introduced French rolls, custards, minced pies, and plum pudding, which they are very fond of. 'Tis impossible to bring them to conform to sillabub, which is so unnatural a mixture in their eyes, they are even shocked to see me eat it. But I expect immortality from the science of butter-making, in which they are become so skilful from my instructions, I can assure you here is as good as in any part of Great Britain. I am afraid I have bragged of this before, but when you

---

[1] In Greek mythology, wife of Hector.

[2] Within two months of her estranged husband's death Lady Orford – Lady Walpole until her father-in-law's death – had married Sewallis Shirley, with whom she had been living. They separated three years later because she refused to settle any money on him.

[3] In Maximilien Misson's popular *Voyage d'Italie* (1691).

do not answer any part of my letters I suppose them lost, which exposes you to some repetitions. Have you received that I wrote on my first notice of the Prince's death?[4]

I shall receive Lord Bute's china with great pleasure.

The pearl necklace for my goddaughter has been long packed up for her; I wish I could say sent. In the meantime give her and the rest of yours my blessing. With thanks and compliments to Lord Bute from your most affectionate mother,

M. Wortley M.

I desire you would order the china to be packed and sent by a skilful man of the trade, or I shall receive it in pieces.

[4] The death of the Prince of Wales, in March 1751, had apparently ended Bute's good fortune at Court.

To Lady Bute

Gottolengo, 8 December 1751

My dear Child,

I received yours of Oct. 24 yesterday, which gave me great pleasure by the account of the good health of you and yours; I need not say how near that is to my heart. I had the satisfaction of an entertaining letter from your father out of Germany, by which I find he has had both benefit and amusement from his travels.[1] I hope he is now with you.

I find you have many wrong notions of Italy, which I do not wonder at. You can take your ideas of it only from books or travellers. The first are generally antiquated or confined to trite observations, and the other yet more superficial. They return no more instructed than they might have been at home by the help of a map. The boys only remember where they met with the best wine or the prettiest women, and the governors (I speak of the most learned amongst them) have only remarked situations and distances or, at most, statues and edifices. As every girl that can read a French novel and boy that can construe a scene in Terence fancies they have attained to the French and Latin languages, when God knows it requires the study of a whole life to acquire a perfect knowledge of either of them, so after a tour (as they call it) of three years round Europe people think themselves qualified to give exact accounts of the customs, policies and interests of the dominions

[1] To Lorraine, Vienna, and Hungary.

they have gone through post, when a very long stay, a diligent inquiry, and a nice observation are requisite even to a moderate degree of knowing a foreign country, especially here, where they are naturally very reserved.

France indeed is more easily seen through, the French always talking of themselves; and the government being the same there is little difference from one province to another. But in Italy the different laws make different customs and manners, which are in many things very particular here from the singularity of the government. Some I do not care to touch upon, and some are still in use here, though obsolete in almost all other places, as the estates of all the great families being unalienable, as they were formerly in England. This would make them very potent if it was not balanced by another law that divides whatever land the father dies possessed of amongst all the sons, the eldest having no advantage but the finest house and best furniture. This occasions numerous branches and few large fortunes, with a train of consequences you may imagine.

But I cannot let pass in silence the prodigious alteration since Misson's writing in regard to our sex. This reformation (or if you please, depravation) begun so lately as the year 1732, when the French overrun this part of Italy, but it has been carried on with such fervour and success that the Italian go far beyond their patterns, the Parisian ladies, in the extent of their liberty. I am not so much surprised at the women's conduct as I am amazed at the change in the men's sentiments. Jealousy, which was once a point of honour amongst them, is exploded to that degree it is the most infamous and ridiculous of all characters, and you cannot more affront a gentleman than to suppose him capable of it.

Divorces are also introduced and frequent enough. They have long been in fashion in Genoa, several of the finest and greatest ladies there having two husbands alive. The constant pretext is impotency, to which the man often pleads guilty, and though he marries again and has children by another wife, the plea remains good by saying he was so in regard to his first; and when I told them that in England a complaint of that kind was esteemed so impudent, no reasonable woman would submit to make it, I was answered we lived without religion, and that their consciences obliged them rather to strain a point of modesty than live in a state of damnation. However, as this method is not without inconvenience (it being impracticable where there is children) they have taken another here: the husband deposes upon oath that he has had a commerce with his mother-in-law, on which the marriage is declared incestuous and nullified, though the children remain legitimate. You will think this hard on the old lady who is scandalized, but it is no scandal at all, nobody supposing it to be true, without circumstances to confirm. But the married couple are set free, to their mutual content, for I believe it would be difficult to get a sentence of divorce if either side made opposition. At least I have heard no example of it.

I am afraid you will think this long letter very tedious, but you tell me you are without company, and in solitude anything amuses, though yours appears to me a sort of paradise. You have an agreeable habitation, a pleasant garden,[2] a man you love and that loves you, and are surrounded with a numerous hopeful progeny. May they all prove comforts to your age; that and all blessings is daily wished you by, my dear child, your most affectionate mother,

M. Wortley

My compliments to Lord Bute and blessing to your little ones.

[2] In 1746 Bute had been given Kenwood House, Hampstead, by his uncle the Duke of Argyll, and later moved there with his family.

To Lady Bute

Gottolengo, 16 February 1752

Dear Child,

I received yesterday, Feb. 15 N.S., the case of books you were so good to send to me. The entertainment they have already given me has recompensed me for the long time I expected them. I begun, by your direction, with *Peregrine Pickle*. I think Lady Vane's memoirs contain more truth and less malice than any I ever read in my life.[1] When she speaks of her own being disinterested I am apt to believe she really thinks herself so, as many highwaymen, after having no possibility of retrieving the character of honesty, please themselves with that of being generous because whatever they get on the road they always spend at the next ale-house, and are still as beggarly as ever. Her history, rightly considered, would be more instructive to young women than any sermon I know. They may see there what mortifications and variety of misery are the unavoidable consequences of gallantries. I think there is no rational creature that would not prefer the life of the strictest Carmelite to the round of hurry and misfortune she has gone through.

Her style is clear and concise, with some strokes of humour which appear to me so much above her I can't help being of opinion the whole has been modelled by the author of the book in which it is inserted, who is some subaltern admirer of hers.[2] I may judge wrong,

[1] At the end of *Peregrine Pickle* (1751) Smollett printed the 'Memoirs of a Lady of Quality' by the notorious Lady Vane (see above, p. 163).

[2] Although Lady Vane may have been acquainted with Smollett, it is uncertain which of them wrote the memoirs; the final version was almost certainly his.

she being no acquaintance of mine, though she has married two of my relations. Her first wedding was attended with circumstances that made me think a visit not at all necessary, though I disobliged Lady Susan by neglecting it;[3] and her second, which happened soon after, made her so near a neighbour that I rather chose to stay the whole summer in town than partake of her balls and parties of pleasure, to which I did not think it proper to introduce you, and had no other way of avoiding it without incurring the censure of a most unnatural mother for denying you diversions that the pious Lady Ferrers permitted to her exemplary daughters.[4] Mr Shirley has had uncommon fortune in making the conquest of two such extraordinary ladies, equal in their heroic contempt of shame, and eminent above their sex, the one for beauty, and the other wealth, both which attract the pursuit of all mankind, and have been thrown into his arms with the same unlimited fondness.[5] He appeared to me genteel, well bred, well shaped and sensible, but the charms of his face and eyes, which Lady Vane describes with so much warmth, were, I confess, always invisible to me, and the artificial part of his character very glaring, which I think her story shows in a strong light.

The next book I laid my hand on was *The Parish Girl*, which interested me enough not to be able to quit it till it was read over, though the author has fallen into the common mistake of romance writers, intending a virtuous character and not knowing how to draw it, the first step of his heroine (leaving her patroness's house) being altogether absurd and ridiculous, justly entitling her to all the misfortunes she met with.[6]

Candles came, and my eyes grown weary I took up the next book merely because I supposed from the title it could not engage me long. It was *Pompey the Little*, which has really diverted me more than any of the others, and it was impossible to go to bed till it was finished.[7] It is a real and exact representation of life as it is now acted in London, as it was in my time, and as it will be (I do not doubt) a hundred years hence, with some little variation of dress and perhaps government. I found there many of my acquaintance. Lady Townshend and Lady Orford are so well painted I fancied I heard them talk, and have heard them say the very things there repeated.

[3] In her memoirs, Lady Vane tells of eloping with Lord William Hamilton, and of being visited the same day by his youngest sister, Lady Susan.

[4] Lady Ferrers, who lived in Twickenham, was widow of the 1st Earl Ferrers; two of her stepson's daughters were Methodists.

[5] Sewallis Shirley, Lady Ferrers's son, became Lady Vane's lover soon after her second marriage in 1735; and in 1751 he married the widowed Lady Orford.

[6] *The History of Charlotte Summers, the Fortunate Parish Girl* (1749) was noticed in the *Monthly Review*: 'All we shall say of this performance, is, that the author has kept his name unknown, which is an instance of his discretion. . . .'

[7] *The History of Pompey the Little: or, The Life and Adventures of a Lap-Dog* (1751) by Francis Coventry.

I also saw myself (as I now am) in the character of Mrs Qualmsick.
You will be surprised at this, no English woman being so free from
vapours, having never in my life complained of low spirits or weak
nerves, but our resemblance is very strong in the fancied loss of appetite, which I have been silly enough to be persuaded into by the physician of this place. He visits me frequently, as being one of the most
considerable men in the parish, and is a grave, sober, thinking great
fool, whose solemn appearance and deliberate way of delivering his
sentiments gives them an air of good sense, though they are often the
most injudicious that ever were pronounced. By perpetual telling me
I eat so little he is amazed I am able to subsist, he had brought me to be
of his opinion, and I begun to be seriously uneasy at it.

This useful treatise has roused me into a recollection of what I ate
yesterday, and do almost every day the same. I wake generally about
seven and drink half a pint of warm ass's milk, after which I sleep two
hours. As soon as I am risen I constantly take three cups of milk coffee,
and two hours after that a large cup of milk chocolate. Two hours more
brings my dinner, where I never fail swallowing a good dish (I don't
mean plate) of gravy soup with all the bread, roots, etc. belonging to it.
I then eat a wing and the whole body of a large fat capon and a veal
sweetbread, concluding with a competent quantity of custard and some
roasted chestnuts. At five in the afternoon I take another dose of ass's
milk, and for supper twelve chestnuts (which would weigh twenty-four
of those in London), one new-laid egg, and a handsome porringer of
white bread and milk. With this diet, notwithstanding the menaces of
my wise doctor, I am now convinced I am in no danger of starving, and
am obliged to *Little Pompey* for this discovery.

I opened my eyes this morning on *Leonora*,[8] from which I defy the
greatest chemist in morals to extract any instruction: the style most
affectedly florid and naturally insipid, with such a confused heap of
admirable characters that never were or can be in human nature. I flung
it aside after fifty pages and laid hold of *Mrs Phillips*, where I expected
to find at least probable, if not true, facts, and was not disappointed.[9]
There is a great similitude in the genius and adventures (the one being
productive of the other) between Madam Constantia and Lady Vane.
The first mentioned has the advantage in birth and (if I am not mistaken)
in understanding. They have both had scandalous law suits with their
husbands and are endowed with the same intrepid assurance.[10] Constantia seems to value herself also on her generosity, and has given the
same proofs of it. The parallel might be drawn out to be as long as any

---

[8] *Leonora: Or, Characters Drawn from Real Life. Containing A Great Variety of
Incidents, Interspersed with Reflections moral and entertaining* (1745).

[9] *An Apology for the Conduct of Mrs T. C. Phillips* (1748–49). Lady Mary wrote
on her copy: 'truly though not finely wrote'.

[10] Teresia Constantia Phillips married Henry Muilman, a Dutch merchant, in
1723; the next year he had the marriage annulled.

of Plutarch's, but I dare swear you are already heartily weary of my remarks and wish I had not read so much in so short a time, that you might not be troubled with my comments. But you must suffer me to say something of the polite Mr S——te, whose name I should never have guessed by the rapturous description his mistress makes of his person, having always looked upon him as one of the most disagreeable fellows about town, as odious in his outside as stupid in his conversation, and I should as soon have expected to hear of his conquests at the head of an army as amongst women; yet he has been (it seems) the darling favourite of the most experienced of the sex, which shows me I am a very bad judge of merit.[11] But I agree with Mrs Phillips that however profligate she may have been she is infinitely his superior in virtue, and if her penitence is as sincere as she says, she may expect their future fate to be like that of Dives and Lazarus.[12]

This letter is of a most immoderate length. I hope it will find you at Kenwood. Your solitude there will permit you to peruse and even to forgive all the impertinence of your most affectionate mother,

M. Wortley

My blessing to your children and compliments to Lord Bute. I enclose a bill to pay the overplus due to you and serve for future little commissions.

[11] Mrs Phillips describes this lover as agreeable, with meaningful eyes and artful tongue; graceful and delicately clean; of dangerous address and robust, lascivious constitution.

[12] One in Heaven and one in Hell.

To Lady Bute

Dear Child,

I have now finished your books, and I believe you'll think I have made quick dispatch. To say truth, I have read night and day. *Mr Loveill* gave me some entertainment,[1] though there is but one character in it that I can find out. I do not doubt Mr Depy is designed for Sir John Rawdon. The adventure mentioned at Rome really happened to him, with this addition, that after he was got quit of his fear of being supected in the interest of the Pretender, he endeavoured to manifest his loyalty by railing at him in all companies with all the warmth imaginable, on which his companions persuaded him that his death was absolutely determined by that Court, and he durst not stir out for some time for fear of being assassinated, nor eat for fear of being poisoned. I saw him at Venice, where on hearing it said I had been at Constantinople, he asked Lord Mansell by what accident I made that journey. He answered, 'Mr Wortley was Ambassador to the Porte.' Sir John replied: 'To what port? The port of Leghorn?'

I could relate many speeches of his of equal beauty, but I believe you are already tired of hearing of him as much as I was with the memoirs of Miss Harriot Stuart,[2] who, being intended for an example of wit and virtue, is a jilt and a fool in every page; but while I was indolently perusing the marvellous figures she exhibits, no more resembling anything in human nature than the wooden cuts in the *Seaven Champions*,[3] I was roused into great surprise and indignation by the monstrous abuse of one of the very, very few women I have a real value for. I mean Lady Bell Finch, who is not only clearly meant by the mention of her library, she being the only lady at Court that has one, but her very name at length, she being christened Cecilia Isabella, though she chooses to be called by the latter. I always thought her conduct in every light so irreproachable I did not think she had an enemy upon earth.[4] I now see 'tis impossible to avoid them, especially in her situation. It is one of the misfortunes of a supposed Court interest (perhaps you may know it by experience), even the people you have obliged hate you if they do not think you have served them to the utmost extent of a power that they fancy you are possessed of, which it may be is only imaginary.

On the other hand I forgive Joe Thompson two volumes of absurdities for the sake of the justice he has done the memory of the Duke of

---

[1] *The Adventures of Mr Loveill, Interspersed with many Real Amours of the Modern Polite World* (1750), attributed to Dr John Hill.

[2] *The Life of Harriot Stuart* (1751) by Charlotte Lennox.

[3] *Famous Historie of the Seaven Champions of Christendom*, a chivalric romance by Richard Johnson, first published in 1597.

[4] Besides mentioning her library, Mrs Lennox castigates Lady Isabella for promising court favours and failing to perform them.

Montagu, who really had (in my opinion) one of the most humane dispositions that ever appeared in the world.[5]

I was such an old fool as to weep over *Clarissa Harlowe* like any milkmaid of sixteen over the *Ballad of the Ladies Fall*.[6] To say truth, the first volume softened me by a near resemblance of my maiden days, but on the whole 'tis most miserable stuff. Miss Howe, who is called a young lady of sense and honour, is not only extreme silly, but a more vicious character than Sally Martin, whose crimes are owing at first to seduction and afterwards to necessity, while this virtuous damsel without any reason insults her mother at home and ridicules her abroad, abuses the man she marries, and is impertinent and impudent with great applause. Even that model of perfection, Clarissa, is so faulty in her behaviour as to deserve little compassion. Any girl that runs away with a young fellow without intending to marry him should be carried to Bridewell or Bedlam the next day. Yet the circumstances are so laid as to inspire tenderness, notwithstanding the low style and absurd incidents, and I look upon this and *Pamela* to be two books that will do more general mischief than the works of Lord Rochester.[7]

There is something humorous in R. *Random* that makes me believe the author is Henry Fielding.[8] I am horridly afraid I guess too well the writer of those abominable insipidities of *Cornelia, Leonora,* and *The Lady's Drawing Room*.[9]

I fancy you are now saying: "Tis a sad thing to grow old. What does my poor mama mean by troubling me with criticisms on books that nobody but herself will ever read over?' You must allow something to my solitude. I have a pleasure in writing to my dear child, and not many subjects to write upon. The adventures of people here would not at all amuse you, having no acquaintance with the persons concerned; and an account of myself would hardly gain credit after having fairly owned to you how deplorably I was misled in regard to my own health, though I have all my life been on my guard against the information conveyed by the sense of hearing – it being one of my earliest observations, the universal inclination of humankind is to be led by the ears, and I am sometimes apt to imagine that they are given to men as they are to pitchers, purposely that they may be carried about by them. This con-

---

[5] *The Life and Adventures of Joe Thompson* (1750) by Edward Kimber. (In vol. i of her copy Lady Mary wrote 'tolerable', and in vol. ii 'intolerable'.) The Duke of Montagu is eulogized as a 'godlike peer' and 'one of the greatest men that ever existed'.

[6] *Clarissa* (1747–48) by Samuel Richardson; *A Lamentable Ballad of the Ladies Fall*, a late seventeenth-century broadside.

[7] Richardson's *Pamela* (1740) had swept Europe. John Wilmot, Earl of Rochester, was a Restoration poet and libertine.

[8] Other readers besides Lady Mary attributed to Fielding *The Adventures of Roderick Random* (1748), Smollett's first important novel.

[9] The author of *The History of Cornelia* was Sarah Scott, of the other two uncertain, Lady Mary's guess was probably Sarah Fielding.

sideration should abate my wonder to see (as I do here) the most astonishing legends embraced as the most sacred truths by those who have always heard them asserted and never contradicted. They even place a merit in complying with their hearing in direct opposition to the evidence of all their other senses.

I am very much pleased with the account you give me of your father's health. I hope your own and that of your family is perfect. Give my blessing to your little ones and my compliments to Lord Bute, and think me ever your most affectionate mother,

M. Wortley

To Lady Bute

Gottolengo, 22 June 1752

My dear Child,

Since you tell me my letters (such as they are) are agreeable to you I shall for the future indulge myself in thinking upon paper when I write to you.

I cannot believe Sir John's advancement is owing to his merit, though he certainly deserves such a distinction, but I am persuaded the present disposers of such dignities are neither more clear-sighted or more disinterested than their predecessors.[1] Ever since I knew the world, Irish patents have been hung out to sale like the laced and embroidered coats in Monmouth Street,[2] and bought up by the same sort of people; I mean those who had rather wear shabby finery than no finery at all, though I don't suppose this was Sir John's case. That good creature (as the country saying is) has not a bit of pride in him. I dare swear he purchased his title for the same reason he used to purchase pictures in Italy, not because he wanted to buy, but because somebody or other wanted to sell. He hardly ever opened his mouth but to say: 'What you please, sir – at your service – your humble servant,' or some gentle expression to the same effect. It is scarce credible that with this unlimited complaisance he should draw a blow upon himself, yet it so happened that one of his own countrymen was brute enough to strike him. As it was done before many witnesses Lord Mansell heard of it, and thinking that if poor Sir John took no notice of it he would suffer daily insults of the same kind, out of pure good nature resolved to spirit him up, at least to some show of resentment, intending to make

---

[1] In 1750 Sir John Rawdon had been raised to the Irish peerage as Baron Rawdon of Moira.

[2] Where secondhand clothes were sold.

up the matter afterwards in as honourable a manner as he could for the poor patient. He represented to him very warmly that no gentleman could take a box o' th' ear. Sir John answered with great calmness: 'I know that, but this was not a box o' th' ear; it was only a slap o' th' face.' I was as well acquainted with his two first wives as the difference of our ages permitted. I fancy they have broke their hearts by being chained to such a companion.[3]

'Tis really terrible for a well-bred virtuous young woman to be confined to the conversation of the object of their contempt. There is but one thing to be done in that case, which is a method I am sure you have observed practised with success by some ladies I need not name. They associate the husband and the lap-dog, and manage so well that they make exactly the same figure in the family. My Lord and Dell tag after Madam to all indifferent places, and stay at home together whenever she goes into company where they would be troublesome.

I pity Lady F. Meadows if the Duke of Kingston marries.[4] She will then know that her mean compliances will appear as despicable to him as they do now to other people. Who would have thought that all her nice notions and pious meditations would end in being the humble companion of Madame de La Touche?[5] I do not doubt she has been forced to it by necessity, and is one proof (amongst many I have seen) of what I always thought, that nobody should trust their virtue with necessity, the force of which is never known till it is felt, and is therefore one of the first duties to avoid the temptation of it. I am not pleading for avarice, far from it. I can assure you I equally contemn Lady Caroline Brand, who can forget she was born a gentlewoman for the sake of money she did not want.[6] That is indeed the only sentiment that properly deserves the name of avarice. A prudential care of one's affairs or (to go further) a desire of being in circumstances to be useful to one's friends is not only excusable but highly laudable, never blamed but by those who would persuade others to throw away their money in hopes to pick up a share of it. The greatest declaimers for disinterestedness I ever knew have been capable of the vilest actions on the least view of profit, and the greatest instances of true generosity given by those who were regular in their expenses and superior to the vanities in fashion.

I believe you are heartily tired of my dull moralities. I confess I am in very low spirits. It is hotter weather than has been known for some

---

[3] His third wife, whom he married in 1752, was the daughter of the Earl of Huntingdon.

[4] Lady Frances, the Duke's sister, lived with him and his mistress at Thoresby. Her husband's income was less than £900 p.a.

[5] Marie Thérèse de Fontaine, illegitimate and married daughter of a Paris banker, abandoned her husband in 1736 to join the Duke in England; their liaison aroused much comment.

[6] Lady Mary's half-sister married Thomas Brand, an M.P. with settled estates worth £1,716 p.a., in January 1749; their marriage was very happy.

years, and I have got an abominable cold, which has drawn after it a troop of complaints I will not trouble you with reciting. I hope all your family are in good health. I am humble servant to Lord Bute. I give my blessing to my grandchildren and am ever your most affectionate mother,

M. Wortley

To Lady Bute

Gottolengo, 28 January 1753

Dear Child,

You have given me a great deal of satisfaction by your account of your eldest daughter. I am particularly pleased to hear she is a good arithmetician; it is the best proof of understanding. The knowledge of numbers is one of the chief distinctions between us and brutes. If there is anything in blood you may reasonable expect your children should be endowed with an uncommon share of good sense. Mr Wortley's family and mine have both produced some of the greatest men that have been born in England. I mean Admiral Sandwich, and my great-grandfather who was distinguished by the name of Wise William.[1] I have heard Lord Bute's father mentioned as an extraordinary genius (though he had not many opportunities of showing it), and his uncle the present Duke of Argyle has one of the best heads I ever knew.[2]

I will therefore speak to you as supposing Lady Mary not only capable but desirous of learning. In that case, by all means let her be indulged in it. You will tell me, I did not make it a part of your education. Your prospect was very different from hers, as you had no defect either in mind or person to hinder, and much in your circumstances to attract, the highest offers. It seemed your business to learn how to live in the world, as it is hers to know how to be easy out of it. It is the common error of builders and parents to follow some plan they think

---

[1] Edward Montagu, 1st Earl of Sandwich, was Wortley's grandfather; the Hon. William Pierrepont was a prominent politician.

[2] The 3rd Duke of Argyll, trained as a lawyer, was (in the opinion of Lady Mary's granddaughter) 'shrewd, penetrating, argumentative – an able man of business.

beautiful (and perhaps is so) without considering that nothing is beautiful that is misplaced. Hence we see so many edifices raised that the raisers can never inhabit, being too large for their fortunes. Vistas are laid open over barren heaths, and apartments contrived for a coolness very agreeable in Italy but killing in the north of Britain. Thus every woman endeavours to breed her daughter a fine lady, qualifying her for a station in which she will never appear, and at the same time incapacitating her for that retirement to which she is destined. Learning (if she has a real taste for it) will not only make her contented but happy in it. No entertainment is so cheap as reading, nor any pleasure so lasting. She will not want new fashions nor regret the loss of expensive diversions or variety of company if she can be amused with an author in her closet. To render this amusement extensive, she should be permitted to learn the languages. I have heard it lamented that boys lose so many years in mere learning of words. This is no objection to a girl, whose time is not so precious. She cannot advance herself in any profession, and has therefore more hours to spare; and as you say her memory is good she will be very agreeably employed this way.

There are two cautions to be given on this subject: first, not to think herself learned when she can read Latin or even Greek. Languages are more properly to be called vehicles of learning than learning itself, as may be observed in many schoolmasters, who though perhaps critics in grammar are the most ignorant fellows upon earth. True knowledge consists in knowing things, not words. I would wish her no further a linguist than to enable her to read books in their originals, that are often corrupted and always injured by translations. Two hours application every morning will bring this about much sooner than you can imagine, and she will have leisure enough beside to run over the English poetry, which is a more important part of a woman's education than it is generally supposed. Many a young damsel has been ruined by a fine copy of verses, which she would have laughed at if she had known it had been stolen from Mr Waller. I remember when I was a girl I saved one of my companions from destruction, who communicated to me an epistle she was quite charmed with. As she had a natural good taste she observed the lines were not so smooth as Prior's or Pope's, but had more thought and spirit than any of theirs. She was wonderfully delighted with such a demonstration of her lover's sense and passion, and not a little pleased with her own charms, that had force enough to inspire such elegancies. In the midst of this triumph I showed her they were taken from Randolph's *Poems*,[3] and the unfortunate transcriber was dismissed with the scorn he deserved. To say truth, the poor plagiary was very unlucky to fall into my hands; that author, being no longer in fashion, would have escaped anyone of less universal reading than myself. You should encourage your daughter to talk over with you what she reads, and as you are very capable of distinguishing, take care she does not mistake pert folly for wit and humour, or rhyme for poetry,

[3] Thomas Randolph, *Poems* (1638).

which are the common errors of young people, and have a train of ill consequences.

The second caution to be given her (and which is most absolutely necessary) is to conceal whatever learning she attains, with as much solicitude as she would hide crookedness or lameness. The parade of it can only serve to draw on her the envy, and consequently the most inveterate hatred of all he and she fools, which will certainly be at least three parts in four of all her acquaintance. The use of knowledge in our sex (beside the amusement of solitude) is to moderate the passions and learn to be contented with a small expense, which are the certain effects of a studious life and, it may be, preferable even to that fame which men have engrossed to themselves and will not suffer us to share. You will tell me I have not observed this rule myself, but you are mistaken; it is only inevitable accident that has given me any reputation that way. I have always carefully avoided it, and ever thought it a misfortune.

The explanation of this paragraph would occasion a long digression, which I will not trouble you with, it being my present design only to say what I think useful for the instruction of my granddaughter, which I have much at heart. If she has the same inclination (I should say passion) for learning that I was born with, history, geography, and philosophy will furnish her with materials to pass away cheerfully a longer life than is allotted to mortals. I believe there are few heads capable of making Sir Isaac Newton's calculations, but the result of them is not difficult to be understood by a moderate capacity. Do not fear this should make her affect the character of Lady ——, or Lady ——, or Mrs ——. Those women are ridiculous not because they have learning but because they have it not. One thinks herself a complete historian after reading Echard's *Roman History*,[4] another a profound philosopher having got by heart some of Pope's unintelligible essays,[5] and a third an able divine on the strength of Whitefield's sermons.[6] Thus you hear them screaming politics and controversy. It is a saying of Thucydides: Ignorance is bold, and knowledge reserved.[7] Indeed it is impossible to be far advanced in it without being more humbled by a conviction of human ignorance than elated by learning.

At the same time I recommend books I neither exclude work nor drawing. I think it as scandalous for a woman not to know how to use a needle, as for a man not to know how to use a sword. I was once extreme fond of my pencil, and it was a great mortification to me when my father turned off my master, having made a considerable progress for the short time I learned. My over-eagerness in the pursuit of it had brought a weakness on my eyes that made it necessary to leave it off, and all the advantage I got was the improvement of my hand. I see by

4 Lawrence Echard, *The Roman History* (1695–98).
5 Alexander Pope's *Essay on Man* (4 epistles: 1733–34).
6 George Whitefield, famous Methodist preacher, published many sermons.
7 'Boldness means ignorance and reflection brings hesitation'; from the *Peloponnesian War*.

hers that practice will make her a ready writer. She may attain it by serving you for a secretary when your health or affairs make it troublesome to you to write yourself, and custom will make it an agreeable amusement to her. She cannot have too many for that station of life which will probably be her fate. The ultimate end of your education was to make you a good wife (and I have the comfort to hear that you are one); hers ought to be, to make her happy in a virgin state. I will not say it is happier, but it is undoubtedly safer than any marriage. In a lottery where there is (at the lowest computation) ten thousand blanks to a prize it is the most prudent choice not to venture.[8]

I have always been so thoroughly persuaded of this truth that notwithstanding the flattering views I had for you (as I never intended you a sacrifice to my vanity) I thought I owed you the justice to lay before you all the hazards attending matrimony. You may recollect I did so in the strongest manner. Perhaps you may have more success in the instructing your daughter. She has so much company at home she will not need seeking it abroad, and will more readily take the notions you think fit to give her. As you were alone in my family, it would have been thought a great cruelty to suffer you no companions of your own age, especially having so many near relations, and I do not wonder their opinions influenced yours. I was not sorry to see you not determined on a single life, knowing it was not your father's intention, and contented myself with endeavouring to make your home so easy that you might not be in haste to leave it.

I am afraid you will think this a very long and insignificant letter. I hope the kindness of the design will excuse it, being willing to give you every proof in my power that I am your most affectionate mother,

M. Wortley

[8] Lady Mary Stuart did in fact marry (Sir James Lowther) in 1761. Elsewhere Lady Mary wrote to her daughter that she was on the alert for possible suitors.

To Lady Bute

Gottolengo, 6 March 1753

I cannot help writing a sort of apology for my last letter, foreseeing that you will think it wrong, or at least Lord Bute will be extremely shocked at the proposal of a learned education for daughters, which the generality of men believe as great a profanation as the clergy would do if the laity should presume to exercise the functions of the priesthood. I desire you would take notice I would not have learning enjoined them as a task, but permitted as a pleasure if their genius leads them naturally to it. I look upon my granddaughters as a sort of lay nuns. Destiny may have laid up other things for them, but they have no reason to expect to pass their time otherwise than their aunts do at present,[1] and I know by experience it is in the power of study not only to make solitude tolerable but agreeable. I have now lived almost seven years in a stricter retirement than yours in the Isle of Bute,[2] and can assure you I have never had half an hour heavy on my hands for want of something to do.

Whoever will cultivate their own mind will find full employment. Every virtue does not only require great care in the planting, but as much daily solicitude in cherishing as exotic fruits and flowers; the vices and passions (which I am afraid are the natural product of the soil) demand perpetual weeding. Add to this the search after knowledge (every branch of which is entertaining), and the longest life is too short for the pursuit of it, which, though in some regards confined to very strait limits, leaves still a vast variety of amusements to those capable of tasting them, which is utterly impossible for those that are blinded by prejudices, which are the certain effect of an ignorant education. My own was one of the worst in the world, being exactly the same as Clarissa Harlowe's, her pious Mrs Norton so perfectly resembling my governess (who had been nurse to my mother) I could almost fancy the author was acquainted with her. She took so much pains from my infancy to fill my head with superstitious tales and false notions, it was none of her fault I am not at this day afraid of witches and hobgoblins, or turned Methodist.

Almost all girls are bred after this manner. I believe you are the only woman (perhaps I might say person) that never was either frighted or cheated into anything by your parents. I can truly affirm I never deceived anybody in my life excepting (which I confess has often happened undesignedly) by speaking plainly. As Earl Stanhope used to say (during his ministry), he always imposed on the foreign ministers by telling them the naked truth,[3] which, as they thought impossible to come from the mouth of a statesman, they never failed to write informations to their respective courts directly contrary to the assurances he gave them, most people confounding the ideas of sense and cunning, though there are really no two things in nature more opposite. It is in part from this false reasoning, the unjust custom prevails of debarring our sex from the advantages of learning, the men fancying the improvement of our understandings would only furnish us with more art to deceive them, which is directly contrary to the truth. Fools are always enterprising, not seeing the difficulties of deceit or the ill consequences

[1] Lord Bute's four sisters, all married, apparently lived in the country.
[2] Because of their small means, the Butes had lived on the Isle of Bute for ten years after their marriage in 1736.
[3] Stanhope, Secretary of State from 1714 to 1721, was noted for his frank, open manner.

of detection. I could give many examples of ladies whose ill conduct has been very notorious, which has been owing to that ignorance which has exposed them to idleness, which is justly called the mother of mischief.

There is nothing so like the education of a woman of quality as that of a prince. They are taught to dance and the exterior part of what is called good breeding, which if they attain they are extraordinary creatures in their kind, and have all the accomplishments required by their directors. The same characters are formed by the same lessons, which inclines me to think (if I dare say it) that nature has not placed us in an inferior rank to men, no more than the females of other animals, where we see no distinction of capacity, though I am persuaded if there was a commonwealth of rational horses (as Doctor Swift has supposed) it would be an established maxim amongst them that a mare could not be taught to pace. I could add a great deal on this subject, but I am not now endeavouring to remove the prejudices of mankind. My only design is to point out to my granddaughters the method of being contented with that retreat to which probably their circumstances will oblige them, and which is perhaps preferable to all the show of public life. It has always been my inclination. Lady Stafford (who knew me better than anybody else in the world, both from her own just discernment, and my heart being ever as open to her as myself) used to tell me my true vocation was a monastery, and I now find by experience more sincere pleasures with my books and garden than all the flutter of a court could give me.

If you follow my advice in relation to Lady Mary, my correspondence may be of use to her, and I shall very willingly give her those instructions that may be necessary in the pursuit of her studies. Before her age I was in the most regular commerce with my grandmother, though the difference of our time of life was much greater, she being past forty-five when she married my grandfather. She died at ninety-six, retaining to the last the vivacity and clearness of her understanding, which was very uncommon.[4] You cannot remember her, being then in your nurse's arms. I conclude with repeating to you, I only recommend but am far from commanding, which I think I have no right to do. I tell you my sentiments because you desired to know them, and hope you will receive them with some partiality as coming from your most affectionate mother,

M. Wortley

I have asked you over and over if you have received my letter to my sister Mar.[5]

---

[4] Lady Denbigh, who died in 1719, was the second wife of Lady Mary's maternal grandfather, and actually her step-grandmother.

[5] Lady Mar, who had been mentally ill since 1727, lived in the country in her daughter's care.

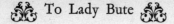

Gottolengo, 3 June 1753

My dear Child,

Y̲ou see I was not mistaken in supposing we should have disputes concerning your daughters if we were together, since we
can differ even at this distance. The sort of learning that I recommended
is not so expensive, either of time or money, as dancing, and in my
opinion likely to be of much more use to Lady Mary, if her memory and
apprehension are what you represented them to me. However, everyone has a right to educate their children after their own way, and I shall
speak no more on that subject.

I was so much pleased with the character you gave her that had there
been any possibility of her undertaking so long a journey I should certainly have asked for her, and I think out of such a number you might
have spared her. I own my affection prevailed over my judgment in this
thought, since nothing can be more imprudent than undertaking the
management of another's child. I verily believe that had I carried six
daughters out of England with me I could have disposed of them all
advantageously. The winter I passed at Rome there was an unusual concourse of English, many of them with great estates, and their own
masters. As they had no admittance to the Roman ladies nor understood
the language they had no way of passing their evenings but in my apartment, where I had always a full drawing-room. Their governors encouraged their assiduities as much as they could, finding I gave them
lessons of economy and good conduct, and my authority was so great
it was a common threat amongst them: 'I'll tell Lady Mary what you
say –.' I was judge of all their disputes, and my decisions always submitted to. While I stayed there was neither gaming, drinking, quarrelling, or keeping. The Abbé Grant (a very honest, good-natured North
Briton, who has resided several years at Rome)[1] was so much amazed at
this uncommon regularity, he would have made me believe I was bound
in conscience to pass my life there for the good of my countrymen. I can
assure you my vanity was not at all raised by this influence over them,
knowing very well that had Lady Charlotte de Roucy been in my place
it would have been the same thing.[2] There is that general emulation in
mankind, I am fully persuaded if a dozen young fellows bred a bear
amongst them and saw no other creature they would everyday fall out
for the bear's favours, and be extremely flattered by any mark of distinction shown by that ugly animal.

Since my last return to Italy (which is now near seven years) I have
lived in a solitude not unlike that of Robinson Crusoe. Excepting my

---

[1] Abbé Peter Grant, who represented the Scottish Mission in Rome for forty-
six years, was popular in all circles there.

[2] A French Protestant refugee at the English Court who (Hervey wrote) was a
miserable, boring drudge.

short trips to Lovere my whole time is spent in my closet and garden, without regretting any conversation but that of my own family. The study of simples is a new amusement to me. I have no correspondence with anybody at London but yourself and your father (whom I have not heard from of a long time). I am much mortified that the post (or perhaps my own servants) take so little care of my letters. By your account there are at least four of mine lost, and some of yours. I have only received a few lines from you since you lay in, till this morning. I have often asked you if you have had the letter I enclosed for my sister Mar. I have wrote to Lord Bute and to my goddaughter, of which you take no notice, which makes me fear they have miscarried. My best wishes attend you and yours, being with great truth your most affectionate mother,

M. Wortley

To Lady Bute

Gottolengo, 23 July 1753

My dear Child,

I have just received two letters from you (though the dates are a month distant). The death of Lady Caroline naturally raises the mortifying reflection on how slender a thread hangs all wordly prosperity. I cannot say I am otherwise much touched at it. It is true she was my sister as it were, and in some sense, but her behaviour to me never gave me any love, nor her general conduct any esteem. I own I cannot forgive her dishonouring her family by her mean marriage. It may be you will call this an old-fashioned way of thinking. The confounding of all ranks and making a jest of order has long been growing in England, and I perceive, by the books you sent me, has made a very considerable progress. The heroes and heroines of the age are cobblers and kitchen wenches. Perhaps you will say I should not take my ideas of the manners of the times from such trifling authors, but it is more truly to be found amongst them than from any historian. As they write merely to get money they always fall into the notions that are most acceptable to the present taste. It has long been the endeavour of our English writers to represent people of quality as the vilest and silliest part of the nation. Being (generally) very low-born themselves, I am not surprised at their propagating this doctrine, but I am much mistaken if this levelling principle does not one day or other break out in fatal consequences to the public, as it has already done in many private families.

You will think I am influenced by living under an aristocratic government, where distinction of rank is carried to a very great height, but I can assure you my opinion is founded on reflection and experience, and I wish to God I had always thought in the same manner. Though I had ever the utmost contempt for misalliances, yet the silly prejudices of my education had taught me to believe I was to treat nobody as an inferior, and that poverty was a degree of merit. This imaginary humility has made me admit many familiar acquaintance of which I have heartily repented every one; and the greatest examples I have known of honour and integrity has been amongst those of the highest birth and fortunes. There are many reasons why it should be so, which I will not trouble you with. If my letter was to be published I know I should be railed at for pride, and called an enemy of the poor, but I take a pleasure in telling you my real thoughts. I would willingly establish the most intimate friendship between us, and I am sure no proof of it shall ever be wanting on my side.

I am sorry for the untimely death of poor Lord Cornbury.[1] He had certainly a very good heart; I have often thought it great pity it was not under the direction of a better head. I had lost his favour sometime before I left England, on a pleasant account. He comes to me one morning with a hat full of paper, which he desired me to peruse and tell him my sincere opinion. I trembled at the proposition, foreseeing the inevitable consequence of this confidence. However, I was not so barbarous to tell him that his verses were extreme stupid (as, God knows, they were) and that he was no more inspired with the spirit of poetry than that of prophecy. I contented myself with representing to him (in the mildest terms) that it was not the business of a man of quality to turn author, and that he should confine himself to the applause of his friends and by no means venture on the press. He seemed to take this advice with good humour, promised to follow it, and we parted without any dispute. But alas, he could not help showing his performance to better judges, who with their usual candour and good nature earnestly exhorted him to oblige the world with this instructive piece, which was soon after published and had the success I expected from it; and Pope persuaded him (poor soul!) that my declaiming against it occasioned the ill reception it met with,[2] though this is the first time I ever mentioned it in my life, and I did not so much as guess the reason I heard of him no more till a few days before I left London. I accidentally said to one of his acquaintance his visits to me were at an end, I knew not why; and I was let into this weighty secret. My journey prevented all explanation between us, and perhaps I should not have thought it worth any if I had stayed.

I am not surprised he has left nothing to the Duchess of Queensbury,[3]

---

[1] Heir of the Earl of Clarendon, he died at the age of forty-three.
[2] When Pope received Cornbury's commendatory verses on his *Essay on Man* he thought them 'fine', and printed them in the 1739 edition of his works.
[3] His sister.

knowing he had no value for her, though I never heard him name her, but he was of that species of mankind who without designing it discover all they think to any observer that converses with them. His desire of fixing his name to a certain quantity of wall is one instance (amongst thousands) of the passion men have for perpetuating their memory.[4] This weakness (I call every sentiment so, that cannot be defended by reason) is so universal it may be looked on as instinct; and as no instinct is implanted but to some purpose I could almost incline to an opinion which was professed by several of the Fathers, and adopted by some of the best French divines, that the punishment of the next life consists not only in the continuance but the redoubling our attachment for this, in a more intense manner than we can now have any notion of. These reflections would carry me very far. For your comfort my paper is at an end, and I have scarce room to tell you a truth which admits of no doubt, that I am your most affectionate mother,

M. Wortley

My compliments to Lord Bute, and blessing to my grandchildren. I have wrote to Lady Mary. Have you received that addressed to my sister Mar?

[4] He is buried in Westminster Abbey.

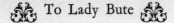

To Lady Bute

This letter will be very dull or very peevish (perhaps both). I am at present much out of humour, being on the edge of a quarrel with my friend and patron the Cardinal.[1] He is really a good-natured and generous man, and spends his vast revenue in (what he thinks) the service of his country. Beside contributing largely to the building a new cathedral, which (when finished) will stand in the first rank of fine churches (where he has already the comfort of seeing his own *busto* finely done both within and without), he has founded a magnificent college for one hundred scholars, which I don't doubt he will endow very nobly, and greatly enlarged and embellished his episcopal palace. He has joined to it a public library, which when I saw it was a very beautiful room. It is now finished and furnished, and open twice in a week with proper attendance.

Yesterday here arrived one of his chief chaplains, with a long compliment which concluded with desiring I would send him my works. Having dedicated one of his cases to English books, he intended my labours should appear in the most conspicuous place. I was struck dumb for some time with this astonishing request. When I recovered my vexatious surprise (foreseeing the consequence) I made answer, I was highly sensible of the honour designed me, but upon my word I had never printed a single line in my life. I was answered in a cold tone, his Eminence could send for them to England but they would be a long time coming and with some hazard, and that he had flattered himself I would not refuse him such a favour, and I need not be ashamed of seeing my name in a collection where he admitted none but the most eminent authors. It was to no purpose to endeavour to convince him. He would not stay dinner, though earnestly invited, and went away with the air of one that thought he had reason to be offended. I know his master will have the same sentiments, and I shall pass in his opinion for a monster of ingratitude, while 'tis the blackest of vices in my opinion, and of which I am utterly incapable. I really could cry for vexation.

Sure nobody ever had such various provocations to print as myself. I have seen things I have wrote so mangled and falsified I have scarce known them. I have seen poems I never read published with my name at length, and others that were truly and singly wrote by me, printed under the names of others. I have made myself easy under all these mortifications by the reflection I did not deserve them, having never aimed at the vanity of popular applause; but I own my philosophy is not proof against losing a friend, and, it may be, making an enemy of one to whom I am obliged.

I confess I have often been complimented (since I have been in Italy)

---

[1] Angelo Maria Querini, Bishop of Brescia and Librarian of the Vatican.

on the books I have given the public. I used at first to deny it with some warmth, but finding I persuaded nobody I have of late contented myself with laughing whenever I heard it mentioned, knowing the character of a learned woman is far from being ridiculous in this country, the greatest families being proud of having produced female writers, and a Milanese lady being now professor of mathematics in the University of Bologna, invited thither by a most obliging letter wrote by the present Pope, who desired her to accept of the chair not as a recompense for her merit but to do honour to a town which is under his protection.[2]

To say truth, there is no part of the world where our sex is treated with so much contempt as in England. I do not complain of men for having engrossed the government. In excluding us from all degrees of power they preserve us from many fatigues, many dangers, and perhaps many crimes. The small proportion of authority that has fallen to my share (only over a few children and servants) has always been a burden and never a pleasure, and I believe everyone finds it so who acts from a maxim (I think an indispensable duty) that whoever is under my power is under my protection. Those who find a joy in inflicting hardships and seeing objects of misery may have other sensations, but I have always thought corrections (even when necessary) as painful to the giver as to the sufferer, and am therefore very well satisfied with the state of subjection we are placed in.

But I think it the highest injustice to be debarred the entertainment of my closet, and that the same studies which raise the character of a man should hurt that of a woman. We are educated in the grossest ignorance, and no art omitted to stifle our natural reason; if some few get above their nurses' instructions, our knowledge must rest concealed and be as useless to the world as gold in the mine. I am now speaking according to our English notions, which may wear out (some ages hence) along with others equally absurd. It appears to me the strongest proof of a clear understanding in Longinus (in every light acknowledged one of the greatest men amongst the ancients) when I find him so far superior to vulgar prejudices as to choose his two examples of fine writing from a Jew (at that time the most despised people upon earth) and a woman.[3] Our modern wits would be so far from quoting, they would scarce own they had read the works of such contemptible creatures, though perhaps they would condescend to steal from them at the same time they declared they were below their notice.

This subject is apt to run away with me; I will trouble you with no more of it. My compliments to Lord Bute and blessing to all yours, which are truly dear to your most affectionate mother,

M. Wortley

[2] Maria Gaetana Agnesi, who published *Instituzioni analitiche* in 1748, was invited to the university post by Benedict XIV in 1750.
[3] Longinus, in *On the Sublime*, mentions Moses and Sappho as writers of the sublime.

Gottolengo, 30 November [?1753]

My dear Child,

I received your agreeable letter of Sept. 24 yesterday, Nov. 29, and am very glad our daughter (for I think she belongs to us both) turns out so much to your satisfaction; may she ever do so. I hope she has by this time received my token. I am afraid I have lost some of your letters. In last April you wrote me word the box directed to me was to set out in a week's time. Since that I have had no news of it, and apprehend very much that the bill which I suppose you sent me has miscarried. If so, I am in danger of losing the cargo.

You please me extremely in saying my letters are of any entertainment to you. I would contribute to your happiness in every shape I can, but in my solitude there are so few subjects present themselves, it is not easy to find one that would amuse you, though as I believe you have some leisure hours at Kenwood, when anything new is welcome, I will venture to tell you a small history in which I had some share.

I have already informed you of the divisions and subdivisions of estates in this country, by which you will imagine there is a numerous gentry of great names and little fortunes. Six of those families inhabit this town. You may fancy this forms a sort of society, but far from it, as there is not one of them that does not think (for some reason or other) they are far superior to all the rest. There is such a settled aversion amongst them, they avoid one another with the utmost care, and hardly ever meet except by chance at the castle (as they call my house), where their regard for me obliges them to behave civilly, but it is with an affected coldness that is downright disagreeable, and hinders me from seeing any of them often.

I was quietly reading in my closet when I was interrupted by the chambermaid of the Signora Laura Bono, who flung herself at my feet, and in an agony of sobs and tears begged me for the love of the Holy Madonna to hasten to her master's house, where the two brothers would certainly murder one another if my presence did not stop their fury. I was very much surprised, having always heard them spoke of as a pattern of fraternal union. However, I made all possible speed thither, without staying for hoods or attendance. I was soon there (the house touching my garden wall) and was directed to the bedchamber by the noise of oaths and execrations, but on opening the door was astonished to a degree you may better guess than I describe, by seeing the Signora Laura prostrate on the ground, melting in tears, and her husband standing with a drawn stiletto in his hand, swearing she should never see tomorrow's sun. I was soon let into the secret.

The good man, having business of consequence at Brescia, went thither early in the morning, but as he expected his chief tenant to pay his rent that day, he left orders with his wife that if the farmer (who lived two mile off) came himself or sent any of his sons, she should take care to make him very welcome, She obeyed him with great punctuality. The money coming in the hand of a handsome lad of eighteen she did not only admit him to her own table and produced the best wine in the cellar, but resolved to give him *chère entière*. While she was exercising this generous hospitality, the husband met midway the gentleman he intended to visit, who was posting to another side of the country. They agreed on another appointment, and he returned to his own house, where, giving his horse to be led round to the stable by the servant that accompanied him, he opened his door with the *passe-partout* key, and proceeded to his chamber without meeting anybody, where he found his beloved spouse asleep on the bed with her gallant. The opening of the door waked them. The young fellow immediately leaped out of the window, which looked into the garden and was open (it being summer), and escaped over the fields, leaving his breeches on a chair by the bedside, a very striking circumstance. In short, the case was such I do not think the Queen of the Fairies herself could have found an excuse, though Chaucer tells us she has made a solemn promise to leave none of her sex unfurnished with one, to all eternity.[1] As to the poor criminal, she had nothing to say for herself but what I dare swear you will hear from your youngest daughter if ever you catch her stealing of sweet-meats: pray, pray, she would do so no more, and indeed it was the first time.

This last article found no credit with me. I can not be persuaded that any woman who had lived virtuous till forty (for such was her age) could suddenly be endowed with such consummate impudence to solicit a youth at first sight, there being no probability, his age and station considered, that he would have made any attempt of that kind. I must confess I was wicked enough to think the unblemished reputation she had hitherto maintained, and did not fail to put us in mind of, was owing to a series of such frolics; and to say truth, they are the only *amours* that can reasonably hope to remain undiscovered. Ladies that can resolve to make love thus *ex tempore* may pass unobserved, especially if they can content themselves with low life, where fear may oblige their favourites to secrecy. There wants only a very lewd constitution, a very bad heart, and a moderate understanding to make this conduct easy, and I do not doubt it has been practised by many prudes beside her I am now speaking of.

You may be sure I did not communicate these reflections. The first word I spoke was to desire Signor Carlo to sheathe his poniard, not being pleased with its glittering. He did so very readily, begging my pardon for not having done it on my first appearance, saying he did not know what he did; and indeed he had the countenance and gesture of a man distracted. I did not endeavour a defence that seemed to me impossible, but represented to him as well as I could the crime of a murder which, if he could justify before men, was still a crying sin before God,

---

[1] In the Merchant's Tale of the *Canterbury Tales*.

the disgrace he would bring on himself and posterity, and irreparable injury he would do his eldest daughter (a pretty girl of fifteen, that I knew he was extreme fond of). I added that if he thought it proper to part from his lady he might easily find a pretext for it some months hence, and that it was as much his interest as hers to conceal this affair from the knowledge of the world. I could not presently make him taste these reasons, and was forced to stay there near five hours (almost from five to ten at night) before I durst leave them together, which I would not do till he had sworn in the most serious manner he would make no future attempt on her life. I was content with his oath, knowing him to be very devout, and found I was not mistaken.

How the matter was made up between them afterwards I know not, but 'tis now two year since it happened, and all appearances remaining as if it had never been. The secret is in very few hands; his brother, being at that time at Brescia, I believe knows nothing of it to this day. The chambermaid and myself have preserved the strictest silence; and the lady retains the satisfaction of insulting all her acquaintance on the foundation of a spotless character that only she can boast in the parish, where she is most heartily hated, from these airs of impertinent virtue, and another very essential reason, being the best dressed woman amongst them, though one of the plainest in her figure.

The discretion of the chambermaid in fetching me, which possibly saved her mistress's life, and her taciturnity since, I fancy appears very remarkable to you, and is what would certainly never happen in England. The first part of her behaviour deserves great praise, coming of her own accord and inventing so decent an excuse for her admittance; but her silence may be attributed to her knowing very well that any servant that presumes to talk of his master will most certainly be incapable of talking at all in a short time, their lives being entirely in the power of their superiors. I do not mean by law but by custom, which has full as much force. If one of them was killed it would either never be inquired into at all or very slightly passed over; yet it seldom happens and I know no instance of it, which I think is owing to the great submission of domestics, who are sensible of their dependence, and the national temper not being hasty and never enflamed by wine, drunkness being a vice abandoned to the vulgar and spoke of with greater detestation than murder, which is mentioned with as little concern as a drinking bout in England, and is almost as frequent. It was extreme shocking to me at my first coming, and still gives me a sort of horror, though custom has in some degree familiarized it to my imagination. Robbery would be pursued with great vivacity and punished with the utmost rigour, therefore is very rare, though stealing is in daily practice; but as all the peasants are suffered the use of firearms the slightest provocation is sufficient to shoot, and they see one of their own species lie dead before them with as little remorse as a hare or a partridge, and when revenge spurs them on, with much more pleasure. A dissertation on this subject would engage me in a discourse not proper for the post.

My compliments to Lord Bute. His kindness to you ought to obtain the friendship of all that love you. My blessing to your little ones. Think of me as ever your most affectionate mother,

M. Wortley

Have you received my letter to my sister Mar?

🎔 To Lady Bute 🎔

Lovere, 23 June 1754

Soon after I wrote my last letter to my dear child, I was seized with so violent a fever, accompanied with so many bad symptoms, my life was despaired of by the physician of Gottolengo, and I prepared myself for death with as much resignation as that circumstance admits. Some of my neighbours (without my knowledge) sent express for the doctor of this place (whom I have mentioned to you formerly as having uncommon secrets). I was surprised to see him at my bedside. He declared me in great danger but did not doubt my recovery if I was wholly under his care, and his first prescription was transporting me hither. The other physician asserted positively I should die on the road. It has always been my opinion that it is a matter of the utmost indifference where we expire, and I consented to be removed. My bed was placed on a brancard, my servants followed in chaises, and in this equipage I set out. I bore the first day's journey of fifteen mile without any visible alteration. The doctor said as I was not worse I was certainly better, and the next day proceeded twenty mile to Iseo, which is at the head of this lake. I lay each night at noblemen's houses which were empty. My cook, with my physician, always preceded two or three hours, and I found my chamber and all necessaries ready prepared with the exactest attention. I was put into a bark in my litter bed, and in three hours arrived here. My spirits were not at all wasted (I think rather raised) by the fatigue of my journey.

I drank the water next morning, and with a few doses of my physician's prescription, in three days found myself in perfect health, which appeared almost a miracle to all that saw me. You may imagine I am willing to submit to the orders of one that I must acknowledge the instrument of saving my life, though they are not entirely conformable to my will and pleasure. He has sentenced me to a long continuance here, which (he says) is absolutely necessary for the confirmation of my health, and would persuade me that my illness has been wholly owing to my omission of drinking the waters these two years past. I dare not contradict him, and must own he deserves (from the various surprising cures I have seen) the name, given him in this country, of the miraculous man.

Both his character and practice are so singular I cannot forbear giving you some account of them. He will not permit his patients to have either surgeon or apothecary. He performs all the operations of the first with great dexterity, and whatever compounds he gives, he makes in his own house. Those are very few, the juice of herbs and these waters being commonly his sole prescriptions. He has very little learning, and professes drawing all his knowledge from experience, which he possesses perhaps in a greater degree than any other mortal, being the seventh doctor of his family in a direct line. His forefathers have all of them left journals and registers solely for the use of their posterity, none of them having published anything, and he has recourse to these manuscripts on every difficult case, the veracity of which (at least) is unquestionable. His vivacity is prodigious, and he is indefatigable in his industry, but what most distinguishes him is a disinterestedness I never saw in any other. He is as regular in his attendance on the poorest peasant, from whom he never can receive one farthing, as on the richest of the nobility; and whenever he is wanted will climb three of four mile in the mountains, in the hottest sun or heaviest rain, where a horse cannot go, to arrive at a cottage where, if their condition requires it, he does not only give them advice and medicines gratis, but bread, wine, and whatever is needful. There never passes a week without one or more of these expeditions. His last visit is generally to me. I often see him as dirty and tired as a foot-post, having eat nothing all day but a roll or two that he carries in his pocket, yet blest with such a perpetual flow of spirits, he is always gay to a degree above cheerfulness. There is a peculiarity in this character that I hope will incline you to forgive my drawing it.

I have already described to you this extraordinary spot of earth, which is almost unknown to the rest of the world, and indeed does not seem to be destined by nature to be inhabited by human creatures, and I believe would never have been so without the cruel civil war between the Guelphs and Ghibellines. Before that time here was only the huts of a few fishermen, who came at certain seasons on account of the fine fish with which this lake abounds, particularly trouts as large and red as salmon. The lake itself is different from any other I ever saw or read of, being the colour of the sea, rather deeper tinged with green, which convinces me that the surrounding mountains are full of minerals, and it may be, rich in mines yet undiscovered, as well as quarries of marble, from whence the churches and houses are ornamented and even the streets paved, which if polished and laid with art would look like the finest mosaic work, being a variety of beautiful colours. I ought to retract the honourable title of street, none of them being broader than an alley, and impassible for any wheel carriage except a wheelbarrow.

This town (which is the largest of twenty-five that are built on the banks of the lake) is near two mile long, in the figure of a semicircle. If it was a regular range of building it would appear magnificent, but being founded accidentally by those who sought a refuge from the violencies of those bloody times it is a mixture of shops and palaces, gardens and houses, which ascend a mile high, in a confusion which is not disagreeable. After this salutary water was found and the purity of the air experienced many people of quality chose it for their summer residence, and embellished it with several fine edifices. It was populous and flourishing till that fatal plague which overran all Europe. In the year 1626 it made a terrible ravage in this place. The poor were almost destroyed, and the rich deserted it. Since that time it has never recovered its former splendour; few of the nobility returned.

It is now only frequented during the water-drinking season, several of the ancient palaces degraded into lodging houses, and others stand empty in a ruinous condition. One of these I have bought. I see you lift up your eyes in wonder at my indiscretion. I beg you to hear my reasons before you condemn me. In my infirm state of health the unavoidable noise of a public lodging is very disagreeable, and there is no private one. Secondly and chiefly, the whole purchase is but one hundred pound, with a very pretty garden in terraces down to the water, and a court behind the house. It is founded on a rock, and the walls so thick they will probably remain as long as the earth.

It is true the apartments are in most tattered circumstances, without doors or windows. The beauty of the great salon gained my affection. It is forty-two foot in length by twenty-five, proportionably high, opening into a balcony of the same length, with marble balusters. The ceiling and flooring are in good repair, but I have been forced to the expense of covering the wall with new stucco, and the carpenter is at this minute taking measure of the windows in order to make frames for sashes. The great stairs are in such a declining way it would be a very hazardous exploit to mount them. I never intend to attempt it. The state bedchamber shall also remain for the sole use of the spiders that have taken possession of it, along with the grand cabinet and some other pieces of magnificence quite useless to me, and which would cost a great deal to make habitable. I have fitted up six rooms, with lodgings for five servants, which are all I ever will have in this place; and I am persuaded that I could make a profit if I would part with my purchase, having been very much befriended in the sale, which was by auction, the owner having died without children, and I believe he had never seen this mansion in his life, it having stood empty from the death of his grandfather. The governor bid for me, and nobody would bid against him; thus I am become a citizen of Lovere, to the great joy of the inhabitants, not (as they would pretend) from their respect for my person, but I perceive they fancy I shall attract all the travelling English; and to say truth the singularity of the place is well worth their curiosity, but as I have no correspondents I may be buried here fifty years and nobody know anything of the matter.

I received the books you were so kind to send me, three days ago, but not the china, which I would not venture amongst the precipices that lead hither. I have only had time to read Lord Orrery's work,[1] which has extremely entertained and not at all surprised me, having the honour of being acquainted with him, and know him for one of those danglers after wit who (like those after beauty) spend their time in humbly admiring, and are happy in being permitted to attend, though they are laughed at, and only encouraged to gratify the insatiate vanity of those professed wits and beauties who aim at being publicly distinguished in those characters. Dean Swift (by his Lordship's own account) was so intoxicated with the love of flattery, he sought it amongst the lowest of people and the silliest of women, and was never so well pleased with any companions as those that worshipped him while he insulted them. It is a wonderful condescension in a man of quality to offer his incense in such a crowd, and think it an honour to share a friendship with Sheridan[2] etc., especially being himself endowed with such universal merit as he displays in these letters, where he shows that he is a poet, a patriot, a philosopher, a physician, a critic, a complete scholar and most excellent moralist, shining in private life as a submissive son, a tender father, and zealous friend. His only error has been that love of learned ease, which he has indulged in a solitude which has prevented the world from being blest with such a general, minister, or admiral, being equal to any of these employments if he would have turned his talents to the use of the public. Heaven be praised, he has now drawn his pen in its service, and given an example to mankind that the most villainous actions, nay, the coarsest nonsense, are only small blemishes in a great genius.

I happen to think quite contrary. (Weak woman as I am!) I have always avoided the conversation of those who endeavour to raise an opinion of their understanding by ridiculing what both law and decency obliges them to revere, but whenever I have met with any of those bright spirits who would be smart on sacred subjects I have ever cut short their discourse by asking them if they had any lights and revelations by which they would propose new articles of faith. Nobody can deny but religion is a comfort to the distressed, a cordial to the sick, and sometimes a restraint on the wicked; therefore whoever would argue or laugh it out of the world without giving some equivalent for it ought to be treated as a common enemy. But when this language[3] comes from a churchman who enjoys large benefices and dignities from that very church he openly despises it is an object of horror for which I want a name, and can only be excused by madness, which I think the Dean was always strongly touched with. His character seems to me a parallel with that of Caligula, and had he had the same power, would have made the same use of it. That Emperor erected a temple to himself, where he was his own high priest, preferred his horse to the highest honours in the state, professed enmity to the human race, and at last

---

[1] *Remarks on the Life and Writings of Swift* (1751) by John Boyle, 5th Earl.

[2] Thomas Sheridan, schoolmaster, grandfather of the playwright.

[3] In *A Tale of a Tub* (1705).

lost his life by a nasty jest on one of his inferiors,[4] which I dare swear Swift would have made in his place.

There can be no worse picture made of the Doctor's morals than he has given us himself in the letters printed by Pope. We see him vain, trifling, ungrateful to the memory of his patron the Earl of Oxford, making a servile court where he had any interested views, and meanly abusive when they were disappointed, and as he says (in his own phrase) flying in the face of mankind in company with his adorer Pope. It is pleasant to consider that had it not been for the good nature of these very mortals they contemn these two superior beings were entitled by their birth and hereditary fortune to be only a couple of link-boys. I am of opinion their friendship would have continued though they had remained in the same kingdom. It had a very strong foundation: the love of flattery on one side and the love of money on the other.

Pope courted with the utmost assiduity all the old men from whom he could hope a legacy: the Duke of Buckingham, Lord Peterborough, Sir Godfrey Kneller, Lord Bolingbroke, Mr Wycherly, Mr Congreve, Lord Harcourt etc.,[5] and I do not doubt projected to sweep the Dean's whole inheritance if he could have persuaded him to throw up his Deanery and come die in his house; and his general preaching against money was meant to induce people to throw it away that he might pick it up. There cannot be a stronger proof of his being capable of any action for the sake of gain than publishing his literary correspondence, which lays open such a mixture of dullness and iniquity that one would imagine it visible even to his most passionate admirers if Lord Orrery did not show that smooth lines have as much influence over some people as the authority of the church in these countries, where it cannot only veil but sanctify any absurdity or villainy whatever.

It is remarkable that his lordship's family have been smatterers in wit and learning for three generations. His great-grandfather[6] has left monuments of his good taste in several rhyming tragedies and the romance of *Parthenissa*. His father begun the world by giving his name to a treatise wrote by Atterbury and his club, which gained him a great reputation,[7] but (like Sir Martin Mar-All, who would fumble with his lute when the music was over)[8] he published soon after a sad comedy

---

[4] Caligula's chief assassin was one of his guards, whom he had provoked with accusations of voluptuousness and effeminacy.

[5] Apparently his only 'legacy' from any of these friends was Peterborough's death-bed gift of a watch presented to him by the King of Sicily.

[6] Roger Boyle, 1st Earl of Orrery, was statesman and soldier as well as dramatist.

[7] Charles, 4th Earl, was assisted in his writing of *Dr Bentley's Dissertations . . . Examined* by Francis Atterbury, later Bishop of Rochester, and by George Smalridge.

[8] In Dryden's comedy *Sir Martin Mar-all*, Sir Martin pretends to serenade a lady; his servant, who supplied the real music, signals that the song is over, but 'Sir Martin continues fumbling'.

of his own, and what was worse, a dismal tragedy he had found amongst the first Earl of Orrery's papers.[9] People could easier forgive his being partial to his own silly works (as a common frailty) than the want of judgment in producing a piece that dishonoured his grandfather's memory. Thus fell into dust a fame that had made a blaze by borrowed fire. To do justice to the present lord, I do not doubt this fine performance is all his own, and is a public benefit if every reader has been as well diverted with it as myself. I verily believe it has contributed to the establishment of my health.

I have wrote two long letters to your father to which I have had no answer. I hope he is well. The prosperity of you and yours is the warmest wish of (my dear child) your most affectionate mother,

M. Wortley

This letter is of a horrible length. I dare not read it over. I should have told you (to justify my folly as far as I can) here is no ground rent to be paid, taxes for church and poor, or any imposition whatever on houses.

I desire in your next parcel you would send me *Lady Frail, The Adventures of G. Edwards,* and *The Life of Lord Stair,*[10] which I suppose very superficial and partly fictitious, but as he was my acquaintance I have some curiosity to see how he is represented.

[9] The 4th Earl wrote a comedy, *As You Find It,* and produced *Altemira* by his grandfather the 1st Earl.

[10] *The Adventures of Lady Frail* (1751) and *The Adventures of Mr George Edwards, A Creole* (1751) were both by Dr John Hill. *The Life of John, Earl of Stair* by Andrew Henderson was published in 1748, a year after Stair's death.

Lovere, 23 July 1754

My dear Child,

I have promised you some remarks on all the books I have received. I believe you would easily forgive my not keeping my word; however, I shall go on. The *Rambler* is certainly a strong misnomer. He always plods in the beaten road of his predecessors, following the *Spectator* (with the same pace a pack-horse would do a hunter) in the style that is proper to lengthen a paper. These writers may perhaps be of service to the public (which is saying a great deal in their favour). There are numbers of both sexes who never read anything but such productions, and cannot spare time from doing nothing to go through a sixpenny pamphlet. Such gentle readers may be improved by a moral hint which, though repeated over and over from generation to generation, they never heard in their lives. I should be glad to know the name of this laborious author.[1]

H. Fielding has given a true picture of himself and his first wife in the characters of Mr and Mrs Booth (some compliment to his own figure excepted) and I am persuaded several of the incidents he mentions are real matters of fact.[2] I wonder he does not perceive Tom Jones and Mr Booth are sorry scoundrels. All these sort of books have the same fault, which I cannot easily pardon, being very mischievous. They place a merit in extravagant passions, and encourage young people to hope for impossible events to draw them out of the misery they choose to plunge themselves into, expecting legacies from unknown relations, and generous benefactors to distressed virtue, as much out of nature as fairy treasures. Fielding has really a fund of true humour, and was to be pitied at his first entrance into the world, having no choice (as he said himself) but to be a hackney writer or a hackney coachman. His genius deserved a better fate, but I cannot help blaming that continued indiscretion (to give it the softest name) that has run through his life, and I am afraid still remains. I guessed R. *Random* to be his, though without his name. I cannot think *Fathom* wrote by the same hand; it is every way so much below it.[3]

Sally Fielding has mended her style in her last volume of *David Simple*, which conveys a useful moral (though she does not seem to have intended it); I mean, shows the ill consequences of not providing against casual losses, which happen to almost everybody. Mrs Orgueil's

---

[1] Samuel Johnson's *Rambler* was collected in six volumes in 1752. His authorship was generally known in London.

[2] In *Amelia* (1751). In her copy of vol. i Lady Mary wrote: 'inferior to himself, superior to most others'.

[3] *Roderick Random* (1748) and *Ferdinand Count Fathom* (1753) were by Tobias Smollett.

character is well drawn, and is frequently to be met with.[4] *TheArt of Tormenting, The Female Quixote*, and *Sir C. Goodville* are all sale work.[5] I suppose they proceed from her pen, and heartily pity her, constrained by her circumstances to seek her bread by a method I do not doubt she despises. Tell me who is that accomplished Countess she celebrates. I left no such person in London; nor can I imagine who is meant by the English Sappho mentioned in *Betsy Thoughtless*, whose adventures, and those of *Jenny Jessamy*, gave me some amusement.[6] I was better entertained by the *Valet*, who very fairly represents how you are bought and sold by your servants.[7] I am now so accustomed to another manner of treatment, it would be difficult for me to suffer them. His adventures have the uncommon merit of ending in a surprising manner.

The general want of invention which reigns amongst our writers inclines me to think it is not the natural growth of our island, which has not sun enough to warm the imagination; the press is loaded by the servile flock of imitators. (Lord Bolingbroke would have quoted Horace in this place.) Since I was born, no original has appeared excepting Congreve, and Fielding, who would I believe have approached nearer to his excellencies if not forced by necessity to publish without correction, and throw many productions into the world he would have thrown into the fire if meat could have been got without money, or money without scribbling. The greatest virtue, justice, and the most distinguishing prerogative of mankind, writing, when duly executed do honour to human nature, but when degenerated into trades are the most contemptible ways of getting bread. I am sorry not to see any more of *Peregrine Pickle*'s performances; I wish you would tell me his name.[8]

I can't forbear saying something in relation to my granddaughters, who are very near my heart. If any of them are fond of reading, I would not advise you to hinder them (chiefly because it is impossible) seeing poetry, plays or romances; but accustom them to talk over what they read, and point to them, as you are very capable of doing, the absurdity often concealed under fine expressions, where the sound is apt to engage the admiration of young people. I was so much charmed at fourteen with the dialogue of *Henry and Emma*,[9] I can say it by heart to this day, without reflecting on the monstrous folly of the story in plain prose,

---

[4] In *The Adventures of David Simple* Mrs Orgueil is a villainous, cruel, and hypocritical character. The novel ends tragically as David and his family suffer a series of misfortunes.

[5] *An Essay on the Art of Ingeniously Tormenting* (1753) by Jane Collier; *The Female Quixote: or, The Adventures of Arabella* (1752) by Charlotte Lennox; *Memoirs of Sir Charles Goodville and His Family* (1753).

[6] *The History of Miss Betsy Thoughtless* (1751) and *The History of Jemmy and Jenny Jessamy* (1753) by Eliza Haywood.

[7] *The Adventures of a Valet. Written by Himself* (1752).

[8] Tobias Smollett.

[9] By Matthew Prior; Lady Mary quoted from it frequently during and after her courtship.

where a young heiress to a fond father is represented falling in love with a fellow she had only seen as a huntsman, a falconer, and a beggar, and who confesses, without any circumstances of excuse, that he is obliged to run his country, having newly committed a murder. She ought reasonably to have supposed him (at best) a highwayman, yet the virtuous virgin resolves to run away with him to live amongst the banditti, and wait upon his trollop if she had no other way of enjoying his company. This senseless tale is, however, so well varnished with melody of words and pomp of sentiments, I am convinced it has hurt more girls than ever were injured by the lewdest poems extant.

I fear this counsel has been repeated to you before, but I have lost so many letters designed for you, I know not which you have received. If you would have me avoid this fault you must take notice of those that arrive, which you very seldom do.

My dear child, God bless you and yours. I am ever your most affectionate mother,

M. Wortley

To Lady Bute

Lovere, 8 December 1754

My dear Child,

This town is at present in a general state, to use their own expression *sotto sopra*,[1] and not only this town but the capital Bergamo, the whole province, the neighbouring Brescian, and perhaps all the Venetian dominion, occasioned by an adventure exactly resembling and, I believe, copied from *Pamela*. I know not under what constellation that foolish stuff was wrote, but it has been translated into more languages than any modern performance I ever heard of.[2] No proof of its influence was ever stronger than this present story, which in Richardson's hands would serve very well to furnish out seven or eight volumes. I shall make it as short as I can.

Here is a gentleman's family [Ardenghi] consisting of an old bachelor and his sister, who have fortune enough to live with great elegance, though without any magnificence, possessed of the esteem of

[1] Topsy-turvy.
[2] Since its publication in 1740, *Pamela* had been translated into Dutch, German, and Danish as well as French and Italian.

all their acquaintance, he being distinguished by his probity, and she by her virtue. They are not only suffered but sought by all the best company, and indeed are the most conversable, reasonable people in the place. She is an excellent housewife, and particularly remarkable for keeping her pretty house as neat as any in Holland. She appears no longer in public, being past fifty, and passes her time chiefly at home with her work, receiving few visitants.

This Signora Diana, about ten years since, saw at a monastery a girl of eight years old who came thither to beg alms for her mother. Her beauty, though covered with rags, was very observable, and gave great compassion to the charitable lady, who thought it meritorious to rescue such a modest sweetness as appeared in her face from the ruin to which her wretched circumstances exposed her. She asked her some questions, to which she answered with a natural civility that seemed surprising, and finding the head of her family (her brother) to be a cobbler who could hardly live by that trade, and her mother too old to work for her maintenance, she bid the child follow her home, and sending for her parent, proposed to her to breed the little Octavia for her servant. This was joyfully accepted, the old woman dismissed with a piece of money, and the girl remained with the Signora Diana, who bought her decent clothes and took pleasure in teaching her whatever she was capable of learning. She learned to read, write, and cast accounts, with uncommon facility, and had such a genius for work that she excelled her mistress in embroidery, point, and every operation of the needle. She grew perfectly skilled in confectionary, had a good insight into cookery, and was a great proficient in distillery. To these accomplishments, she was so handy, well-bred, humble and modest, that not only her master and mistress but everybody that frequented the house took notice of her.

She lived thus near nine years, never going out but to church. However, beauty is as difficult to conceal as light; hers begun to make a great noise. Signora Diana told me she observed an unusual concourse of peddling women that came on pretext to sell penn'orths of lace, china, etc., and several young gentlemen, very well powdered, that were perpetually walking before her door and looking up at the windows. These prognostics alarmed her prudence, and she listened very willingly to some honourable proposals that were made by many honest thriving tradesmen. She communicated them to Octavia, and told her that though she was sorry to lose so good a servant, yet she thought it right to advise her to choose a husband. The girl answered modestly that it was her duty to obey all her commands, but she found no inclination to marriage, and if she would permit her to live single she should think it a greater obligation than any other she could bestow. Signora Diana was too conscientious to force her into a state from which she could not free her, and left her to her own disposal.

However, they parted soon after. Whether (as the neighbours say) Signor Aurelio Ardenghi, her brother, looked with too much attention on the young woman or that she herself (as Diana says) desired to seek a place of more profit, she removed to Bergamo, where she soon found preferment, being strongly recommended by the Ardenghi family. She was advanced to be first waiting woman to an old Countess, who was so well pleased with her service, she desired on her death-bed Count Jeronimo Sozzi, her son, to be kind to her. He found no repugnance to this act of obedience, having distinguished the beautiful Octavia from his first sight of her, and during the six months that she had served in the house had tried every art of a fine gentleman accustomed to victories of that sort, to vanquish the virtue of this fair virgin. He has a handsome figure and has had an education uncommon in this country, having made the tour of Europe and brought from Paris all the improvements that are to be picked up there, being celebrated for his grace in dancing and skill in fencing and riding, by which he is a favourite amongst the ladies and respected by the men. Thus qualified for conquest, you may judge of his surprise at the firm yet modest resistance of this country girl, who was neither to be moved by address nor gained by liberality, nor on any terms would be prevailed on to stay as his housekeeper after the death of his mother.

She took that post in the house of an old judge, where she continued to be solicited by the emissaries of the Count's passion, and found a new persecutor in her master, who, after three months endeavour to corrupt her, offered her marriage. She chose to return to her former obscurity, and escaped from his pursuit without asking any wages, and privately returned to the Signora Diana. She threw herself at her feet, and kissing her hands begged her with tears to conceal her at least some time, if she would not accept of her service. She protested she had never been happy since she left it.

While she was making these submissions Signor Aurelio entered. She entreated his intercession on her knees, who was easily persuaded to consent she should stay with them, though his sister blamed her highly for her precipitate flight, having no reason from the age and character of her master to fear any violence, and wondered at her declining the honour he offered her. Octavia confessed that perhaps she had been too rash in her proceedings, but said that he seemed to resent her refusal in such a manner as frighted her; she hoped that after a few days' search he would think no more of her, and that she scrupled entering into the holy bands of matrimony where her heart did not sincerely accompany all the words of the ceremony. Signora Diana had nothing to say in contradiction to this pious sentiment, and her brother applauded the honesty which could not be perverted by any interest whatever. She remained concealed in their house, where she helped in the kitchen, cleaned the rooms, and redoubled her usual diligence and officiousness. Her old master came to Lovere on pretence of adjusting a lawsuit three days after and made private enquiry after her, but hearing from her mother and brother (who knew nothing of her being here) that they had never heard of her he concluded she had taken another route, and returned to Bergamo; and she continued in this retirement near a fortnight.

Last Sunday, as soon as the day was closed, arrived at Signor Aurelio's door a handsome equipage in a large bark attended by four well armed servants on horseback. An old priest stepped out of it, and desiring to speak with Signora Diana, informed her he came from the Count Jeronimo Sozzi to demand Octavia, that the Count waited for her at a village four mile from hence, where he intended to marry her, and had sent him, who was engaged to perform that divine rite, that Signora Diana might resign her to his care without any difficulty. The young damsel was called for, who entreated she might be permitted the company of another priest with whom she was acquainted. This was readily granted, and she sent for a young man that visits me very often, being remarkable for his sobriety and learning. Meanwhile a valet de chambre presented her with a box in which was a complete genteel undress for a lady. Her laced linen and fine nightgown were soon put on, and away they marched, leaving the family in a surprise not to be described.

Signor Aurelio came to drink coffee with me next morning. His first words were, he had brought me the history of *Pamela*. I said, laughing, I had been tired with it long since. He explained himself by relating this story, mixed with great resentment for Octavia's conduct. Count Jeronimo's father had been his ancient friend and patron, and this escape from his house (he said) would lay him under a suspicion of having abetted the young man's folly, and perhaps expose him to the anger of all his relations for contriving an action he would rather have died than suffered if he had known how to prevent it. I easily believed him, there appearing a latent jealousy under his affliction that showed me he envied the bridegroom's happiness at the same time he condemned his extravagance.

Yesterday noon, being Saturday, Don Joseph returned (who has got the name of Parson Williams by this expedition).[3] He relates that when the bark which carried the coach and train arrived they found the amorous Count waiting his bride on the bank of the lake. He would have proceeded immediately to the church, but she utterly refused it till they had each of them been at confession, after which the happy knot was tied by the parish priest. They continued their journey and came to their palace at Bergamo in a few hours, where everything was prepared for their reception. They received the communion next morning, and the Count declares that the lovely Octavia has brought him an inestimable portion, since he owes to her the salvation of his soul. He has renounced play, at which he had lost a great deal of time and money. She has already retrenched several superfluous servants and put his family into an exact method of economy, preserving all the splendour necessary to his rank. He has sent a letter in his own hand to her mother,

---

[3] In *Pamela* the parson tries to help the heroine escape from her would-be seducer.

inviting her to reside with them, and subscribing himself her dutiful
son; but the Countess has sent another privately by Don Joseph, in
which she advises the old woman to stay at Lovere, promising to take
care she shall want nothing, accompanied with a token of twenty sequins, which is at least nineteen more than ever she saw in her life. I
forgot to tell you that from Octavia's first serving the old lady there
came frequent charities in her name to her poor parent, which nobody
was surprised at, the lady being celebrated for pious works, and
Octavia known to be a great favourite with her. It is now discovered
that they were all sent by the generous lover, who has presented Don
Joseph very handsomely, but he has brought neither letter nor message
to the house of Ardenghi, which affords much speculation.

I am afraid you are heartily tired with this tedious tale. I will not
lengthen it with reflections; I fancy yours will be the same with mine.
All these adventures proceed from artifice on one side and weakness on
the other. An honest, open, tender mind is betrayed to ruin by the
charms that make the fortune of a designing head, which when joined
with a beautiful face can never fail of advancement, except barred by a
wise mother who locks up her daughters from view till nobody cares to
look on 'em. My poor friend the Duchess of Bolton was educated in
solitude, with some choice books, by a saint-like governess. Crammed
with virtue and good qualities she thought it impossible not to find
gratitude, though she failed to give passion, and upon this plan threw
away her estate, was despised by her husband, and laughed at by the
public. Polly, bred in an alehouse and produced on the stage, has obtained wealth and title and found the way to be esteemed.[4] So useful is
early experience; without it half of life is dissipated in correcting the
errors that we have been taught to receive as indisputable truths.

Make my compliments to Lord Bute. I am out of humour with Lady
Mary for neglecting to answer my letters. However, she shares my
blessing with her brothers and sisters. I have a little ring for Lady Jane,
but God knows when I shall have an opportunity to send it. I am ever
your truly affectionate mother,

M. Wortley

It is a long time since I have heard from your father, though I have
wrote several times.

[4] The first wife of the Duke of Bolton had been rejected by him soon after their
marriage. Lavinia Fenton, famous as the original Polly Peachum of *The
Beggar's Opera*, became his mistress, and he married her in 1751, soon after his
first wife's death. Both as mistress and wife her conduct was notably discreet.

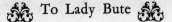

Lovere, 1 January 1755

My dear Child,

I wish you many New Years, accompanied with every blessing that can render them agreeable, and that it was in my power to send you a better New Year's gift than a dull letter. You must however accept it as well meant though ill performed. I am glad you have found a house to please you.[1] I know nothing of that part of the town you mention. I believe London would appear to me as strange as any place I have passed in my travels, and the streets as much altered as the inhabitants.

I did not know Lady H. Wentworth was married, though you speak of her children;[2] you see my total ignorance. It would be amusing to me to hear various things that are as indifferent to you as an old almanac.

I am sorry my friend Smollett loses his time in translations. He has certainly a talent for invention, though I think it flags a little in his last work. *Don Quixote* is a difficult undertaking.[3] I shall never desire to read any attempt to new dress him; though I am a mere piddler in the Spanish language I had rather take pains to understand him in the original than sleep over a stupid translation.

I thank you for your partiality in my favour. It is not my interest to rectify mistakes that are so obliging to me. To say truth, I think myself an uncommon kind of creature, being an old woman without superstition, peevishness or censoriousness. I am so far from thinking my youth was passed in an age of more virtue and sense than the present, I am of opinion the world improves every day. I confess I remember to have dressed for St James's Chapel with the same thoughts your daughters will have at the opera, but am not of the *Rambler*'s mind that the church is the proper place to make love in;[4] and the peepers behind a fan, who divided their glances between their lovers and their Prayer Book, were not at all modester than those that now laugh aloud in public walks. – I tattle on, and forget you're in town and consequently I ought to shorten my letters, knowing very well that the same letter that would be read thrice over in the country will be crammed into the pocket before 'tis half gone through when people are in a hurry to go to the Court or playhouse.

My compliments to Lord Bute and blessing to you and yours, to whom I am ever a most affectionate mother,

M. Wortley

1 Bute had moved to South Audley Street, Mayfair.
2 Married to Henry Vernon in 1743, Lady Henrietta had, in all, three sons and five daughters.
3 In calling him her friend, Lady Mary refers only to her fondness for Smollett's writings; they had never met. His translation, previously advertised, was not published until February 1755. Whether he translated it himself or plagiarized from Charles Jervas's version (1742) is disputed.
4 *The Rambler* of 19 February 1751, by Samuel Richardson.

❧ To Lady Bute ❧

Lovere, 23 January 1755

I am very sorry for your past indisposition and, to say truth, not heartily glad of your present condition;[1] but I neither do nor will admit of your excuses for your silence. I have already told you some ten or twelve times over that you should make your eldest daughter your secretary; it would be an ease to yourself and highly improving to her in every regard. You may, if you please, at once oblige your mother and instruct your daughter by only talking half an hour over your tea in a morning.

The Duchess of Queensbury's misfortune would move compassion in the hardest heart, yet all circumstances coolly considered I think the young lady deserves most to be pitied, being left in the terrible situation of a young (and I suppose) rich widowhood, which is (as I have already said of Lady M. Coke)[2] walking blindfold upon stilts amidst precipices, though perhaps as little sensible of her danger as a child of a quarter old would be in the paws of a monkey leaping on the tiles of a house.

I believe (like all others of your age) you have long been convinced there is no real happiness to be found or expected in this world. You have seen a Court near enough to know neither riches nor power can secure it, and all human endeavours after felicity are as childish as running after sparrows to lay salt on their tails; but I ought to give you another information which can only be learned by experience: that liberty is an idea equally chimerical, and has no real existence in this life. I can truly assure you I have never been so little mistress of my own time and actions as since I have lived alone. Mankind is placed in a state of dependency, not only on one another (which all are in some degree); but so many inevitable accidents thwart our designs and limit our best laid projects, the poor efforts of our utmost prudence and political schemes appear (I fancy) in the eyes of some superior beings like the pecking of a young linnet to break a wire cage or the climbing of a squirrel in a hoop. The moral needs no explanation. Let us sing as cheerfully as we can in our impenetrable confinement and crack our nuts with pleasure from the little store that is allowed us.

My old friend the Cardinal is dead of an apoplectic fit, which I am sorry for, notwithstanding the disgust that happened between us on the ridiculous account of which I gave you the history a year ago.[3] His memory will probably last as long as this province, having embellished it with so many noble structures, particularly a public library well

---

[1] Lady Bute was, her mother thought, too frequently pregnant.
[2] Lord Drumlanrig, son and heir of the Duke of Queensbury, accidentally shot himself three months after his marriage in July 1754 to Lady Elizabeth Hope. Lady Mary Coke had been separated from her husband, who died on 31 August 1753.
[3] Cardinal Querini (see above, p. 245).

furnished and richly adorned, and a college built for one hundred scholars, with salaries for masters, and plentifully endowed many charitable foundations; and so large a part of the new cathedral (which will be one of the finest churches in Lombardy) has been built at his expense he may be almost called the founder of it. He has left a considerable annuity to continue it, and deserves an eminent place amongst the few prelates that have devoted what they received from the church to the use of the public, which is not here (as in some countries) so ungrateful to overlook benefits. Many statues have been erected and medals cast to his honour, one of which has the figures of piety, learning and munificence on the reverse in the attitude of the three graces. His funeral has been celebrated by the city with all the splendour it was capable of bestowing, and waited on by all the ranks of the inhabitants.

You told me some months since that a box was made up for me. I have never had the bill of lading, and know not whether you have received the little bill of exchange sent by your most affectionate mother,

M. Wortley

🌺 To Lady Bute 🌺

Lovere, 22 September 1755

My dear Child,

I received two days ago the box of books you were so kind to send, but I can scarce say whether my pleasure or disappointment was greatest. I was much pleased to see before me a fund of amusement, but heartily vexed to find your letter consisting of only three lines and a half. Why will you not employ Lady Mary as secretary if it is troublesome to you to write? I have told you over and over, you may at the same time oblige your mother and improve your daughter, both which I should think very agreeable to yourself. You can never want something to say. The histories of your nursery, if you had no other subject to write on, would be very acceptable to me. I am such a stranger to everything in England I should be glad to hear more particulars relating to the families I am acquainted with – if Miss Liddell marries the Lord Euston I knew or his nephew who has succeeded him; if Lord Berkeley has left children,[1] and several trifles of that sort that would be a satisfaction to my curiosity.

I am sorry for Henry Fielding's death, not only as I shall read no

[1] The Lord Euston known to Lady Mary had died in 1747; Anne Liddell married his nephew in January 1756. Berkeley left four children.

more of his writings, but I believe he lost more than others, as no man enjoyed life more than he did, though few had less reason to do so, the highest of his preferment being raking in the lowest sinks of vice and misery.[2] I should think it a nobler and less nauseous employment to be one of the staff officers that conduct the nocturnal weddings. His happy constitution (even when he had, with great pains, half demolished it) made him forget everything when he was before a venison pasty or over a flask of champagne, and I am persuaded he has known more happy moments than any prince upon earth. His natural spirits gave him rapture with his cookmaid, and cheerfulness when he was fluxing in a garret.[3] There was a great similitude between his character and that of Sir Richard Steele. He had the advantage both in learning and, in my opinion, genius. They both agreed in wanting money in spite of all their friends, and would have wanted it if their hereditary lands had been as extensive as their imagination, yet each of them so formed for happiness, it is a pity they were not immortal.

I have read *The Cry*,[4] and if I would write in the style to be admired by good Lord Orrery I would tell you *The Cry* made me ready to cry, and *The Art of Tormenting* tormented me very much. I take them to be Sally Fielding's, and also *The Female Quixote*. The plan of that is pretty, but ill executed. On the contrary, the fable of *The Cry* is the most absurd I ever saw, but the sentiments generally just, and I think (if well dressed) would make a better body of ethics than Bolingbroke's. Her inventing new words that are neither more harmonious or significant than those already in use is intolerable.[5] The most edifying part of the *Journey to Lisbon* is the history of the kitten.[6] I was the more touched by it, having a few days before found one in deplorable circumstances in a neighbouring vineyard. I did not only relieve her present wants with some excellent milk, but had her put into a clean basket and brought to my own house, where she has lived ever since very comfortably.

I desire to have Fielding's posthumous works with his *Memoirs of Jonathan Wild* and *Journey to the Next World*; also the *Memoirs of Versorand, a Man of Pleasure*, and those of a young lady.[7] You will call all this trash, trumpery etc. I can assure you I was more entertained by

2. He died in October 1754 in Portugal, where he had gone for his health. He had been a Justice of the Peace for Westminster.

3. As his second wife, Fielding married Mary Daniel, described by Lady Mary's granddaughter as his first wife's maid.

4. Subtitled *A New Dramatic Fable*, a collaboration by Sarah Fielding and Jane Collier.

5. Portia, the heroine, proposes introducing three new words into the language: *turba* (angry passions), and *dextra* and *sinistra* (rightness and wrongness of mind).

6. In Fielding's *Journal of a Voyage to Lisbon* a kitten falls into the sea, and is rescued and revived, but some time later is found suffocated under a feather bed.

7. Probably *The Memoirs of a Young Lady of Quality, A Platonist* (1756), which Lady Mary asked for again in 1757 and received.

G. Edwards than H. St John, of whom you have sent me duplicates.[8] I see new story books with the same pleasure your eldest daughter does a new dress, or your youngest a new baby. I thank God I can find play-things for my age. I am not of Cowley's mind that this world is

> a dull ill acted comedy,

nor of Mrs Philips's that it is

> a too well acted tragedy.[9]

I look upon it as a very pretty farce for those that can see it in that light. I confess a severe critic that would examine by ancient rules might find many defects, but 'tis ridiculous to judge seriously of a puppet show. Those that can laugh and be diverted with absurdities are the wisest spectators, be it of writings, actions, or people.

The Stage-Coach has some grotesque figures that amuse. I place it in the rank of *Charlotte Summers,* and perhaps it is by the same author. I am pleased with *Sir Herald* for recording a generous action of the Duke of Montagu (which I know to be true, with some variation of circum-stances). You should have given me a key to *The Invisible Spy,* particu-larly to the catalogue of books in it; I know not whether the conjugal happiness of the Duke of B. is intended as a compliment or an irony.[10]

This letter is as long and as dull as any of Richardson's. I am ashamed of it, notwithstanding my maternal privilege of being tiresome.

I return many thanks to Lord Bute for the china, which I am sure I shall be very fond of, though I have not yet seen it. I send you a third bill of exchange, supposing the second, sent last June, has not reached you. In the next box put up *The History of London,*[11] and also three of Pinchbeck's watches, with shagreen cases and enamelled dial plates. When I left England they were five guineas each; I do not now know the price. Whatever it is, pray take it of Mr Samuel Child.[12] You may imagine they are for presents; one for my doctor, who is exactly Parson Adams[13] in another profession, and the other for two priests to whom I have some obligations.

---

[8] Henry St John, Lord Bolingbroke's *Letters on the Study and Use of History.*

[9] From Abraham Cowley's *The Mistress* and Katherine Philips's 'A Revery', *Poems* (1669).

[10] *The Stage-Coach: containing the character of Mr Manly and the History of his Fellow-Travellers* (1753) by Miss Smythies. In *The History of Sir Harry Herald and Sir Edward Haunch* (1754), a gentleman identified as the D—— of M–nt–g–u gives money and an army commission to a poor, worthy man. *The Invisible Spy by Exploralibus* (1755), by Eliza Haywood.

[11] Probably *The History of an Old Lady and Her Family* (1754), evidently a satire on the recent elections.

[12] Member of the banking firm, he had died in 1752.

[13] In Fielding's *Joseph Andrews.*

This Richardson is a strange fellow. I heartily despise him and eagerly read him, nay, sob over his works in a most scandalous manner. The two first tomes of *Clarissa* touched me as being very resembling to my maiden days. I find in the pictures of Sir Thomas Grandison and his lady what I have heard of my mother and seen of my father.[14]

This letter is grown (I know not how) into an immeasurable length. I answer it to my conscience as a just judgment on you for the shortness of yours. Remember my unalterable maxim: where we love we have always something to say. Consequently my pen never tires when expressing to you the thoughts of your most affectionate mother,

M. Wortley

My compliments to Lord Bute and blessing to all your dear young ones, even the last-comer.

[14] In *Sir Charles Grandison* (1753).

PART VII

❧

Venice and Home Again
1756–1762

❧

As her ultimate refuge Lady Mary chose Venice, where she had lived so agreeably fifteen years before. She resumed her friendship with Algarotti, who had retired from court life to live in Bologna. She also acquired a new and trusted friend in the elderly General William Graeme, commander of the Venetian army. To avoid the busy social life of Venice when she wished, she took a house in Padua, and passed much of her time there reading the boxloads of books and pamphlets sent from England by Lady Bute.

The felicity of her life was embittered during these years by her enmity with John Murray, British Resident in Venice. For a brief time she enjoyed the company of Sir James and Lady Frances Steuart, whom she enthusiastically befriended soon after they visited there. Her other friends were Venetians and travelling English, particularly the well-born young men on the Grand Tour whom she assessed as possible matches for her numerous granddaughters.

Her son, who had been elected to Parliament at his father's expense, could now return to England with immunity from arrest by the creditors of his considerable debts; he did not succeed, however, in persuading his parents of his reformation. In January 1761 Wortley died, leaving relatively modest annuities to Lady Mary and their son and his vast fortune to Lady Bute's second son (who was to assume the name of Wortley). In her distress and agitation at the news of her widowhood Lady Mary turned to Bute's brother, Mackenzie, recently appointed envoy to Turin. She prepared to return to England, and in September started on the long overland route. After being detained in Rotterdam by brutal weather she arrived in England at the end of January 1762, ending an expatriation of almost twenty-three years.

In London she settled down in a small house near Hanover Square that had been rented for her. Because of her own fame as well as her importance as mother-in-law of the prime minister (which Bute became in May) she led a busy life, receiving and paying visits. But she was not happy, and probably would have returned to Italy had she not been ill of breast-cancer. She died in August 1762, aged seventy-three, and was buried in Grosvenor Chapel.

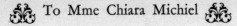

Padua, 4 November 1756

Very dear and kind Madam,

I have received with inexpressible pleasure the kind letter with which you have honoured me. I am delighted that you have done my language the honour of taking the trouble to learn it. You are endowed with a marvellous facility to learn all that you wish. I flatter myself that we have some books worthy of entertaining you, and perhaps my small library may be of some use to you. I should be very proud of that.

I am hastening to Venice to embrace you, since it is permitted.[1] As soon as I arrive, I shall not fail to pay my respects to you, and on every occasion you will find me, with an eternal devotion, madam, your very humble and obedient servant,

M. W. Montagu

I have not written in English; I am very glad, in case my letter is opened, to have people see the innocence of our correspondence. If it were known how much I hate and scorn politics I would never be suspected.

[translation]

[1] Mme Michiel had been confined to her house and denied visitors after breaking a Venetian law forbidding patricians to converse with foreign ambassadors.

❧ To Francesco Algarotti ❧

You have not yet received the insults which I sent you, and I receive from you a letter capable of calming all my anger. Here I am mollified to the point of believing myself obliged to thank you for the precious waters, which come very much apropos, after my spending the night at the Regina d'Inghilterra.[1]

You see that I plunge headlong into all the debaucheries of the carnival. I confess that I no longer have the right to make fun of monarchs who dissipate their treasures and diminish their subjects for a phantom of ambition.[2] I who dissipate my health and diminish my few remaining days pursuing a phantom of pleasure which I seek through blood and destruction, I can say to excuse myself (you know that one always believes one can find something to say in favour of one's stupidities) that pheasants and partridges are hatched to be the prey of men, that they are made for our nourishment, that they may be prepared in any sauce, and that such a short space of time is curtailed by depriving them of life that it is not worth thinking about. A hero could justify his conduct, perhaps, with more reason. He will say that the human race is born to die, and when they perish by sword or fire they escape diseases a thousand times more cruel, to which nature has destined them, not to mention the pleasure that they ought to find in dying for the glory of their master, and that among a hundred thousand one will not find ten who have not deserved the noose for their crimes. The innocent birds are created to enjoy a sweet and peaceful life, without vice or ambition. They limit their purposes to populating the woods with their posterity, and it is depriving them of a true blessing to plunge them into nothingness. I am struck with this truth, and I regard conquerors as the avengers of the beasts which are sacrificed so ruthlessly to our caprices and our lust. Is it right to look with horror on a battlefield strewn with dead bodies, and with joy on a supper for which hundreds of different species have been massacred?

If I were inclined to write I would compose an epistle in the name of all the animals to the greatest warrior of the century, to encourage him to the slaughter of these tyrants, who imagine themselves privileged to exercise the most enormous cruelty.

You will admit that debauchery inspires me to beautiful moralizing. If anyone wanted to have the thoughts after a victory that I have on leaving table, he would agree with me that friendship alone can bring happiness. Firm in this sentiment, judge what friendship I feel for you.

[*translation*]

---

[1] An elegant hotel, now called the Hotel Vittoria.
[2] Frederick the Great had invaded Saxony in 1756; the Seven Years War resulted.

To Francesco Algarotti

Venice, 12 March 1757

Farewell philosophy; here are the fine beginnings of dotage. I gave proof of it last night at the academy of M. Barbarigo in the presence of three or four hundred people. I must tell you the story. There was excellent music. Perhaps you do not know that I love music to the point of hatred. I could not listen to it with impunity; I am as sensitive as Alexander, and another Timotheus would make me run, torch in hand, to set fire to the city. But since I have not won enough battles to make my follies respected I have kept myself as distant as I could from that charming seductress, and I flattered myself that my weakness was not known. Poor human wisdom! it is your last effort; you can hide the passions, never will you succeed in exterminating them. This reflection smells terribly of Marivaux.[1]

Let us return to my story. I abandoned myself to the pleasure of listening to enchanting sounds which stir the soul, thinking mine frozen enough by time to be able to resist even the Sirens. Mademoiselle Barbarigo with her angelic face joins her voice with the instruments, the applause is deserved and general, her mother's eyes sparkle with joy. A certain Chevalier Sagramoso[2] (whom I shall hate all my life) whispers to me, out of an accursed politeness, that he had heard my daughter sing in London. A thousand pictures present themselves at the same time to my mind, the impression becomes too strong, and, fool that I am, I burst into tears, and am obliged to leave in order not to disturb the concert by my sobs. I return home, exasperated at having drawn public scorn on myself deservedly: a sentimental old woman, what a monster!

I feel this ridicule in all its force. Defend me, if you can, against the jokes which people will not fail to make. I should like still to keep a little corner in your esteem. If that is impossible, keep in mind at least that it is in your interest to save me from pitiless mockers. My friendship, which is entirely yours, would lose all value if I fall into disrepute for stupidity. You would be as imprudent to make fun of my weakness, as a painter to admit the uselessness of pictures.

[translation]

[1] Pierre de Marivaux, dramatist and novelist, whose delicate analysis and affected style are termed *marivaudage*.

[2] Ambassador to Venice from the Order of Malta.

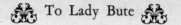

30 September 1757

My dear Child,

Lord Bute has been so obliging as to let me know your safe delivery and the birth of another daughter; may she be as meritorious in your eyes as you are in mine. I can wish nothing better to you both, though I have some reproaches to make you. Daughter, daughter, don't call names. You are always abusing my pleasures, which is what no mortal will bear. Trash, lumber, sad stuff, are the titles you give to my favourite amusements. If I called a white staff a stick of wood, and gold key gilded brass, and the ensigns of illustrious orders coloured strings, this may be philosophically true, but would be very ill received. We have all our playthings; happy are they that can be contented with those they can obtain. Those hours are spent in the wisest manner that can easiest shade the ills of life, and are the least productive of ill consequences. I think my time better employed in reading the adventures of imaginary people, than the Duchess of Marlborough's, who passed the latter years of her life in paddling with her will, and contriving schemes of plaguing some and extracting praise from others, to no purpose, eternally disappointed and eternally fretting.[1]

The active scenes are over at my age. I indulge, with all the art I can, my taste for reading. If I would confine it to valuable books, they are almost rare as valuable men. I must be content with what I can find. As I approach a second childhood I endeavour to enter into the pleasures of it. Your youngest son is, perhaps, at this very moment riding on a poker with great delight, not at all regretting that it is not a gold one, and much less wishing it an Arabian horse, which he would not know how to manage; I am reading an idle tale, not expecting wit or truth in it, and am very glad it is not metaphysics to puzzle my judgment or history to mislead my opinion. He fortifies his health by exercise, I calm my cares by oblivion. The methods may appear low to busy people, but if he improves his strength and I forget my infirmities we attain very desirable ends.

I shall be much pleased if you would send your letters in Mr Pitt's packet.[2]

I have not heard from your father of a long time. I hope he is well, because you do not mention him.

I am ever, dear child, your most affectionate mother,

M.W.M.

My compliments to Lord Bute and blessing to all yours.

[1] Sarah, Duchess of Marlborough died in 1744; twenty-six wills which she drew up still survive.
[2] William Pitt was Secretary of State for the Southern Department.

13 May 1758

It was with great pleasure I received my dear child's letter of April 15th this day, May 13th. Do not imagine I have had hard thoughts of you when I lamented your silence. I think I know your good heart too well to suspect you of any unkindness to me. In your circumstances many unavoidable accidents may hinder your writing, but having not heard from you of many months my fears for your health made me very uneasy.

I am surprised I am not oftener low spirited, considering the vexations I am exposed to by the folly of Murray. I suppose he attributes to me some of the marks of contempt he is treated with, without remembering that he was in no higher esteem before I came. I confess I have received great civilities from some friends that I made here so long ago as the year '40, but upon my honour have never named his name or heard him mentioned by any noble Venetian whatever; nor have in any shape given him the least provocation to all the low malice he has shown me, which I have overlooked as below my notice, and would not trouble you with any part of it at present if he had not invented a new persecution which may be productive of ill consequences.

Here arrived a few days ago Sir James Steuart with his lady. That name was sufficient to make me fly to wait on her. I was charmed to find a man of uncommon sense and learning, and a lady that without beauty is more amiable than the fairest of her sex. I offered them all the little good offices in my power, and invited them to supper, upon which our wise minister has discovered that I am in the interest of popery and slavery. As he has often said the same thing of Mr Pitt, it would give me no mortification if I did not apprehend that his fertile imagination may support this wise idea by such circumstances as may influence those that do not know me. It is very remarkable that after having suffered all the rage of that party at Avignon for my attachment to the present reigning family I should be accused here of favouring rebellion, when I hoped all our odious divisions were forgotten.

I return you many thanks, my dear child, for your kind intention of sending me another set of books. I am still in your debt nine shillings and send you enclosed a note on Child to pay for whatever you buy; but no more duplicates – as well as I love nonsense, I do not desire to have it twice over in the same words – no translations, no periodical papers, though I confess some of *The World* entertained me very much, particularly Lord Chesterfield, and Hory Walpole, whom I knew at Florence; but whenever I met Dodsley I wished him out of the world with all my heart.[1] The title was a very lucky one, being as you see productive of puns world without end, which is all the species of wit some people can either practise or understand.

---

[1] *The World* (1753–56) was collected in 1756 and 1757. Robert Dodsley, its publisher, wrote only one paper.

I beg you would direct the next box to me without passing through the hands of Smith. He makes so much merit of giving himself the trouble of asking for it that I am quite weary of him, beside that he imposes on me in everything. He has lately married Murray's sister, a beauteous virgin of forty, who after having refused all the peers in England because the nicety of her conscience would not permit her to give her hand when her heart was untouched, she remained without a husband till the charms of that fine gentleman Mr Smith, who is only eighty-two, determined her to change her condition.[2] In short, they are (as Lord Orrery says of Swift and company) an illustrious group, but with that I have nothing to do. I should be sorry to ruin anybody or offend a man of such strict honour as Lord Holdernesse, who like a great politician has provided for a worthless relation without any expense.[3] It has long been a maxim not to consider if a man is fit for a place, but if the place is fit for him, and we see the fruit of these Machiavellian proceedings. All I desire is that Mr Pitt would require of this noble minister to behave civilly to me, the contrary conduct being very disagreeable. I will talk further on this subject in another letter if this arrives safely. Let me have an answer as soon as possible, and think of me as your most affectionate mother,

M. Wortley

My compliments to Lord Bute and blessing to all yours, who are very near my heart.

[2] Joseph Smith had been consul since 1744. Lady Mary does not exaggerate his age.

[3] Holdernesse had been appointed Secretary of State in March, and Murray as Resident in Venice in July 1754. Murray's wife was first cousin to Holdernesse.

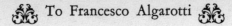

To Francesco Algarotti

I received yours by General Graeme with great pleasure, but as I am destined never to taste pleasure without a strong dash of mortification I am very sorry to find my two letters miscarried, and also the copy of the ode you desired.[1] Here is another, which I hope may reach you, notwithstanding the mountains between us. If we ever meet, the memory of Lord Hervey shall be celebrated; his gentle shade will be pleased in Elysium with our gratitude.[2] I am insensible to everything but the remembrance of those few friends that have been dear to me.

[1] Probably the 'Hymn to the Moon', which Algarotti printed as Lady Mary's accompanied by a eulogy of her abilities.
[2] Hervey had died in 1743.

To Lady Bute

Padua, 21 August 1758

I am much obliged to you (my dear child) for the concern you express for me in yours of July 10th, which I received yesterday, August 20th, but I can assure you I lose very little in not being visited by the English, boys and governors being commonly (not always) the worst company in the world. I am no other ways affected by it, [but] that it has an ill appearance in a strange country, though hitherto I have not found any bad effect from it amongst my Venetian acquaintance.

I was visited two days ago by my good friend Cavalier Antonio Mocenigo,[1] who came from Venice to present to me the elected husband of his brother's great grand-daughter, who is a noble Venetian (Signor Zeno) just of age, heir to a large fortune, and is one of the most agreeable figures I ever saw: not beautiful, but has an air of so much modesty and good sense, I could easily believe all the good Signor Antonio said of him. They came to invite me to the wedding. I could not refuse such a distinction, but hope to find some excuse before the solemnity, being unwilling to throw away money on fine clothes, which are as improper for me as an embroidered pall for a coffin, but I durst not mention age before my friend, who told me he is eighty-six. I thought him four years younger. He has all his senses perfect and is as lively as a man of thirty. It was very pleasing to see the affectionate respect of the young man and

[1] Procurator of St Mark; Lady Mary referred to him in an earlier letter as 'one of my best friends at Venice'.

the fond joy that the old one took in praising him. They would have persuaded me to return with them to Venice. I objected that my house was not ready to receive me. Signor Antonio laughed and asked me if I did not think he could give me an apartment (in truth it was very easy, having five palaces on a row on the great canal, his own being the centre, and the others inhabited by his relations). I was reduced to tell a fib (God forgive me) and pretend a pain in my head, promising to come to Venice before the marriage, which I really intend. They dined here; your health was the first drank. You may imagine I did not fail to toast the bride. She is yet in a convent, but is to be immediately released, and receive visits of congratulation on the contract till the celebration of the church ceremony, which perhaps may not be this two months, during which time the lover makes a daily visit, and never comes without a present, which custom (at least sometimes) adds to the impatience of the bridegroom and very much qualifies that of the lady.

You would find it hard to believe a relation of the magnificence, not to say extravagance, on these occasions. Indeed, it is the only one they are guilty of, their lives in general being spent in a regular handsome economy, the weddings and the creation of a procurator being the only occasions they have of displaying their wealth, which is very great in many houses, particularly this of Mocenigo, of which my friend is the present head. I may justly call him so, giving me proofs of an attachment quite uncommon at London, and certainly disinterested, since I can no way possibly be of use to him. I could tell you some strong instances of it if I did not remember you have not time to listen to my stories; and there is scarce room on my paper to assure you I am (my dear child) your most affectionate mother,

M. Wortley

Compliments to Lord Bute and blessing to all yours.

San Massimo,[1] *Padua, 4 September 1758*

My dear Lady Fanny,

I have been sometime in pain for your silence, and at last begun to fear that either some accident had befallen you or you had been so surfeited with my dullness at Padua you resolved not to be plagued with it when at a distance. These melancholy ideas growing strong upon me, I wrote to Mr Duff to inquire after your health. I have received his answer this morning; he tells me you are both well and safely arrived at Tübingen, and I take the liberty to put you in mind of one that can never forget you and the cheerful hours we have passed together. The weather favoured you according to your prayers; since that time we have had storms, tempests, pestilential blasts, and at this moment such suffocating heat the doctor[2] is sick in bed, and nobody in health in my family excepting myself and my Swiss servants, who support our constitutions by hearty eating and drinking, while the poor Italians are languishing on their salads and lemonade. I confess I am in high spirits, having succeeded in my endeavour to get a promise of assisting some very worthy people whom I am fond of. You know I am enthusiastic in my friendships.[3]

I also hear from all hands of my daughter's prosperity; you, madam, that are a mother, may judge of my pleasure in her happiness, though I have no taste for that sort of felicity. I could never endure with tolerable patience the austerities of a court life. I was saying everyday from my heart (while I was condemned to it), 'the things that I would do, those do I not, and the things I would not do, those do I daily'; and I had rather be a Sister of St Clare than lady of the bedchamber to any queen in Europe.[4] It is not age and disappointment that has given me these sentiments; you may see them in a copy of verses sent from Constantinople in my early youth to my uncle Fielding and by his (well intended) indiscretion shown about, copies taken, and at length miserably printed.[5] I own myself such a rake, I prefer liberty to chains of diamonds, and when I hold my peace (like King David) it is pain and grief to me.

> No fraud the poet's sacred breast can bear,
> Mild are our manners and our hearts sincere.

---

[1] A church in Padua; Lady Mary's house may have been in the parish.
[2] Dr Julio Moro, her secretary since 1755.
[3] Lady Mary had begun a campaign, which she pursued for the rest of her life, to assist the Steuart family by having Sir James pardoned.
[4] Lady Mary never held any Court appointment.
[5] 'Verses Written in the Chiosk at Pera', printed in Anthony Hammond's *A New Miscellany of Original Poems . . .* (1720).

Rude and unpolished in the courtier's school,
I loathe a knave and tremble at a fool.[6]

With this rusticity of manners I do not wonder to see my company avoided by all great men and fine ladies. I could tell your ladyship such a history of my calamities since we parted, you will be surprised to hear I have not despaired and died like the sick lion in Æsop's fables, who so pathetically cries out – *Bis videor mori*[7] – when he was kicked by a certain animal I will not name because it is very like a paw word.

Vale.

I desire this letter (innocent as it is) may be burnt. All my works are consecrated to the fire for fear of being put to more ignoble uses, as their betters have been before them. I beg an immediate answer.

[6] The first couplet is quoted from Congreve, the second adapted from Lord Lansdown.

[7] 'I seem to die twice.'

❧ To Lady Bute ❧

Padua, 5 September 1758

I wrote to you very lately (my dear child) in answer to that letter Mr Hamilton brought me. He was so obliging to come on purpose from Venice to deliver it, as I believe I told you. But I am so highly delighted with this, dated August 4th, giving an account of your little colony, I cannot help setting pen to paper to tell you the melancholy joy I had in reading it. You would have laughed to see the old fool weep over it.

I now find that age, when it does not harden the heart and sour the temper, naturally returns to the milky disposition of infancy. Time has the same effect on the mind as on the face; the predominant passion and the strongest feature become more conspicuous from the others' retiring. The various views of life are abandoned from want of ability to pursue them, as the fine complexion is lost in wrinkles; but as surely as a large nose grows larger and a wide mouth wider the tender child in your nursery will be a tender old woman, though perhaps reason may have restrained the appearance of it till the mind relaxed is no longer capable of concealing its weakness. For weakness it is, to indulge any attachment at a period of life when we are sure to part with life itself at a very short warning; according to the good English proverb, young people may die, but old must. You see I am very industrious in finding comfort to myself in my exile, and to guard as long as I can against the peevishness which makes age miserable in itself and contemptible to others. 'Tis surprising to me that with the most inoffensive conduct I should meet enemies, when I cannot be envied for anything, and have pretentions to nothing.

Is it possible the old Colonel Duncombe I knew should be Lord Feversham and married to a young wife?[1] As to Lord Ranelagh, I confess it must be a very bitter draught to submit to take his name, but his lady has had a short purgatory and now enjoys affluence with a man she likes and who, I am told, is a man of merit, which I suppose she thinks preferable to Lady Selina's nursery.[2]

Here are no old people in this country, neither in dress or gallantry. I know only my friend Antonio who is true to the memory of his adored lady.[3] Her picture is always in his sight, and he talks of her in the style of *Pastor Fido*.[4] I believe I owe his favour to having shown him her miniature by Rosalba[5] which I bought at London; perhaps you remember it in my little collection. He is really a man of worth and sense. Hearing it reported (I need not say by whom)[6] that my retirement was owing to having lost all my money at play at Avignon, he sent privately for my chief servant and desired him to tell him naturally if I was in any distress, and not only offered but pressed him to lay 3,000 sequins on my *toilette*. I don't believe I could borrow that sum without good security amongst my great relations. I thank God I had no occasion to make use of this generosity, but I am sure you will agree with me that I ought never to forget the obligation. I could give some other instances in which he has shown his friendship in protecting me from mortifications invented by those that ought to have assisted me, but 'tis a long tiresome story.

You will be surprised to hear the General does not yet know these circumstances. He arrived at Venice but few days before I left it, and promising me to come to Padua at the fair I thought I should have time sufficient to tell him my history. Indeed, I was in hopes he would have accepted my invitation of lodging in my house, but his multiplicity of affairs hindered him from coming at all; and 'tis only a few days since that he made me a visit in company with Mr Hamilton, before whom I did not think it proper to speak my complaints. They are now gone to drink the waters at Vicenza. When they return I intend removing to Venice, and then shall relate my grievances, which I have more reason to do than ever. I have tired you with this disagreeable subject. I will

---

[1] Anthony Duncombe was created Lord Feversham in 1747. In August 1758 he took a third wife, aged twenty-two; he was sixty-three.

[2] Selina, daughter of Peter Bathurst and Lady Selina Shirley, married Lord Ranelagh in 1748. He died in 1754; a year later she married Sir John Elwill.

[3] Antonio Mocenigo's wife had been a celebrated beauty.

[4] A pastoral play by Guarini.

[5] Rosalba Carriera, famous woman painter.

[6] Murray, British Resident.

release you and please myself in repeating the assurance of my being ever (while I have a being) your most affectionate mother,

M. Wortley

My dear child, do not think of reversing nature by making me presents. I would send you all my jewels and my *toilette* if I knew how to convey them, though they are in some measure necessary in this country, where it would be (perhaps) reported I had pawned them if they did not sometimes make their appearance. I know not how to send commissions for things I never saw; nothing of price I would have. As I would not new furnish an inn I was on the point of leaving, such is this world to me. Though china is in such high estimation here I have sometimes an inclination to desire your father to send me the two large jars that stood in the windows in Cavendish Square. I am sure he don't value them and believe they would be of no use to you. I bought them at an auction for two guineas before the Duke of Argyle's example had made all china (more or less) fashionable. My compliments to Lord Bute and blessing to our dear children.

❧ To Lady Bute ❧

Venice, 8 November 1758

My dear Child,

You are extremely good to take so much care of my trifling commissions in the midst of so many important occupations. You judge very right on the subject of Mr Walpole. I saw him often both at Florence and Genoa,[1] and you may believe I know him. I am not surprised at the character of poor Charles Fielding's sons. The epithet of fair and foolish belonged to the whole family, and as he was over-persuaded to marry an ugly woman I suppose his offspring may have lost the beauty and retained the folly in full bloom.[2] Colonel Otway, younger brother to Lady Bridget's spouse, came hither with

---

[1] Horace Walpole, in Florence 1740 and in Genoa 1741.

[2] Charles Fielding, son of 4th Earl of Denbigh, was a cousin of Lady Mary's; his two sons were William, who entered the army, and Charles, who distinguished himself in the navy.

Lord Mandeville.[3] He told me that she has a daughter with the perfect figure of Lady Winchilsea. I wish she may meet with as good friends as I was to her aunt;[4] but I won't trouble you with old stories. I have indeed my head so full of one new one that I hardly know what I say. I am advised to tell it you though I had resolved not to do it. I leave it to your prudence to act as you think proper. Commonly speaking, silence and neglect is the best answer to defamation, but this is a case so peculiar that I am persuaded it never happened to anyone but myself.

Some few months before Lord W. Hamilton married[5] there appeared a foolish song said to be wrote by a poetical great lady who I really think was the character of Lady Arabella in *The Female Quixote* (without the beauty).[6] You may imagine such a conduct at Court made her superlatively ridiculous. Lady De La Warr, a woman of great merit with whom I lived in much intimacy, showed this fine performance to me. We were very merry in supposing what answer Lord William would make to these passionate addresses. She begged me to say something for a poor man who had nothing to say for himself. I wrote extempore on the back of the song some stanzas that went perfectly well to the tune. She promised they should never appear as mine, and faithfully kept her word. By what accident they have fallen into the hands of that thing Dodsley I know not, but he has printed them as addressed by me to a very contemptible puppy, and my own words as his answer.[7]

I do not believe either Job or Socrates ever had such a provocation. You will tell me it cannot hurt me with any acquaintance I ever had, it is true, but 'tis an excellent piece of scandal for the same sort of people that propagate with success that your nurse left her estate, husband, and family to go with me to England, and then I turned her to starve after defrauding her of God knows what. I thank God witches are out of fashion, or I should expect to have it deposed by several credible witnesses that I had been seen flying through the air on a broomstick etc.

I am really sick with vexation, but ever your most affectionate mother,

M. Wortley

[3] Lady Bridget, daughter of Denbigh, married James Otway. His younger brother Francis was governor to Lord Mandeville, son and heir of the Duke of Manchester.

[4] Miss Otway's aunt, Lady Frances, was wife of the Earl of Winchilsea. Lady Mary had described her as 'really the prettiest woman in town'.

[5] In May 1733 Lord William married the future Lady Vane, who describes him rapturously in her 'Memoirs of a Lady of Quality'.

[6] Frances, Lady Hertford. In *The Female Quixote* by Charlotte Lennox, Arabella, an avid reader of romances, imagines every man she meets is in love with her.

[7] Robert Dodsley included the verses in his *Collection of Poems*, vol. vi (March 1758) entitled 'Lady Mary W——, to Sir W[illiam] Y[onge]', and under it 'Sir W—— Y——'s Answer'. Yonge, the Whig politician, had been an acquaintance of Lady Mary's in London.

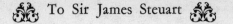

14 November 1758

This letter will be solely to you, and I desire you would not communicate it to Lady Fanny. She is the best woman in the world, and I would by no means make her uneasy; but there will be such strange things in it that the Talmud or the Revelations are not half so mysterious. What these prodigies portend, God knows; but I never should have suspected half the wonders I see before my eyes, and am convinced of the necessity of the repeal of the Witch Act (as it is commonly called).[1] I mean, to speak correctly, the tacit permission given to witches, so scandalous to all good Christians, though I tremble to think of it for my own interests. It is certain the British Islands have always been strangely addicted to this diabolical intercourse, of which I dare swear you know many instances; but since this public encouragement given to it I am afraid there will not be an old woman in the nation entirely free from suspicion. The Devil rages more powerfully than ever: you will believe me when I assure you the great and learned English minister is turned Methodist, several duels have been fought in the Place of Saint Mark for the charms of his excellent lady, and I have been seen flying in the air in the figure of Julian Cox, whose history is related with so much candour and truth by the pious pen of Joseph Glanvill, chaplain to King Charles.[2] I know you young rakes make a jest of all those things, but I think no good body can doubt of a relation so well attested. She was about seventy years old (very near my age), and the whole sworn to before Judge Archer (1663), very well worth reading but rather too long for a letter.

You know (wretch that I am), 'tis one of my wicked maxims to make the best of a bad bargain; and I have said publicly that every period of life has its privileges, and that even the most despicable creatures alive may find some pleasures. Now observe this comment: who are the most despicable creatures? Certainly, old women. What pleasure can an old woman take? Only witchcraft. I think this argument as clear as any of the devout Bishop of Cloyne's[3] metaphysics; this being decided in a full congregation of saints only such atheists as you and Lady Fanny can deny it. I own all the facts, as many witches have done before me, and go every night in a public manner astride upon a black cat to a meeting where you are suspected to appear. This last article is not sworn to, it being doubtful in what manner our clandestine midnight correspondence is carried on. Some think it treasonable, others lewd (don't tell Lady Fanny), but all agree there was something very odd and unaccountable in such sudden likings. I confess, as I said before, it is witch-

---

[1] The Witch Act punished persons convicted of witchcraft.
[2] Glanvill tells the story of Julian Cox, a woman accused of being a witch, who was executed.
[3] George Berkeley.

craft. You won't wonder I do not sign (notwithstanding all my impudence) such dangerous truths. Who knows the consequence? The Devil is said to desert his votaries.

P.S. Fribourg, who you inquire after so kindly, is turned *beau garçon* and actually kept by the finest lady in Venice; Doctor Moro robs on the highway; and Antonio sings at the opera.[4] Would you desire better witchcraft?

This to be continued.

Nota bene. You have dispossessed me of the real devils who haunted me; I mean the nine Muses.

---

[4] In this jesting passage Lady Mary refers to Fribourg, her servant, Dr Moro, her secretary, and Antonio Mocenigo, her friend and octogenarian head of a great Venetian family.

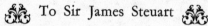

To Sir James Steuart

Venice, 13 January 1759

I have indulged myself some time with daydreams of the happiness I hoped to enjoy this summer in the conversation of Lady Fanny and Sir James Steuart, but I hear such frightful stories of precipices and hovels during the whole journey, I begin to fear there is no such pleasure allotted me in the book of fate. The Alps were once molehills in my sight when they interposed between me and the slightest inclination; now age begins to freeze, and brings with it the usual train of melancholy apprehensions. Poor humankind! We always march blindly on. The fire of youth represents to us all our wishes possible; and, that over, we fall into despondency that prevents even easy enterprises: a stove in winter, a garden in summer bounds all our desires, or at least our undertakings. If Mr Steuart would disclose all his imaginations I dare swear he has some thoughts of emulating Alexander or Demosthenes, perhaps both; nothing seems difficult at his time of life, everything at mine. I am very unwilling, but am afraid I must submit to the confinement of my boat and my easy chair, and go no farther than they can carry me. Why are our views so extensive and our power so miserably limited? This is among the mysteries which (as you justly say) will remain ever unfolded to our shallow capacities. I am much inclined to think we are no more free agents than the queen of clubs when she victoriously takes prisoner the knave of hearts, and all our efforts (when we rebel against destiny) as weak as a card that sticks to a glove when the gamester is determined to throw it on the table. Let us then (which is the only true philosophy) be contented with our chance, and make the best of that very bad bargain of being born in this vile planet, where we may find however (God be thanked!) much to laugh at though little to approve.

I confess I delight extremely in looking on men in that light. How many thousands trample under foot honour, ease and pleasure, in pursuit of ribands of certain colours, dabs of embroidery on their clothes, and gilt wood carved behind their coaches in a particular figure! others breaking their hearts till they are distinguished by the shape and colour of their hats; and, in general, all people earnestly seeking what they do not want while they neglect the real blessings in their possession – I mean the innocent gratification of their senses, which is all we can properly call our own. For my part, I will endeavour to comfort myself for the cruel disappointment I find in renouncing Tübingen by eating some fresh oysters on the table. I hope you are sitting down with dear Lady Fanny to some admirable red partridges, which I think are the growth of that country. Adieu! Live happy, and be not unmindful of your sincere distant friend, who will remember you in the tenderest manner while there is any such faculty as memory in the machine called

M. W. Montagu

🎕 To Lady Bute 🎕

Venice, 22 May 1759

My dear Child,

I am always pleased to hear from you but particularly so when I have any occasion of congratulation. I sincerely wish you joy of your infant's having gone happily through the smallpox.

I had a letter from your father before he left London. He does not give so good an account of his spirits as you do, but I hope his journeys will restore them. I am convinced nothing is so conducive to health and absolutely necessary to some constitutions. I am not surprised, as I believe you think I ought to be, at Lord Leicester's leaving his large estate to his lady, notwithstanding the contempt with which he always treated her,[1] and her real inability of managing it. I expect you should laugh at me for the exploded notion of predestination, yet I confess I am inclined to be of the opinion that nobody makes their own marriage or their own will. It is what I have often said to the Duchess of Marlborough when she has been telling me her last intentions, none of which she has performed, choosing Lord Chesterfield for her executor, whose

---

[1] For an example (when he was Mr Coke) see above, p. 125.

true character she has many times enlarged upon.[2] I could say much more to support this doctrine if it would not lengthen my letter beyond a readable size.

Building is the general weakness of old people. I have had a twitch of it myself, though certainly 'tis the highest absurdity, and as sure a proof of dotage as pink-coloured ribands, or even matrimony. Nay, perhaps there is more to be said in defence of the last – I mean in a childless old man. He may prefer a boy born in his own house, though he knows it is not his own, to disrespectful or worthless nephews or nieces. But there is no excuse for beginning an edifice he can never inhabit or probably see finished. The Duchess of Marlborough used to ridicule the vanity of it by saying one might always live upon other people's follies, yet you see she built the most ridiculous house I ever saw,[3] since it really is not habitable from the excessive damps.

So true it is, the things that we would do, those do we not, and the things we would not do, those do we daily. I feel in myself a proof of this assertion, being much against my will at Venice. Though I own it is the only great town where I can properly reside, yet here I find so many vexations that in spite of all my philosophy and (what is more powerful) my phlegm I am oftener out of humour than amongst my plants and poultry in the country. I cannot help being concerned at the success of iniquitous schemes, and grieve for oppressed merit. You, who see these things everyday, think me as unreasonable in making them matter of complaint as if I seriously lamented the change of seasons. You should consider I have lived almost a hermit ten years, and the world is as new to me as to a country girl transported from Wales to Covent Garden. I know I ought to think my lot very good, that can boast of some sincere friends amongst strangers.

Sir Wyndham Knatchbull and his governor, Mr Devismes, are at length parted.[4] I am very sorry for them both. I cannot help wishing well to the young man, who really has merit and would have been happy in a companion that sincerely loved him and studied his interest.– My letter is so long I am frighted at it myself. I never know when to end when I write to you. Forgive it, amongst the other infirmities of your affectionate mother,

M. Wortley

If my things are at sea, I am afraid they are lost. Here has been such storms these three days as never were known at this season. I shall regret nothing so much as your father's present. Perhaps my token to you is also at the bottom of the ocean. That I sent by land to Lady Mary is fallen into the French hands, as I am told.

[2] The Duchess left Chesterfield £20,000; it was notorious that she wished to reward him for his opposition to Walpole, whom she detested.

[3] Blenheim Palace, the extravagant baroque creation of Vanbrugh.

[4] Sir Wyndham Knatchbull-Wyndham and his tutor, Louis Devismes, had met Lady Mary at Padua the previous year.

To Lady Bute

My dear Child,

I have this minute received yours of May 24th. I am glad the little picture pleases Lady Mary. It is a true representation of the summer dishabille of the Venetian ladies. You have taken no notice of the box I sent by Captain Munden. If it is lost I will venture nothing more at sea.

I have had a letter from Mr Mackenzie informing me that he has sent my books. I have not yet received them but hope to have that pleasure in a short time. I could heartily wish to see Lady Betty and your brother-in-law; I fancy I have a thousand questions to ask in relation to their nephews and nieces. Whatever touches you is important to me.[1] I fear I must not expect that satisfaction; they are obliged to reside at Turin, and I cannot resolve to appear in a court, where old people always make an ill figure even when they have business there.

I am not surprised at Lady Waldegrave's good fortune; beauty has a large prerogative. Her mother's was the most remarkable I have ever heard of.[2] Being taken notice of by Mrs Secker[3] (who told it me) when she was in the humble position of sitting on a dust cart before the Bishop's door, that lady had the curiosity to call her in, merely to see her nearer, and assured me that, in all her rags and dirt, she never saw a more lovely creature. Some time after she heard she was in the hands of a Covent Garden milliner, who transferred her to Neddy Walpole, who doated on her till the day of her death.

Lord Fordwich arrived here three days ago. He made me a visit yesterday, and appears a well disposed youth. Lord Brudenell continues here and seems to have no desire of seeing his native land.[4] Here are beside a large group of English gentlemen who will all disperse in a short time. General Graeme has promised to oblige me with his company a few days, though his charge finds him so much employment it may (perhaps) be impossible for him to leave Venice. I suppose you are now at Kew, with all your rising family about you.[5] May they ever be blessings to you. I believe you that see them every day scarce think of them oftener than I do.

---

[1] Mackenzie, Bute's brother, had married his cousin Lady Betty Campbell, in 1749. He had been at Turin since November 1758 as British Envoy.

[2] Maria Walpole was the daughter of Sir Edward, 2nd son of Sir Robert Walpole, and Dorothy Clement, daughter of a postmaster in Co. Durham, who became his mistress when she was fifteen. In May 1759 Maria married Earl Waldegrave.

[3] Wife of Thomas Secker, ultimately Archbishop of Canterbury. From 1727 to 1732 he was a prebendary of Durham.

[4] Fordwich was Earl Cowper's son and heir, and Brudenell was the Earl of Cardigan's; both were on the Grand Tour.

[5] The Prince of Wales (later George III), to whom Lord Bute was Groom of the Stole, lived at Kew during the summer.

This town is at present very full of company. Though the opera is not much applauded I have not yet seen it, nor intend to break my rest for its sake; it begins about the hour I go to sleep. I continue my college hours, by which I am excluded many fashionable amusements. In recompense I have better health and spirits than many younger ladies, who pass their nights at the ridotto and their days in spleen for their losses there. Play is the general plague of Europe. I know no corner of it entirely free from the infection. I do not doubt the familiarities of the gaming table contribute very much to that decay of politeness of which you complain. The pouts and quarrels that naturally rise from disputes must put an end to all complaisance or even goodwill towards one another.

I am interrupted by a visit from Mr Hamilton. He desires me to make his compliments to you and Lord Bute. I am to you both a most affectionate mother,

M. Wortley

My hearty blessing to all yours.

To Sir James Steuart

Padua, 19 July 1759

Your letters always give me a great deal of pleasure, but particularly this, which has relieved me from the pain I was in from your silence.

I have seen the Margrave of Baden–Durlach;[1] but I hope he has forgot he has ever seen me, being at that time in a very odd situation, of which I will not give you the history at present, being a long story, and you know life is too short for a long story.

I am extremely obliged for the valuable present you intend me.[2] I believe you criticize yourself too severely on your style; I do not think that very smooth harmony is necessary in a work which has a merit of a nobler kind. I think it rather a defect, as when a Roman Emperor (as we see him sometimes represented on a French stage) is dressed like a *petit-maître*. I confess the crowd of readers look no further; the tittle-

---

[1] Steuart was a friend of the Margrave, whom Lady Mary confuses with the Prince of Baden–Durlach; she had met the Prince in 1746 when she was travelling across northern Italy and he was with the Imperial army there.

[2] Steuart's book, *Inquiry into the Principles of Political Economy*, not published until 1767.

tattle of Madame de Sévigné and the *clinquant* of *Télémaque*[3] have found admirers from that very reason. Whatever is clearly expressed is well wrote in a book of reasoning. However, I shall obey your commands in telling you my opinion with the greatest sincerity.

I am extremely glad to hear Lady Fanny has overcome her disorder; I wish I had no apprehensions of falling into it. Solitude begets whimsies; at my time of life one usually falls into those that are melancholy, though I endeavour to keep up a certain sprightly folly that (I thank God) I was born with. But alas! What can we do with all our endeavours? I am afraid we are little better than straws upon the water; we may flatter ourselves that we swim when the current carries us along.

Thus far I have dictated for the first time of my life, and perhaps it will be the last, for my amanuensis is not to be hired, and I despair of ever meeting with another. He is the first that could write as fast as I talk, and yet you see there are so many mistakes, it wants a comment longer than my letter to explain my insignificant meaning, and I have fatigued my poor eyes more with correcting it than I should have done in scribbling two sheets of paper. You will think, perhaps from this idle attempt, that I have some fluxion on my sight. No such matter; I have suffered myself to be persuaded by such sort of arguments as those by which people are induced to strict abstinence or to take physic – fear, paltry fear, founded on vapours rising from the heat, which is now excessive and has so far debilitated my miserable nerves that I submit to a present displeasure by way of precaution against a future evil that possibly may never happen. I have this to say in my excuse, that the evil is of so horrid a nature, I own I feel no philosophy that could support me under it, and no mountain girl ever trembled more at one of Whitefield's pathetic lectures[4] than I do at the word blindness, though I know all the fine things that may be said for consolation in such a case; but I know also they would not operate on my constitution.

'Why then,' say my wise monitors, 'will you persist in reading or writing seven hours in a day?'[5] – 'I am happy while I read and write.' – 'Indeed one would suffer a great deal to be happy,' say the men sneering; and the ladies wink at each other and hold up their fans. A fine lady of threescore had the goodness to add, 'At least, madam, you should use spectacles; I have used them myself these twenty years. I was advised to it by a famous oculist when I was fifteen. I am really of opinion they have preserved my sight, notwithstanding the passion I always had both for reading and drawing.' This good woman, you must know, is half blind and never read a larger volume than a newspaper. I will not trouble you with the whole conversation, though it would make an excellent scene in a farce. But after they had, in the best-bred way in the

---

[3] A didactic romance by Fénelon, published in 1699.

[4] George Whitefield, the famous Methodist preacher.

[5] Here Lady Mary abruptly begins her account of an afternoon at the 'court' of John Murray, British Resident in Venice.

world, convinced me that they thought I lied when I talked of reading without glasses, the foresaid matron obligingly said she should be very proud to see the writing I talked of, having heard me say formerly I had no correspondents but my daughter and Mr Wortley. She was interrupted by her sister, who said, simpering, 'You forget Sir James Steuart.' I took her up something short, I confess, and said in a dry stern tone, 'Madam, I do write to Sir James Steuart, and will do it as long as he will permit that honour.'

This rudeness of mine occasioned a profound silence for some minutes, and they fell into a good-natured discourse of the ill consequences of too much application, and remembered how many apoplexies, gouts and dropsies had happened amongst the hard students of their acquaintance. As I never studied anything in my life, and have always (at least from fifteen) thought the reputation of learning a misfortune to a woman I was resolved to believe these stories were not meant at me. I grew silent in my turn, and took up a card that lay on a table and amused myself with smoking it over a candle. In the meantime (as the song says)

> Their tattles all run, as swift as the sun,
> Of who had won, and who was undone,
> By their gaming and sitting up late.

When it was observed I entered into none of these topics, I was addressed by an obliging lady who pitied my stupidity. 'Indeed, madam, you should buy horses to that fine machine you have at Padua; of what use is it standing in the portico?' 'Perhaps,' said another wittily, 'of as much use as a standing dish.' – A gaping schoolboy added with still more wit, – 'I have seen at a country gentleman's table a venison pasty made of wood.' – I was not at all vexed by said schoolboy, not because he was (in more senses than one) the highest of the company, but knowing he did not mean to offend me. I confess (to my shame be it spoken) I was grieved at the triumph that appeared in the eyes of the king and queen of the company, the court being tolerably full.[6]

His majesty walked off early with the air befitting his dignity, followed by his train of courtiers, who like courtiers were laughing amongst themselves as they followed him; and I was left with the two queens, one of whom was making ruffles for the man she loved,[7] and the other slopping tea for the good of her country. They renewed their generous endeavours to set me right, and I (graceless beast that I am) take up the smoked card which lay before me, and with the corner of another write –

---

[6] Murray, his wife, and their friends.
[7] Consul Smith's wife, *née* Murray.

> If ever I one thought bestow
> On what such fools advise,
> May I be dull enough to grow
> Most miserably wise –[8]

and flung down the card on the table and myself out of the room in the most indecent fury. A few minutes on the cold water convinced me of my folly, and I went home as much mortified as my Lord Edgecumbe when he has lost his last stake at hazard. Pray don't think (if you can help it) this is an affectation of mine to enhance the value of a talent I would be thought to despise, as celebrated beauties often talk of the charms of good sense, having some reason to fear their mental qualities are not quite so conspicuous as their outside lovely form.

Apropos of beauties:

> I know not why, but Heaven has sent this way
> A nymph fair, kind, poetical and gay;
> And what is more (though I express it dully),
> A noble, wise, right honourable cully;
> A soldier worthy of the name he bears,
> As brave and senseless as the sword he wears.[9]

You will not doubt I am talking of a puppet show, and indeed so I am, but the figures (some of them) bigger than the life, and not stuffed with straw like those commonly shown at fairs. I will allow you to think me madder than Don Quixote when I confess I am governed by the *que dira-t-on* of these things, though I remember whereof they are made and know they are but dust. Nothing vexes me so much as that they are below satire. (Between you and me) I think there are but two pleasures permitted to mortal man, love and vengeance, both which are, in a peculiar manner, forbidden to us wretches who are condemned to petticoats. Even vanity itself, of which you daily accuse us, is the sin against the Holy Ghost, not to be forgiven in this world or the next.

> Our sex's weakness you expose and blame,
> Of every prating fop the common theme;
> Yet from this weakness you suppose is due
> Sublimer virtue than your Cato knew.
> From whence is this unjust distinction shown?
> Are we not formed with passions like your own?
> Nature with equal fire our souls endued,
> Our minds as lofty and as warm our blood.
> O'er the wide world your wishes you pursue,
> The change is justified by something new;
> But we must sigh in silence and be true.

[8] Adapted from 'Song' by the Earl of Dorset.
[9] Lady Mary's summary of this letter names the persons in the verse: 'Mrs Wright, Lord Brudenelle, Col. Hamilton'.

How the great Dr Swift would stare at this vile triplet!

And then what business have I to make apologies for Lady Vane, who I never spoke to, because her life is writ by Dr Smollett, who I never saw? Because my daughter fell in love with Lord Bute am I obliged to fall in love with the whole Scots nation? 'Tis certain I take their quarrels upon myself in a very odd way; and I cannot deny that (two or three dozen excepted), I think they make the first figure in all arts and sciences, even in gallantry, in spite of the finest gentlemen that have finished their education at Paris.

You will ask me what I mean by all this nonsense, after having declared myself an enemy to obscurity to such a degree that I do not forgive it to the great Lord Viscount Bolingbroke, who professes he studied it. I dare swear you will sincerely believe him when you read his celebrated works. I have got them for you and intended to bring them. – *Oime! l'huomo propone, Dio dispone.* – I hope you won't think this dab of Italian that slid involuntarily from my pen an affectation like his gallicisms, or a rebellion against Providence in imitation of his Lordship, who I never saw but once in my life: he then appeared in a corner of the Drawing-Room in the exact similitude of Satan when he was soliciting the Court of Heaven for leave to torment an honest man.

There is one honest man lately gone off of the stage, which (considering the great scarcity of them) I am heartily sorry for: Dr Irwin, who died at Rome with as much stoicism as Cato at Utica, and less desperation, leaving a world he was weary of with the cool indifference you quit a dirty inn to continue your journey to a place where you hope for better accommodation. He took part of a bowl of punch with some Englishmen of my acquaintance the day before his death, and told them with a firm tone of voice: by God! he was going. I am afraid neither Algarotti nor Vallisnieri[10] will make their exit with so good a grace. I shall rejoice them both by letting them know you honour them with a place in your memory when I see them, which I have not done since you left Padua. Algarotti is at Bologna, I believe, composing panegyrics on whoever is victor in this uncertain war;[11] and Vallisnieri gone to make a tour to add to his collection. Which do you think the best employed? I confess I am woman enough to think the naturalist who searches after variegated butterflies, or even the lady who adorns her grotto with shades of shells, nay, even the devout people who spend twenty years in making a magnificent *presepio* at Naples,[12] throw away time in a more rational manner than any hero, ancient or modern. The lofty Pindar who celebrated the Newmarket of those days, or the divine

---

[10] Antonio Vallisnieri the younger held the chair of Natural History at Padua University.

[11] The Seven Years War, which Algarotti's former patron Frederick II had begun.

[12] Models of Christ's manger.

Homer who recorded the bloody battles the most in fashion, appear to me either to have been extremely mistaken or extremely mercenary.

This paragraph is to be dead secret between Lady Fanny and yourself. You see I dare trust you with the knowledge of all my defects in understanding. Mine is so stupefied by age and disappointment, I own I have lost all taste for worldly glory. This is partly your fault: I experienced last year how much happiness may be found with two amiable friends at a *léger repas*, and 'tis as hard to return to political or gallant conversations as it would be for a fat prelate to content himself with the small beer he drank at college. You have furnished me with a new set of notions; you ought to be punished for it, and I fancy you will (at least in your heart) be of opinion that I have very well revenged myself by this tedious unconnected letter. Indeed I intend no such thing, and have only indulged the pleasure everybody naturally feels when they talk to those they love; as I sincerely do yourself and dear Lady Fanny, and your young man because he is yours.

To Sir James Steuart

Venice, 7 April 1760

I have now with great pleasure and, I flatter myself, with some improvement read over again your delightful and instructive treatise; you have opened to me several truths of which I had before only a confused idea. I confess I cannot help being a little vain of comprehending a system that is calculated only for a thinking mind and cannot be tasted without a willingness to lay aside many prejudices which arise from education and the conversation of people no wiser than ourselves. I do not only mean my own sex when I speak of our confined way of reasoning; there are very many of yours as incapable of judging otherwise than they have been early taught, as the most ignorant milkmaid. Nay, I believe a girl out of a village or a nursery more capable of receiving instruction than a lad just set free from the university. It is not difficult to write on blank paper, but 'tis a tedious if not an impossible task to scrape out nonsense already written, and put better sense in the place of it. Mr Steuart is very happy to be under the direction of a father who will not suffer him to entertain errors at an age when 'tis hard to distinguish them. I often look back on my past life in the light in which old Montaigne considered it; it is perhaps a more useful study than it is generally imagined. Mr Locke, who has made the best dissection of the human mind of any author I have ever read, declares that he has drawn all his observations from reflecting on the progression of his own ideas. It is true a very small proportion of knowledge is allowed us in this world, few truths permitted, but those truths are plain; they may be overseen or artfully obscured from our sight, but when pointed out to us it is impossible to resist the conviction that accompanies them. I am persuaded your manuscript would have the same effect on every candid reader it has on me, but I am afraid their number is very small.

I think the omission you desire in the Act of Indemnity cannot fail of happening.[1] I shall take every opportunity of putting people of my acquaintance in mind of it; at present the real director (at least of home affairs) is a countryman of yours, but you know there are certain circumstances that may disincline him from meddling in some nice matters.[2] I am always with gratitude and the truest esteem both to Lady Frances and yourself a faithful humble servant,

M. W. Montagu

[1] Steuart, exiled for joining the Jacobite rebellion, had not been pardoned in the Act of Indemnity.
[2] Lord Mansfield had himself been accused of Jacobitism earlier in his career.

To Sir James Steuart

Venice, 25 January 1761

Sir,

I have not returned my thanks for your obliging letter so soon as both duty and inclination prompted me, but I have had so severe a cold, accompanied with a weakness in my eyes, that I have been confined to my stove for many days. This is the first use I make of my pen. I will not engage in a dispute with you, being very sure that I am unable to support it against you; yet I own I am not entirely of your opinion in relation to the Civil List. I know it has long been a custom to begin every reign with some mark of the people's love exceeding what was shown to the predecessor; I am glad to see this distinguished by the trust and affection of the King to his people, and am persuaded it will have a very good effect on all our affairs, foreign and domestic.[1] It is

[1] Parliament customarily granted an annual revenue to the new sovereign, from which he was expected to pay the cost of the civil government. George III surrendered his hereditary revenues in return for £800,000 a year.

possible my daughter may have some partiality; the character of his present Majesty needs only be half so perfect as she describes it to be such a monarch as has never existed but in romances.

Though I am preparing for my last and longest journey, and stand on the threshold of this dirty world, my several infirmities like post horses ready to hurry me away, I cannot be insensible to the happiness of my native country, and am glad to see the prospect of a prosperity and harmony that I never was witness to. I hope my friends will be included in the public joy; and I shall always think Lady Fanny and Sir James Steuart in the first rank of those I wish to serve. Your conversation is a pleasure I would prefer to any other; but I confess even that cannot make me desire to be in London, especially at this time when the shadow of credit that I should be supposed to possess would attract daily solicitations, and gain me a number of enemies who would never forgive me the not performing impossibilities. If all people thought of power as I do, it would be avoided with as much eagerness as it is now sought. I never knew any person that had it who did not lament the load, though I confess (so infirm is human nature) they have all endeavoured to retain it at the same time they complained of it.

You are above any view of that kind. I hope every post to hear news of your return to your native country, where that you may long enjoy a happiness superior to any a court can give is the most ardent desire of, sir, your grateful and faithful humble servant,

M. W. Montagu

❦ To Sir James Steuart ❦

Venice, 12 April 1761

Sir,

I received your obliging letter yesterday and make haste to answer it the first post. I am very sincere in assuring you all your interests are mine, consequently I share with you the concern you feel for Lady Fanny's disorders.

You observe justly there is no happiness without an alloy, nor indeed any misfortune without some mixture of consolation, if our passions permitted us to perceive it. But alas! we are too imperfect to see on all sides; our wisest reflections (if the word wise may be given to humanity) are tainted by our hopes and fears: we all indulge views almost as extravagant as those of Phaeton, and are angry when we do not succeed in projects that are above the reach of mortality. The happiness of

domestic life seems the most laudable as it is certainly the most delightful of our prospects, yet even that is denied, or at least so mixed 'we
think it not sincere or fear it cannot last'.[1] A long series of disappointments have perhaps worn out my natural spirits and given a melancholy
cast to my way of thinking. I would not communicate this weakness to
any but yourself, who can have compassion even where your superior
understanding condemns.

I confess that though I am (it may be) beyond the strict bounds of
reason pleased with my Lord Bute's and my daughter's prosperity I am
doubtful whether I will attempt to be a spectator of it. I have so many
years indulged my natural inclinations to solitude and reading, I am
unwilling to return to crowds and bustle, which would be unavoidable
in London. The few friends I esteemed are now no more; the new set
of people who fill the stage at present are too indifferent to me even to
raise my curiosity.

I now begin (very late, you'll say) the worst effects of age, blindness
excepted: I am grown timorous and suspicious; I fear the inconstancy
of that goddess so publicly adored in ancient Rome and so heartily in-
wardly worshipped in the modern. I retain, however, such a degree of
that uncommon thing called commonsense not to trouble the felicity
of my children with my foreboding dreams, which I hope will prove as
idle as the croaking of ravens or the noise of that harmless animal distinguished by the odious name of screech-owl. You will say, why then
do I trouble you with my old wives' prophecies? Need I tell you that it
is one of the privileges of friendship to talk of our own follies and infirmities? You must then, nay you ought to, pardon my tiresome tattle in
consideration of the real attachment with which I am unalterably, sir,
your obliged and faithful humble servant,

M. W. Montagu

My best compliments to dear Lady Fanny and congratulation to the
young gentleman.[2] I do not doubt he is sorry to leave her, but if it be
necessary for his advancement you will teach him to suffer it at least
with patience.

[1] From Matthew Prior, *Henry and Emma*.
[2] James Steuart the younger had entered the British army as cornet.

❧ To James Stuart Mackenzie ❧

Venice, 6 June 1761

Your Excellency is dead, but as I do not doubt it is only a removal to a better life I ought rather to congratulate than condole. I wish you would take Venice in your way when you make your journey.[1] I almost despair of being able to undertake mine; the infirmities of age come fast upon me, and sometimes I am inclined to think with Shakespeare, 'tis better to endure the ills I have, than fly to others that I know not of.

I should be glad to see Lord Titchfield[2] if he intends coming this road when he returns to England.

I will not trouble you with a long letter; you are in a hurry sufficient to tire any spirits but yours. I only beg you to be assured that while I exist you will have a sincere and faithful friend.

M. W. Montagu

[1] Mackenzie had been recalled from his post at Turin.
[2] Grandson of Lady Oxford.

❧ To Sir James and Lady Frances Steuart ❧

Rotterdam, 20 November 1761

Sir,

I received yesterday your obliging and welcome letter by the hands of Mr Simpson. I tried in vain to find you at Amsterdam; I began to think we resembled two parallel lines, destined to be always near and never to meet. You know there is no fighting (at least no overcoming) destiny. So far I am a confirmed Calvinist, according to the notions of the country where I now exist.

I am dragging my ragged remnant of life to England. The wind and tide are against me; how far I have strength to struggle against both I know not. That I am arrived here is as much a miracle as any in the Golden Legend;[1] and if I had foreseen half the difficulties I have met with I should not certainly have had courage enough to undertake it. I have scrambled through more dangers than his Majesty of Prussia, or even my well-beloved cousin (not counsellor) Marquis Granby;[2] but my

[1] The thirteenth-century collection of saints' lives.
[2] A distant relation of Lady Mary, Granby was commander-in-chief of the British contingent in the Seven Years War and famous for his military exploits and daring.

spirits fail me when I think of my friends risking either health or happiness. I will write to Lady Fanny to hinder your coming to Rotterdam, and will sooner make one jump more myself to wait on you at Antwerp. I am glad poor D. has sold his medals; I confess I thought his buying them a very bold stroke. I supposed that he had already left London, but am told that he has been prevented by the machinations of that excellent politician and truly great man, Murray, and his ministry.

My dear Lady Fanny, I am persuaded that you are more nearly concerned for the health of Sir James than he is himself; I address myself to you to insist on it to him not to undertake a winter progress in the beginning of a fit of the gout. I am nailed down here by a severe illness of my poor Marianne, who has not been able to endure the frights and fatigues that we have passed. If I live to see Great Britain, you will have there a sincere and faithful servant that will omit no occasion of serving you; and I think it almost impossible I should not succeed. You must be loved and esteemed wherever you are known.

Give me leave however, dear madam, to combat some of your notions, or more properly speaking, your passions. Mr Steuart is in a situation that opens the fairest prospect of honour and advancement. We mothers are all apt to regret the absence of children we love. Solomon advises the sluggard to go to the ant and be wise; we should take the example of the innocent inhabitants of the air: when their young are fledged they are delighted to see them fly and peck for themselves. Forgive this freedom. I have no other receipt for maternal fondness, a distemper which has long afflicted your ladyship's obliged and obedient humble servant,

M. W. Montagu

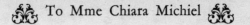

To Mme Chiara Michiel

London, April 1762

I swear to you (my beautiful lady) that the greatest pleasure I have received in London has been your kind letter of the tenth of last month. What you said about the fine marriage of our friend Rosenberg is incomparable.[1] It has finesse, justice, and nobility, and all that; only you could express yourself so well in a foreign language. Alas, I have the gibberish of the Tower of Babel in my poor head, and I speak with as little clarity as an antediluvian. My heart at least is sincere, and always at your service to sell and pledge.

If your gentlemen have not left I shall beg them to allow my little coffers which are in the Convent to come with their baggage.[2] You know that good company is very useful on journeys. The Earl of Northampton is very eager to see your beautiful city; he is bringing with him a charming wife, of the first rank in England.[3]

I am, besides, sincerely grieved at the conduct of madam your daughter-in-law. We have a proverb: my son is my son till he has a wife. You are fortunate in having a mother truly worthy of you; she is doubly so in living with a daughter as perfect as the Signora Chiara M. B. May this union last for ever! and may your grandchildren recompense you for all the griefs you have received elsewhere![4]

These are the most ardent wishes of your ailing but sincere, very humble and obedient servant,

M. Wortley Montagu

[translation]

[1] The elderly Count von Rosenberg–Orsini, Imperial Ambassador to Venice, had married Giustiniana Wynne, formerly one of Casanova's many mistresses.
[2] Lady Mary had left some belongings at a convent in Venice, and wished them to be brought to London by the Venetian ambassadors.
[3] Northampton, married (1759) to a daughter of the Duke of Beaufort, was newly appointed Ambassador to Venice.
[4] Mme Michiel was asked to leave her son's house by her daughter-in-law; she found refuge with her mother.

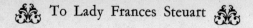

London, 2 July 1762

Dear Madam,

I have been ill a long time, and am now so bad I am little capable of writing, but I would not pass in your opinion as either stupid or ungrateful. My heart is always warm in your service and I am always told your affairs shall be taken care of.[1] You may depend, dear madam, nothing shall be wanting on the part of your ladyship's faithful humble servant,

M. W. Montagu

[1] Sir James's pardon and permission to return to Scotland were granted the following year.

Index

Note: This index excludes the Introduction and the seven brief prefatory sections. It uses LM as an abbreviation for Lady Mary (Pierrepont) Wortley Montagu, and W for Edward Wortley Montagu.